THE CONCORDE CLUB

CLUB

The First 50 Years!

COLE MATHIESON
with **Norman Giller**

Archive material compiled by Maureen Chapman

NMG

NMG

**A NormanMichaelGillerEnterprises publication
in association with Cole Mathieson**

© Cole Mathieson and Norman Giller 2008

First published in 2008 by NMG Enterprises
PO Box 3386, Ferndown, BH22 8XT

A CIP catalogue for this title is available from the British Library
ISBN 978-0-9543243-2-2

Typeset and designed by NMG Enterprises, Dorset, UK
Printed and bound in the United Kingdom by Antony Rowe Limited
Bumper's Farm, Chippenham, Wiltshire SN14 6LH

MANY OF THE PHOTOGRAPHS IN THIS BOOK HAVE BEEN KINDLY PROVIDED
BY GORDON SAPSED, STUART McWILLIAM, KEN NUTLEY AND JIM BUDD, AND
SEVERAL ARE FROM COLE MATHIESON'S PRIVATE COLLECTION. BEST EFFORTS
HAVE BEEN MADE TO CLEAR COPYRIGHTS.
THANKS TO MICHAEL GILLER, JACKIE JONES, CHRISTOPHER JONES, GEOFF
FISHER AND LIBBY RODGER FOR PRODUCTION ASSISTANCE.

CONTENTS

Humphrey Lyttelton (left) playing at the original Concorde Club at the Bassett Hotel in 1964 ... and more than 40 years on (above) relaxing at the 'new' Concorde, with me looking suitably respectful of a man who was a legend in his own lifetime. Sadly, my old friend 'left the building' on the very day this book was being printed. I pay my tribute on Page 10. We will not see or hear his like again.

THE CONCORDE CLUB: The First 50 Years
Introduction by Humphrey Lyttelton

IT was the Autumn of 1964 when I first played the Concorde. Back then it was little more than a large room at the rear of a pub in Southampton where you could swing a tune but not a cat. It says much for the entrepreneurial skills and ambition of Cole Mathieson that he persuaded me to bring my band and our star guest Buck Clayton to play at what was then very much a jazz outpost.

Over the following four decades I have watched in wonderment as Cole has quietly transformed the Concorde into what is unquestionably one of the finest jazz venues in Europe, and he has expanded it beyond even his wildest dreams into a huge entertainment complex, including a fine hotel and as good a restaurant as you will find anywhere in the jazz world.

The list of musicians who have played the Concorde reads like a veritable *Who's Who* of post-war jazz, including giants of the genre like Coleman Hawkins, Ben Webster, Bud Freeman, Wild Bill Davison, Benny Carter, Bud Shank, Barney Kessel and Big Joe Turner, who sang with my band on our second visit to the old Concorde in 1964.

In all the years I have known Cole he has remained the same modest, unflappable, welcoming character, and as time has passed by he has begun to look more and more like the friendly captain of an exclusive golf club. It takes somebody of great taste and vision to create a club that is not only ideal for jazz but also for so many other forms of entertainment. Where else in the world would you find a place of such elegance and class that rewards its artistes with a huge plate of gorgeous chips after the show? And where else would you be entertained by a large congenial dog capable of pilfering a pair of socks from the bags of unsuspecting musicians?

I have played the club many times, and also made a broadcast from there when appearing on a radio quiz called *Jazz Score*. My only slight and very personal reservation about playing at the Concorde is that the final few strides to the stage are an increasing challenge to my size thirteen and a halfs as I start to creak a bit. But then, mountaineering was never my forte.

Cole asked me for a signature to use with this introduction. I hope my autographed sketch suffices. The full-size original will be auctioned, with proceeds going to the Wessex Cancer Trust – the charity that will benefit from sales of this book. I will sign off by saying that the world of jazz owes Cole a debt of gratitude for giving us a splendid platform for our music. This is his story of the first fifty years. Here's to the next fifty.

A study of what 50 years of clubbing can do to a man

This is me (left) as I reach the autumn of my years, and that's me above in the springtime of my life when I started the Concorde Club at the Bassett Hotel, with no plans for where I was going. It's been quite a journey.

YES, if you ask me I could write a book. And here it is: The First 50 Years of The Concorde Club. I have written it reluctantly, because I am not comfortable talking about myself. If I sound arrogant on any of the following pages, I apologise. Those who know me well will be relieved to learn that the book is not so much about me as about the Concorde, the Club that started out as a hobby and became my life.

It was with great sadness that I learned on the very day we were going to press with this book that my good friend Humphrey Lyttelton had gone to the great bandstand in the sky. He was always encouraging me to write the history of the Concorde. "It's our duty," he said, "to keep jazz history alive for the next generation."

While the book has its roots deep in the jazz world, there is much that will keep non-jazz lovers amused and entertained. I have written the book in harness with Norman Giller, a sports historian, jazz disciple, Concorde Club member and author of seventy-eight previous books. He persuaded me to write the book more for posterity than prosperity, and the clincher is that £1 for every book signed by me will go to the Wessex Cancer Trust. I will be very happy for you to help give me writer's cramp.

The Wessex Cancer Trust is one of my favourite charities, and Norman has a special reason to want to support them. Shortly before we agreed to work together on the book he had a cancerous tumour removed by Southampton surgeon Nicholas Beck. Norman vowed he would give something back, so he will be working hard to boost the fund by making this a best seller.

And Norman says he has a lot for which to thank the Concorde. It was there (in the Moldy Fig wine bar) that he met his partner and long-time Concorde member Jackie Jones. When you read the Members' Memories chapter you will discover that Cupid has often struck in the Concorde, and it's no exaggeration to say that the Club has been the springboard for many romances and marriages. There may have been a few break-ups too, but as I want this to be a happy book I will sweep them out of sight.

The book is in two parts, first my story and then the memories of my family, close friends, staff, members and musicians. A big thank you to all those who have provided us with their personal memories, making this as much your book as mine; just as it is YOUR Club as much as mine. It has been a long partnership of pleasure.

This is not just a jazz book. It is the story of how the Club has grown to take in all forms of musical and corporate entertainment, the delights of eating and drinking and generally making merry. The book mirrors the six decades since I first had the idea for the Club back in the Fifties when there were no such things as personal computers, mobile phones, breathalysers, decimalised currency, motorways, colour televisions or micro chips. The only chips we knew about came with fish, and we would drink two-bob (10p) pints of beer in smoke-filled pubs and clubs, tell pre-PC mother-in-law jokes, ogle pictures of Marilyn Monroe and Jane Russell, and moan about footballers earning too much money (£20 a week!).

As a jazz fanatic, there will obviously be a big emphasis on my favourite music and musicians. I also have stories to tell about rock 'n' rhythm stars like Rod Stewart, Georgie Fame, Joe Cocker, Ginger Baker, Eric Clapton, Robert Plant, Alan Price, and a young pianist who appeared at the Concorde when known as Reg Dwight and before he became fairly famous as Elton John.

There are stories about the chaos and comedy at our charity pantomimes, wine tasting anecdotes and tales about summer balls, tribute nights, hotel fun and games, comical cabaret evenings and DJ shows.

I will also be telling about the mountain I've climbed to get the Concorde as established as it is today. Believe me, there have been many times when I have been close to falling off.

The climb could not have been completed without the help of scores of people who have supported me over the years. In particular I want to thank my wife and partner Pauline, daughters Fiona and Kirstie, and my son Jamie, all of whom play a vital part in the running of the Club.

Norman and I bow the knee to Maureen Chapman, without whose archive treasures this book would not have been half as interesting or informative. And a grateful nod in the direction, too, of my secretary/PA Pat Masom and her successor Lynne Wicks for organising me, and especially 'Jim'll Fixit' Budd, who has been there with me almost every step of the way, making sure everything works.

There are many others who know they are special to me, and I have attempted to mention as many as possible in the 'Last Word' Acknowledgements page. If I have forgotten anybody, please, please forgive me. I have reached that stage in my life when I cannot remember what I had for breakfast but can clearly recall the first gigs at the original Concorde Club at the Bassett Hotel more than fifty years ago.

As a lover of black and white films, I can also recall old movies like treasured memories, which is why I paraphrase Bette Davis in *All About Eve*: "Fasten your safety belts, we could be in for a bumpy ride ..."

Now come back with me to the summer of 1950, and the start of all that jazz.

Part One

Cole's story

This Book is dedicated to the memory of my loving parents Leslie and Edith, and to the futures of Fiona, Kirstie, Jamie and Michael. And also remembering my good friend and giant of jazz Humphrey Lyttelton

MY FRIEND HUMPH
Cole remembers a giant of jazz and comedy

MY dear old friend Humphrey Lyttelton's famous sense of humour would have been tickled pink by the timing of his exit from this mortal coil. He 'left the building' on the very day that we pushed the button for the first print run of this book.

If you think I am being irreverent and disrespectful about the passing of one of the all-time kings of jazz and comedy, it will mean you did not know or begin to understand Humph and his unique wit.

He would expect nothing less than laughter (and just a few tears) at news of his passing. I know of nobody else who could match the eventful and entertaining times that Humph packed into his 86 years. And I am very proud that the Concorde Club played quite a part in his extraordinary life.

We decided not to tinker with the introduction he wrote for the book, and the illustrated autograph was the very last cartoon that the man of so many talents drew.

Humph, elderly man with the horn. The innuendo is deliberate and would have won the approval of the Master of Double Entendre.

He made his final stage appearance at the Concorde two weeks before he passed on, just as his idol Nat Gonella had ten years earlier. Humph, with his wonderfully loyal manager Susan, ate as usual in the Moldy Fig before the concert. Then, in front of a packed house, he played beautifully. Called back for the inevitable encore, he – with typical off-the-wall humour – had the entire audience joining in with choruses of *Mairzy Doats and Dozy Doats*, Alan Barnes decorating it with Charlie Parker-style riffs. It was surreal and the great man's final song.

That night Humph confided to me that he was going into hospital for "a little heart surgery, nothing serious." We talked about his upcoming plans, including his tour with the *I'm Sorry I Haven't A Clue* roadshow. I asked him for a signature to accompany his introduction to this book, and in a blinking of an eye he had not only produced his autograph but a cartoon to go with it. He gave the go-ahead for me to auction it for charity, and we agreed to try to meet up on publication of the book. It is a meeting that will never take place, but I have a bookful of memories of a giant of jazz, a giant of comedy and a giant among men. Thanks, Humph.

IT all started with George Formby. As silly as it sounds, it was one of his records that turned me on to a life-long love of jazz and an ambition to start a club of my own that I'm proud to say has become popular, famous even, as The Concorde Club.

I know that George Formby has as much to do with jazz as Sir John Dankworth with ladies' hairdressing, so I had better explain. In 1950 – when I was twelve, coming up thirteen – my father bought a '78' record on which George, with his little ukulele in his hands, performed *Do-De-Oh-Do*. In the middle of the song there was a 30-second trumpet solo that sounded magical to my schoolboy ears.

The rented, terraced house where I lived in Newtown, Southampton, with my parents, brother Derek and sister Janet, resounded to the constant playing of the record as I listened to it time and time again on our wind-up gramophone. It got to the stage where I wore a huge groove in the record at the in and out point of the solo, and I blunted a procession of needles.

For those of the iPod generation who may have stumbled on this book, the ten and twelve inch 78s were made of vinyl and circled 78.26 revolutions a minute on the gramophone turntables. Veterans like me will talk about their '78' collections with a lot of emotion; our records back in those days were like friends and almost had a personality, unlike today's sanitised music without the crackle and scratches of our beloved old vinyl.

Excuse me wandering. I had better warn you now that I have a grasshopper mind that jumps from one subject to another and back again, and I am just relying on my writing partner to keep me on a tight rein.

Back to George Formby. I played the record so loudly and so frequently that a neighbour called me on one side and asked why I kept playing the same record over and over again.

I explained about the trumpet solo, and he said (words that were to set the path of my life): "Oh you should listen to the *real* thing. You can borrow my Louis Armstrong records."

Louis Armstrong! This kid had found the keys to his future. I was quickly immersed in the sounds and history of New Orleans jazz, and took every opportunity to listen to or read about what was for me a new phenomenon. I bought Rudi Blesh's famous history of jazz, *Shining Trumpets*, and digested every word and fact.

My father, Leslie, was a painter and decorator who in his spare time played accordion and pub-style piano. As you can guess from his taste in George Formby records, he was not a great jazz lover. But he and my mother, Edith, did not complain as I began to monopolise the gramophone with my growing collection of Armstrong, Kid Ory, King Oliver, Bunk Johnson, George Lewis and Johnny Dodds records. This, incidentally, when I was known as Col, short for Colin, rather than the more sophisticated Cole that I later adopted as the name by which I wanted to be known. If it was good enough for Cole Porter, it was good enough for me.

I was always told that Scotsman Tommy McQuater played the trumpet solo that first captured me on the George Formby record. He was then a session musician famous for his duets with trombonist George Chisholm, another Scot. There has always been a strong jazz tradition in Scotland, and perhaps the rhythm got into my blood through my Scottish grandfather.

For years I have been giving the credit to McQuater, but when I got round to researching for this book, imagine my surprise and pleasure to discover that the trumpet solo was in fact the work of one of my all-time jazz heroes and somebody who became a good friend, Nat Gonella. More of him later.

I was a bit of a dummy at my Secondary Modern school in Newtown, and when I left in 1952 at fifteen I had only two ambitions: to become a photographer and to play and listen to as much jazz as possible. My friendly neighbour, Jim, who introduced me to Louis Armstrong, also showed me how to play the drums.

It just happened that he was a left-handed drummer, so when I got my first drum kit I set it up the same way he did. I am right handed, so from day one I had given myself a handicap. I was playing the bass drum with my left foot and the high-hat with my right. I was never going to become another Buddy Rich!

By this time in the mid-1950s I had discovered there was much more to jazz than New Orleans music. I used to religiously tune into the AFN (American Forces Network) broadcasts from Germany, which was about the only jazz you could hear on the wireless because the BBC virtually ignored it. The alternative was the awful 'pop' music on Radio Luxembourg. Sorry, but no thanks. Jazz won my ears outright, with just enough space left for a growing interest in opera arias and soothing classical music. But the 'beat' stuff of the pop world never got through to me.

Suddenly I was being carried away on a magic carpet ride by the likes of Benny Goodman, Count Basie, Duke Ellington and I found myself getting engulfed by the modernists such as Charlie Parker, Dizzy Gillespie, Gerry Mulligan and all the be-bop giants of the 1950s American jazz scene. I consider myself so lucky to enjoy jazz right across the board, and I cannot understand the traditionalists who shut their ears to modern jazz and vice versa. For me, good music is good music regardless of the label. Mind you, I do shut off post-John Coltrane. I can't stand the jazz where they seem to play cascades of notes for the sake of it. I like my jazz to have a beginning, a middle and an end, and some respect shown to the composer by not drifting too far away from the original melody. But each to his own.

Yes, I'm wandering again. Back to my drumming. There was a lovely old pub called White's Home in Northam where they encouraged jam sessions. It was mostly New Orleans jazz and I used to take my drums along and join in with my cack-handed playing.

During the day I was working in the development and print department of the Southampton-based Eucryl toothpaste company, thinking it was going to lead me into a hoped-for career as a photographer. By then, 1955, I was seventeen and had got myself married to a local girl called Mary Hagens. We were both much too young to know what we were doing and the marriage was short-lived, but it did have the bonus of producing, in 1962, my lovely eldest daughter, Fiona, who now assists with the running of the Concorde and is in charge of the Human Resources department.

Jazz was dominating my thoughts and spare time (perhaps one of the reasons the marriage didn't work), and when the quaint White's Home pub was demolished as part of a redevelopment programme I took my drums to the Portswood Hotel at Bevois Valley in Southampton, today better known as The Hobbit.

Traditional jazz was then becoming huge in Southampton, with dozens of bands ranging from the good to the appalling filling pubs and clubs throughout the city. We decided to climb on board the bandwagon so to speak, and in 1956 took over from the hugely popular Gerry Brown Band in the Portswood. When I say "we" I mean our band at the time that, after a brief spell as the Climax Jazz Band, eventually became the Yellow Dog Stompers. A typical early line-up would have been Pete Passant trumpet, Brian Leake clarinet, Don Gordon trombone, 'Bo-Bo' Barlett banjo, George Lane or cartoonist extraordinaire Toni Goffe bass, and me on my wrong-way-round drums. How good were we? Well I have a poster in my office advertising the Climax Jazz Band. In front of Climax, somebody has scrawled the word 'Anti.' So I guess we were not as hot as we thought we were, but the Yellow Dog Jazz Club that we formed quickly became very popular – Yellow Dog, of course, after the blues composed by W.C. Handy and beautifully played and sung by Satchmo Armstrong.

As I always arrived first at our gigs to set up my drums, I automatically also set up the cash desk. It was a natural succession to become secretary and administrator, including among my duties a weekly typewritten newsletter to our hundreds of members. The bug had bitten.

I also later organised some sessions at the Red Lion in Totton for the Ronnie Horler Band and various guests like Jimmy Skidmore, and where a young Southampton singer called Shirley Alexander made a great impression with her Ella-like tones. More than fifty years on she is still singing beautifully for me at the Concorde, known now to one and all as Shirley Morgan! I also played occasionally at the Southampton Rhythm Club based in the Cliff Hotel in Woolston, where I first met the great Nat Gonella and got to play with him a few times. That was pretty close to the pinnacle for Cole the drummerman!

Jazz fan Lord Montagu got to hear about the Yellow Dog and promoted an open-air concert presenting many of the local jazz bands, with the Avon Cities Jazz band from Bristol as the major attraction. It was compered by Johnny Morris, of *Animal Magic* fame. I played with the Climax Jazz Band, and in the programme I was described as Col. Mathieson. If I had been bright like Elvis Presley's manager Colonel Tom Parker, I would have carried it on as my title. Colonel Mathieson has a nice ring to it. Tom Parker, of course, was as much a Colonel as Duke Ellington and Count Basie were titled people.

We were back at Beaulieu the following year with a concert organised "under the auspices

I am playing the poseur here on the snare drum for a staged photograph with the original Yellow Dog Stompers, circa 1957. The line-up here is Don Gordon trombone, Mick Erridge trumpet, Loz Garfield clarinet, Jim McConnell bass, and to my left is banjoist Harry Fry.

of the Yellow Dog Jazz Club." Among the topliners at the Palace House were French violin virtuoso Stephane Grappelli and Welsh piano genius Dill Jones. I was blown away by the keyboard wizardry of Dill, and I asked him what were the chances of him appearing at the Yellow Dog. Much to my astonishment he agreed, and we got a packed house for his gig even though we were charging, at five shillings (25p), twice the usual admittance money.

The landlord of the Portswood Hotel – impressed that we had sold out the night well in advance -– insisted I immediately book Dill for a second gig, but I thought this was far too ambitious. He told me that if I incurred any loss he would make it up. As popular as the club was it couldn't sustain two nights at a fee of five shillings, which was a lot of money at that time and I took a heavy loss. "That's your hard luck," the landlord said, or words to that effect and refused to put his hand in his pocket.

I was fuming and made up my mind there and then to find another venue. So it was in September 1957 that I launched a new club at the Bassett Hotel in Burgess Road on a hill at the northwest corner of Southampton Common. It was to be called The Concorde Club.

The Bassett was picked out as an ideal location by guitarist John Fanner, who was heavily into the music of the Modern Jazz Quartet. They released a record in the mid-1950s called Concorde, inspired by the Place de la Concorde in Paris. It seemed an ideal name for our club, and I was even more taken by it when I found the following quote in Shakespeare's *The Merchant of Venice:*

'The man that hath no music in himself,
Nor is not moved with concord of sweet sounds,
Is fit for treason, stratagems and spoils ...'

I hung this up on a board over the entrance to the Bassett, which I thought gave it an appropriate touch of class, and I'm proud to say we thought of the name years ahead of the launch of the supersonic Concorde.

John Fanner was too involved in his career in the insurance business to help with the running of the club, but I was indebted to him for finding the Bassett because the venue was just about perfect for what I needed at the time.

It had an excellent upright piano by the standards of pub pianos, and a separate entrance from the main hotel. There was a domed roof that gave it superb acoustics, and – perhaps more important, certainly to the musicians – it had a bar in the room! Watneys, the brewers, were fully supportive, and we could not have had a more helpful and encouraging landlord than the giant 'Tiny' Smith. He was the old-style landlord, upright and dependable and always ready with a good word of advice. I made the mistake early on of trying to keep pace with his drinking, but was quickly out of my depth. Tiny sank spirits with alarming speed, and after several sessions getting completely sozzled in his thirsty company I made a mental note to stick in future to beer and wine.

Tiny, supported by his wife, Elsie, and son, David, was very happy with the general behaviour of our members. There was no need for bouncers (sorry, greeters!). In fact I was always able to employ willing girls on the cash desks – and continue to do so without cause for concern.

The hotel had large grounds that were once used as a zoo, and behind the main bar was a huge stuffed bear who, when alive, had been a main attraction at the zoo. The bear's name was Mischka, and local legend had it that he escaped from the zoo and was shot on Southampton Common. Now he was an attraction cased in glass and still behind bars.

In an earlier life, the room we had converted into our club had been the 'Old Colonial Restaurant.' There was an old-fashioned feel to it, and one of our early members, an interior

Dill Jones playing to a packed house at the Yellow Dog Jazz Club in 1957. We re-booked him too quickly, and it changed my life. Dill, as hot a pianist as the UK has ever produced, was resident keyboard man on the Queen Mary, and so a regular visitor to Southampton. He eventually emigrated to the United States in 1961, a huge loss to our jazz scene. I was delighted to welcome him in to the 'new' Concorde 20 years after his last appearance at the Basssett. That's Danny Craig on the drums.

designer called Roland Tucker, suggested ways we could improve the look of the place, and a crowd of volunteers got to work with paintbrushes, hammers and nails, wallpaper and paste. Roland, a life-long friend who developed into one of the country's finest designers, later drew up proper plans and we completely changed the look of the place, with some help from Watneys brewers. Roland will become a frequent visitor to my memoirs, along with Jim Budd who has been with me nearly every step of the way in his role as a fixer of all things.

People often refer to the Concorde as 'Cole's place.' But I could never ever have got it off the ground without the help and support of dozens of wonderful friends and club members who were always willing to give their time and energy to make the club work. I was the weakest link in the chain. I am the Charlie Chaplin of Do It Yourself, a complete clown.

Within six months of opening in October 1957 we had attracted 1,000 members, concentrating mostly on mainstream and modern jazz and also featuring the revivalist New Orleans style of music that had first captured my ears. Elsewhere in Southampton the fare was mainly Trad or 'beat' music, and the Top Rank Ballroom drew a lot of couples dancing to the music of an orchestra made up mainly of jazz musicians supplementing their income. The Ballroom manager was a friendly rival of mine called Colin Bull, and we competed for the same customers.

In those early formative years I was so lucky to have the careful bookkeeping work of Gordon Ricketts, with whom I set up a jazz and variety promotions agency called Mathieson and Ricketts. People thought we were a disabled tap-dancing double act.

Gordon, whose parents ran the Lamb Inn in the New Forest, emigrated to Australia and we lost touch with each other. A short while ago I found myself wondering how he had got on with his new life. The next day I was standing in the reception area at the Concorde when who should walk up and tap me on the shoulder but Gordon, who was on a visit home from Oz! He came to the jazz concert that evening with a photograph of a crowd of us from the old days at the Bassett, and astonishingly – this nearly 50 years on, remember – six of the seven people in the picture were in the club that night! The only one missing was Kenny Harrison, who had also emigrated to Australia to carry on his drumming career, later briefly returning to play at the 'new' Concorde with the Sydney-based Graeme Bell Band.

Among those in the photograph was journalist and jazz and folk music buff John Edgar Mann. I must mention here the magnificent support we have always had from the *Daily Echo* and in particular from John, a walking record book on jazz whose intelligent, considered reporting for the *Echo* over the years has been instrumental in our success. Anybody reading this and considering starting up an entertainment club of any kind must make sure they get a friendly reporter on their side. John Edgar Mann was vital to us and to all Southampton jazz and folk clubs in those early days. Duncan Eaton, another excellent *Echo* journalist, is equally important to us today, and carrying on the JEM tradition of intelligent, trustworthy reporting.

Before the club was even in the planning stage I had to concentrate on the little matter of my National Service. My two years' duty to Queen and Country fell neatly between the Korean War and the invasion of Suez, so the nearest I got to action was watching the occasional warship steer out of Southampton Water.

When I got my 'Call Up' the Royal Army Medical Corps were seeking volunteers for psychiatric orderlies in the sprawling Netley Hospital by the shore of Southampton Water. I volunteered simply because of the word 'Southampton.' It meant I generally worked 'regimental hours' – nine to five, so each evening I could keep my eyes and ears tuned to the vibrant local jazz scene and I managed to keep on running the Yellow Dog Club. The White's Home pub was still staging jam sessions, and I was able to play thanks to the help of my younger brother Derek, who was in his last year at school. He used to collect my drums from home, put them into a big case and then, using his pedal bike, would transport them to the pub in Northam. Once I had finished I would pack the drums and wave Derek off before preparing to return to my duties at the hospital.

I have rarely seen such an amazing building as the Netley Hospital. It was built on the orders of Queen Victoria to nurse the wounded from the Crimean War, and at one stage was under the direction of Florence Nightingale.

It was a quarter of a mile long, and in its peak years had 138 wards and more than 1,000 beds. From the outside it looked like a huge, three-storey baronial home, and the corridors were so wide that when the Yanks took it over in the latter part of the Second World War they drove their jeeps up and down them. I saw some disturbing cases of servicemen suffering from shell shock and nervous exhaustion, even during what was virtually peacetime.

The vast hospital was being run down by the time I worked there, and ten years after my demob the place caught fire and virtually burned to the ground. All that was left standing after the bulldozers had been called in was a psychiatric wing, the hospital chapel and the Officers' Mess (since converted into luxury apartments). I was not sorry to see the hospital go because, to be honest, the interior was depressing and almost haunting, and hardly the place to take somebody suffering from psychological problems.

Looking back, I can now say with some certainty that the RAMC training I received in treating patients has helped me handle difficult people throughout all my years running the Concorde Club. Whenever potential troublemakers make an appearance (we call them PITAs, for Pains In The Arse) I talk to them the way I was taught to speak to disturbed soldiers, using a calming, controlled voice and talking them round, before quietly persuading them to leave.

To give you a flavour of what was happening in the world following my National Service, Prime Minister Harold Macmillan was telling us "you've never had it so good" and was preparing his prophetic "Winds of Change" speech to the South African Parliament. Dwight Eisenhower was President of the United States, the first bricks of the Berlin Wall were being planned as the Cold War with Russia hit freezing point, the average price of a semi-detached house was £2,200, you could buy a Morris Minor for £400, petrol cost 4s 6d (22.5p) a gallon, Elvis was recording *Jailhouse Rock*, Leonard Bernstein had just completed *West Side Story* and Jerry Lee Lewis had gone to No 1 in the hit parade with *Great Balls of Fire*. ITV had been running for just a couple of years and introduced *Oh Boy!* to compete with *Six-Five Special* on the BBC. Tommy Steele was *Rocking with the Caveman*, Cliff Richard was changing his name from Harry Webb and Terry Nelhams-Wright was about to become Adam Faith. The Cavern Club had just opened in Liverpool, but there was no sight or sound yet of The Beatles.

I had given up my printing and developing job to focus on running the Concorde, but kept my clickety-click ambitions alive by doing camera freelance work at weddings for Concorde member Reggie Harris, an amusing and unconventional character who had a photographic business.

I was only making pennies in profits, and – to keep myself fed and watered and my council

I am drumming along with John Fanner, he of the luxuriant moustache and controlled guitar. It was John who discovered the Bassett, which could not have been a better first home for the Concorde Club. Keen observationalists will notice that I have the snare drum upside down!

flat rent paid – I took an early-morning job as a bakery roundsman in the New Forest. What should have been a quick morning tour started to become a marathon, because there were so many club members and other people on the route who wanted to talk about the bands we were putting on. I used to get through about a dozen cups of tea as I stopped off chatting.

Gradually the gruelling schedule began to tell on me. I was having late-nights at the club

This is where it all started in 1957, the annexe room of the Bassett Hotel in Burgess Road at the north-west corner of Southampton Common. It became a regular magnet for hundreds of jazz and rhythm and blues followers, and was like a second home for me. Retirement apartments now stand on the site, but the memories live on.

and then getting up early the next morning to do the round of the forest. Feeling exhausted, I just had to surrender the bakery duties to concentrate full time on running the club.

In the earliest days I was not just organising the gigs but also playing in various bands. I had a few try-out sessions, playing the drums in support to gifted all-round musician Mike Vickers, who would play an important part in the development of the club.

When eventually launching in October 1957 we featured the Terry Colane Quintet, with Terry Shaw on piano, George Lane on bass and me playing the drums. So it is not too difficult to work out how we came by our name, a mix of Terry, Cole and Lane. Terry Colane. We must have put a lot of thought into that!

Our jazz was mainstream bordering on contemporary, with Terry and George far advanced of me with their technique and feeling for ultra-modern stuff that demanded greater expertise than I ever needed when playing New Orleans jazz. Superb local trumpeter Mick Erridge, with whom I had played in the Solent City, Climax and Yellow Dog Jazz Bands, had politely told me I was too modernist to continue playing with him, and Mike Vickers later suggested I move out of the drumming chair because I was not modern enough. I quickly realized that my future lay in promoting rather than playing jazz.

I shared my promotional dreams with fellow drummer Kenny Harrison in unusual circumstances. He and I were good mates, and in the least productive of times collected our dole money together from the local benefit office. While standing in the dole queue I used to tell him of my plan to get the jazz club up and running in Southampton to which I would bring a featured soloist from London. "You can be in the group supporting the celebrity player," I would say. This daydreaming used to help us pass the time, but with neither of us truly believing that I could turn my ramblings into reality.

Amazingly, by the start of 1958 I was able to start putting action where my mouth and imagination had been. Kenny Harrison had developed into an excellent drummer and he was part of our new resident group, with graphic artist Ron Andrews on bass and the two of them supporting the multi-talented Spike Bamsey, who was equally at home on piano, guitar and vibes. They played some red-hot stuff, and I had no qualms about inviting top jazzmen to make the trek to Southampton to play with them.

Within a few months they were joined by Adrian Lightfoot, a fine local trombonist and bassist who in his other life was a young solicitor following in his father's footseps. I mention this because Adrian's father, Raymond, could have been the inspiration for Rumpole of the Bailey.

Adrian recommended me to use Raymond when somebody living one hundred yards from the Bassett Hotel complained about the "racket from the Jazz club." They got up a local petition (poorly supported I hasten to add) to try to get the club shut down.

Raymond Lightfoot invited the main complainants to his office, along with their solicitor, a Mr Biddles. I sat at the back of the room watching as Raymond steamrollered the unfortunate Mr Biddles.

Imagine Horace Rumpole, with the waistcoat, gold watch chain, immaculate black jacket, pinstripe trousers and slightly rotund, and you have Raymond Lightfoot. The one difference was that instead of a cigar he was smoking a cigarette that hardly left his mouth.

"I am surprised your client has taken the matter this far, Mr Fiddles," he said as his opening shot.

"It's Biddles," said Biddles.

"There are at least twenty people living closer to the Bassett Hotel, Mr Diddles ..."

"It's Biddles," said Biddles, this time with an edge to his voice.

" ... and not one of their names appears on your client's petition, Mr Biggles."

"It's Biddles," complained Biddles, now very bothered and spelling out his name slowly and deliberately. "B-I-D-D-L-E-S. Biddles."

"Thank you for that, Mr Piddles," said Raymond, "but I don't think we should let misunderstandings over your name get in the way of what is a serious and ungrounded complaint against my client."

All the time he was talking, he was leaving his lighted cigarette in his mouth, and the sight of his ash getting longer and longer transfixed all of us in the room.

"What my client would like to offer as a gesture of peace and goodwill," Raymond continued, as we wondered what would be his next concoction of Biddles' name, "... is that he will improve the soundproofing of the music room and that all windows will be shut while the classical jazz concerts are underway. Would your clients agree that is a fair response to this poorly supported petition, Mr ... (a deliberate pause) Biddles?"

By now Biddles was so concerned about the juggling around of his name that his concentration had been broken, and his embarrassed clients nodded their heads in acceptance of the peace offering. Then the tension was released as at last the ash fell from the cigarette to be expertly caught in an ashtray by the cunningly clever Raymond Lightfoot.

From that day on the Lightfoots, father and son, were my legal advisers.

The next person to try to get the club closed was the new Chief Inspector of police, who came marching into the Bassett Hotel one day and told me bluntly: "I don't want a jazz club on my patch. You're trouble. If I get my way I will have you closed down."

Jazz in those days had a bad image, but it was unjustified. I argued that there had been virtually no trouble at all since starting the club eighteen months earlier, and the few members who had caused minor problems were no longer welcome.

"Well I'm watching you," the police inspector said threateningly, leaving me in a deep depression.

I thought we might have a problem with the licence a short while later following an incident that was really disturbing. A chap who had drunk himself silly in a pub on the other side of the Common came crashing through the doors into the club and started throwing punches at everyone. It finally took three of us sitting on him to restrain the drunken intruder. Of course we had to call the police, but in the end nothing came of the dramatic episode. Police later told me that the guy shouldn't even have been alive with the amount of alcohol he had consumed. How he had managed to get across the Common in his legless state was a complete mystery.

Because of the top-flight musicians we were booking, the club was becoming so popular that we often had queues that stretched right around the corner into Butterfield Road. Several times people trying to beat the queue got themselves stuck in the toilet window that opened out on to the garden side of the club.

I have to go forward six or seven years for the only really serious incident. It involved American tenor saxophonist Don Byas, who was guesting with the Bruce Turner Jump Band.

We had a young regular member at the club, an extremely handicapped lad called Skip Conway, who was totally obsessed by jazz. This particular night the likeable lad tried to approach the stage to talk to the musicians at the end of their gig. Don Byas, who had single handedly got through almost a bottle of brandy during the set, misunderstood his motives for suddenly trying to come to the stage and pulled a flick knife on him.

It was a really scary moment before we got him under control and explained his misinterpretation of an innocent affair. Just by chance a policeman on his beat called into the club moments later, and we were convincing him that everything was fine when the heavily intoxicated Byas drew his knife again. We calmed him down, and the young policeman accepted that he was too drunk to know what he was doing and he was happy to hear he would be returning to London that night.

My other brush with the law revolved around Monty Worlock, a marvellous classically trained pianist who was the last person you would have expected to feature with the crazy variety orchestra Sid Millward and his Nitwits. Monty took over from Spike Bamsey as our regular piano man, and as he did not live far away I used to give him a lift to and from the gig. He was an astonishing character who had written tunes for ragtime queen Winifred Atwell and had a brother who was Archbishop of Liverpool, and here he was playing for me at the Bassett for a fiver a session and thoroughly content.

This particular night he and his wife, Peggy, kept me talking in his home and showing me scrapbooks with pictures and reports of his antics with the Millward band. Monty also enthralled me with a collection of gripping wartime poems he had penned while serving in North Africa. Suddenly I realised we were running late, and when we went out to my car – a tired old 1940s Hillman – the battery was flat. We started pushing it out into the road, intending to make a jump start when a policeman appeared with Monty out of sight on the far side.

“So what are you up to?” asked the policeman.

“I’ve got a flat battery,” I replied.

“Can you prove it’s your car?”

“Of course it’s my car,” I said. “I wouldn’t steal it by pushing it.”

“So what’s the registration?”

I had a complete blank, mainly because it was dawning on me that my tax was overdue. “Uh, I can’t remember,” I mumbled.

Just then Monty appeared from the other side of the car.

The policeman’s face lit up. “Monty! I haven’t seen you for ages,” he said. “How are you?”

It turned out they were old neighbours, and Monty explained that he was late for a gig at the Concorde and that we were trying to get the car started. It ended with Monty and the policeman pushing the untaxed car with me at the wheel and finally getting the ignition to spark.

This was the same Hillman I used to drive to and from London to keep a personal check on the musicians who might be available for appearances at the Concorde. One of my early ideas was to get trumpeter Ken Colyer down. Gordon Ricketts wrote to his agent, who replied that Colyer would be delighted to come down to Southampton to play for us. His fee: £75!

Gordon and I almost fainted, because this would have been our budget for three gigs. This,

As this is a book about the history of the Concorde Club rather than my life story, I have refrained from giving too many personal details. But I just have to make glowing reference to my Dad, Leslie (above left) who, with my mother, Edith, was always supportive and encouraging as I set off on my adventure as a jazz club owner.

remember, when the average take-home pay was £9 a week and footballers were on a maximum £20 a week. Thank goodness other musicians were not this demanding, otherwise the Concorde would not have survived.

In fairness to Ken I should repeat that it was his agent who put the price on his head, and we said, "Thanks but no thanks." It was more than twenty years before Ken finally appeared at the Concorde, and his personal share of the band fee would not have been much more than £75!

Among the venues I used to visit regularly, and indeed played at in London, was Humphrey Lyttelton's club in Oxford Street, which in later years became The 100 Club run by Roger Horton and his wife Pat, who became very good friends. Now they are retired I see them frequently at the Concorde and we occasionally visit London jazz haunts together. Unfortunately we seem to meet up most often these days at various funerals of musicians, but jazzmen being jazzmen it usually ends up as some sort of party.

I also used to visit the Flamingo in Wardour Street where the modernists were in full swing, and Cy Laurie's club in Great Windmill Street, often for all-night jazz after which I would sleep in my car in Soho Square – in the days before parking meters and traffic wardens. The Marquee was another regular haunt, where I used to listen to the Dankworth band, with young university graduate Dudley Moore on piano and doing a comedy scat-singing act during the interval. The contrasts were extraordinary. Down at Cy Laurie's basement club under Jack Solomons' boxing gymnasium the dress was scruffy in a Bohemian way, with duffle coats almost a uniform and hair unkempt and often reaching the shoulders; while at the Flamingo most of the guys were sharp-suited, with polished shoes and hair that was cut short in what was known as college-boy style. As anybody who knows me will testify, I took the Flamingo look (apart from a short spell with style-of-the-day shoulder-length hair some time in the 1970s).

It was at the Flamingo that I first heard Georgie Fame, not thinking of him in terms of jazz. I was knocked out by his performance, and vowed one day to get him down to the Concorde. It was the start of a near-50 years association.

Back in the 1950s, there was quite a lot of hostility between modernists and traditionalists. I always bridged the two forms of jazz, but there was a lot of unnecessary rivalry between the camps. I remember one session at the Concorde when modernist baritone player Harry Klein was guesting, and a trad heckler in the audience kept loudly complaining about his choice of tunes. The pianist/compere Alec Andrews put him down beautifully. "For the gentleman at the back with more volume than taste," he said, "the band will now play *When the Saints*, though don't be too surprised if it sounds like *Perdido*."

That shut him up.

Our policy, as I had outlined to Kenny Harrison in the dole queue, was to bring down a special guest from London each week, with our resident group in support. The first 'name' player to make the trek was West Indian altoist Joe Harriott, quickly followed by a queue of major

The Jazzmakers live at the original Concorde Club in November 1959, left to right: Ronnie Ross (baritone sax), Keith Christie (trombone), Stan Wasser (bass), Art Ellefson (tenor) and Allan Ganley (drums). For Allan, it was the start of a near-50 year association with the Concorde. And he never missed a beat. Sadly, this wonderful man and great drummer died aged 78 in March 2008. At the Concorde, we looked on him almost as family.

players that read like a Who's Who of British Jazz in the '50s: Tommy Whittle, Vic Ash, Jimmy Skidmore, Ronnie Ross, Kenny Baker, Red Price, Bill Le Sage, Harry Klein, Tubby Hayes, Ronnie Scott, Don Rendell, Benny Green, Eddie Thompson, our old friend Dill Jones, Diz Disley, Betty Smith, Bert Courtley and his wife Kathy Stobart. We all fell in love with Kathy and installed her as the club president.

Don Rendell, one of the all-time great saxophonists, took me on one side after his gig, and talked to me for ages. I was flattered that a jazzman of his stature should show so much interest in me. It was almost as if he was interviewing me, wanting to know all about my family and background. He produced pictures of his family and told me how they had all found true happiness and contentment. It then dawned on me that he was trying to recruit me for the Jehovah's Witnesses! I had been brought up as a Salvationist, but long ago drifted towards being a sort of freelance Christian although I will always have deep respect for all that the Salvation Army do. They really put something back into this world.

The first time we dared book a band rather than a soloist threatened to end in a financial disaster, and believe me I have faced a few cash crises during the 50 years of building the Concorde. As Ronnie Scott once said to me when we were comparing club notes: "Promoting jazz is a very enjoyable way of losing money!"

We decided to bring the Jazzmakers down in November 1959, and had a sell-out crowd waiting to greet them. The impressive line-up was Art Ellefson, Keith Christie, Ronnie Ross,

Stan Wasser, Eddie Harvey and drumming master Allan Ganley, who became a regular visitor to the Club. We felt we had lost a member of the Concorde family when he died in March 2008 at the age of 78. There have been few better drummers, and few nicer human beings.

Half of the band decided to come by train, which got held up by one of those British Rail incidents on the line. The other half chose to drive, and got caught in a standstill jam on the A3 (this was, of course, pre-motorway days). They arrived an hour later than planned, with me reduced to a nervous wreck. But they eventually blew the roof off and gave one of those performances that make your skin tingle.

Tenor king Tubby Hayes was, of course, a great favourite when he used to come to play, but I will always have painful memories of him. I called a cab to take him to Southampton Central following one of his gigs, and after giving me a friendly bear hug he climbed into the taxi and slammed the door ... with my right hand in it. For weeks afterwards my throbbing right hand looked like a bunch of blackened bananas.

My staff at the Concorde are always complaining that they can't read my writing and I tell them to blame Tubby Hayes. I have not been able to hold a pen properly since the taxi incident. That's my story, and I'm sticking to it.

Some of our most memorable evenings in those innocent yet exciting 1950s were when legendary 'Father of British Jazz' Nat Gonella used to drop in to jam with whichever players were appearing. He lived in Southampton and then Gosport in the last decade of his life, and became a regular visitor. Even after having his teeth out in the 1980s and unable to blow that magical trumpet of his, he thrilled the audience with his scat singing.

I have rarely known a performer with such magnetism as Nat. Late in his life he used to come and improvise with the Teddy Layton Quartet in the Moldy Fig, and the second he stepped in front of the microphone the audience would suddenly be in his grasp, hanging on every note as he sang in his Louis-style growl.

Campbell Burnap – trombonist, broadcaster, jazz historian – told me a story that captures just what a major star Nat was in his heyday in the 1930s. "When Nat came to the Concorde to see American clarinettist Kenny Davern, I was in the band and took the opportunity to talk to the great man," Campbell recalled. "I asked him what sort of car he drove during his peak pre-war years. His face lit up and he said, 'Oh, a lovely Alvis Speed 20.' I replied that he must have felt pretty excited going to the showroom to pick up such a beautiful machine. 'Oh no,' he said, 'they delivered it to my West End apartment.' Yes, Mr. Gonella really was a big star!"

I am very proud of the fact that Nat made his final recording at the Concorde Club in 1998 just six months before he died at the age of 90. Even at his advanced age, Nat was still able to swing. Backed by a band of admirers including Kenny Baker, Digby Fairweather, Teddy Layton, Diz Disley, Martin Litton and Jack Fallon, dear old Nat sang his heart out on nine tracks: *I Can't Give You Anything But Love, Shine, Satchmo Blues, Margie, Slow Boat to China, Stormy Weather, Just A Gigolo, Jeepers Creepers* and *When You're Smiling.*

It was all organised by the innovative Dave Bennett, and there was not a soul in the house

We are moving from the Fifties into the Sixties with the world at our feet, left to right front: me, Spike Bamsey, John Edgar Mann, and behind: Kenny Harrison, Ron Andrews (with Ralph Seymour peeping over his shoulder) and my dear old friend Gordon Ricketts. They scattered all over the world, Kenny and Gordon going to Australia and Spike and Ralph to the United States.

who was unmoved by the highly emotional session. We all knew that it would be the master's last stand.

In a way, it completed a circle for me, because, as I have now discovered, it was Nat's solo on the George Formby record that turned me on to jazz. And he went right back to the start of the Concorde, sitting in with Dill Jones for an impromptu session way back in 1957. Also, we once gave him what he described as the "best birthday party of my life." Yes, he is etched into Concorde history.

When they buried Nat in Gosport in 1998 he was given the greatest send-off I have ever seen. It was a New Orleans-style funeral on a grand scale, with just about every major jazz musician in Britain taking part. I must remember to put it in my will that it's the sort of farewell I would like when my time comes. I want to go out to the sounds of the music that has meant so much to me. What Nat once told me should be engraved on the minds of every jazz musician: "Jazz players should make the music into words and 'speak' them on their instrument as they would in conversation, with a pause here, an inflection there, an accentuation here, and so on. Most of all – put some *feeling* into it."

And now you has jazz. He made it seem so easy. There will never be another quite like Nat Gonella.

Now, as the Monty Python team would say, for something completely different ... the swinging Sixties, and the realisation that I had to sell something more than just jazz.

THEY say that if you can remember the Sixties, you weren't there. Well I was there every inch of the way, working all hours at building the Concorde into a club that was buzzing and bursting with music every night of the week. For all of us who were regulars at the Bassett Hotel-based club they were literally the Swinging Sixties.

As the decade dawned there was a sudden shift of musical tastes. Jazz took something of a back seat, with rhythm and blues and rock 'n' roll fighting for the main market place. Little did I know it, but I was about to help give a foundation to the careers of young 'unknowns' who are now legends in their own lifetimes.

My blinkered reluctance to have anything to do with music outside the world of jazz was gradually chipped away by public demand. It was Mike Vickers who first convinced me to open my ears to other than out-and-out jazz musicians.

Mike and another Hampshire lad, Andover-born Mike Hugg, had both been playing jazz at the Concorde since our opening sessions, and they were persuaded to go to London to team up with a chap called Manfred Mann. It was history in the making.

I have never known a young man with as much musical talent as Mike Vickers. His output was prodigious. He had been playing alto sax at the Concorde, a few times with me on the drums. Mike was also a genius on the flute and even in his teens he was an accomplished composer and arranger (some years later both the John Dankworth and Ted Heath bands played his arrangements, as did The Beatles). He arrived forty-five minutes ahead of one gig while Jim Budd and I were setting up the tables and chairs. Before we had everything ready he had written three arrangements for the band to be played that night! One was for a tune he had composed inspired by Prince Charles. Always a witty guy, he called it *Proper Charlie.*

His Quintet included Derek Harris on trumpet and Adrian Lightfoot on trombone and bass. Mike blew such a sweet alto that I was convinced he was going to become one of our great jazzmen. Imagine my surprise when he informed me that he was playing lead guitar rather than a wind instrument with a group called Manfred Mann, named after their South African-born leader.

A little unwillingly I coughed up £30 to feature Manfred Mann at the Concorde in 1962, and their rhythm and blues style went down a storm with our members. They had Manfred on organ, Mike Hugg on drums and vibes, Dave Richmond bass, Mike Vickers playing lead guitar and occasional alto, and actor/singer Paul Jones as vocalist and harmonica player. They were sensational!

It was enough to convince me that I should not close my ears to the R&B revolution, and I started to book bands who specialised in the style of music that was, to me, like a cousin of jazz.

We installed Manfred Mann as the resident band, and in 1963 cameras from Southern Television accompanied the group, using their gig as the background for a documentary on local-lads-made-good Mike Hugg, Mike Vickers and Portsmouth-born Paul Jones. To this day, I have rarely seen as much excitement as generated by the Manfred Mann band. It was Southampton's equivalent of Beatlemania, and – to coin a jazz phrase – *the joint was really jumpin'!* You could not squeeze a cat in let alone swing it, and every inch of the floor was taken. While there was a definite sway towards the commercial music world, they still had a strong jazz foundation in their sessions.

I could see they were going to appeal way beyond domestic boundaries and I promoted them for several concerts at Kimbell's Ballroom in Portsmouth, hugely successful shows that had fans clamouring for tickets. I also staged shows featuring Alex Harvey and Jimmy Powell.

Remember that at this stage I had no grounding whatsoever in business matters, but I was learning quickly and took photographer Reg Harris's advice to "get an accountant." I used Reg's man, Bill Elliott, who got my books in order and saved me from a problem with the taxman.

If there has been a secret to my success (excuse the arrogance), I discovered early on that you needed to cater for all tastes. Going down just the jazz road would have bankrupted me in no time at all. I devoted each day of the week to a different sound. This was a typical week's menu in 1963:

SUNDAY
Manfred Mann-Mike Hugg, rhythm and blues
MONDAY
Gerry Brown's Jazzmen, New Orleans
TUESDAY
Hampshire Jazz Appreciation Society
WEDNESDAY
The Balladeer Club, folk music
THURSDAY
Alexis Korner Blues Incorporated
FRIDAY
Slim Newton Band, rags, stomps and syncopations
SATURDAY
Tony Coe, with our resident band, mainstream

It sounds astonishing now that I once had Robert Plant and the Band of Joy playing at the Concorde for a fee of £30. John Bonham was on drums. This was on March 7 1968, the year that Plant and Bonham became founder members of what was to be the phenomenally successful Led Zeppelin. I will send a copy of this book to Robert to remind him that he owes me two quid. They did not have enough money to pay for their petrol for the drive back home to Birmingham in their beaten up old van, so I lent them two pounds.

Humphrey Lyttelton plays a muted solo as trumpet legend Buck Clayton takes a breather during their 1964 gig at the original Concorde. It set me back a then record fee of £180, but was worth every penny. Note the poster advertising 'open every night.' The graphic artwork was by bassist Ron Andrews.

"You'll get it back, Cole," promised Robert. I have not seen him since.

While jazz remained my number one priority, I had to admit that it was rhythm and blues that was really pulling the people in. As Manfred Mann started to catch on nationally as well as locally it became close to bedlam at the Bassett. We had queues snaking right up the road, and I had to remove many of our tables because so many couples wanted to dance. This was in the days when they danced with each other!

Paul Jones was hugely popular with his singing and jazz-based harmonica playing, and the atmosphere was always sizzling when he was performing within touching distance of his audience. Paul singing *I Got My Mojo Working* to adoring fans just a couple of feet away was about as exciting as it could get, and I remember a similar electric atmosphere when the energetic and exciting Jimmy James and the Vagabonds hit town.

When The Cream played for us in 1966, including Eric Clapton performing wonders on a chrome-plated guitar, Ginger Baker sat at the drums wearing a duffel coat. One brave punter, steaming-hot like the rest of us, asked: "Why are you wearing your duffel coat?" Always in a universe of his own, Ginger replied: "'Cos I'm f****** cold, a***hole!"

Good old Ginger, as ever smart and witty with his choice of words. Noël Coward eat your heart out.

One of my preferred visiting bands was Jimmy Powell and the Dimensions. Could that boy sing! He had a powerful voice that was famously said could "take the paper off the walls." He and Rod Stewart shared vocals for a short while, but Powell blew him away and Rod wisely went solo.

Guitar guru Bert Weedon was a lovely man but had a straight-laced stage presence, and the club was not even a quarter full for his visit in 1960. The few of us there sat around while Bert chatted away between tunes. We were all drinking, and somehow the atmosphere slowly transformed from gig to party! What had started out as a dull evening developed into a great bash, with Bert suddenly coming alive and throwing off his inhibitions. I lost a packet that night, yet I look back on it fondly as one of my most memorable sessions at the Bassett. I think the alcohol may have had something to do with it.

For a time in the mid-60s the splendid Mike Pyne was our resident pianist before London and Ronnie Scott called. Mike didn't drive then, and one night after a gig I offered to take him home to Weymouth. The chariot I had awaiting him was my ancient Morris Oxford, which was just about clapped out. We got as far as the centre of Bournemouth when there was a snapping sound beneath us, and I jammed my foot on the brake. The springs on the bench seat had given up the ghost, and it suddenly and dramatically tilted backwards – leaving Mike and I trapped looking up helplessly at the roof, unable to move. Mike resisted saying: "That's another fine mess you've gotten me into ..." After what seemed ages a passerby helped straighten us up, and – shaken and stirred – we continued on our way to Weymouth, with Mike holding on to the dashboard for dear life. Before I could get back home to Southampton I had to have the seat lashed with rope.

While all the music was going on, romances were blossoming all over the dance floor under dimmer-switch lighting set up by the irreplaceable Jim Budd. Bernie Thomason, a long-time member and our respected insurance broker, reminded me that one of the main lights was a fluorescent purple and it made dancers look as if they had transparent teeth and showed up dandruff on collars and shoulders as if it were snow. "Despite all that," said Bernie, "I fell in love on the dance floor of the Concorde, and Mo and I have now been married forty-something years."

Our wildest party nights at the Bassett were New Year's eve celebrations, when we would go right over the top with our decorations. One year we had huge polystyrene stars hanging from the ceiling, and as our very happy customers staggered off into the New Year they had the stars in tow and were last seen trying to squash them into cars for the journey home.

Another time our friendly landlord Tiny Smith was so envious of our Christmas decorations that the following year he asked Jim and I to put up the same type in his public bar. It consisted of inch rolls of aluminium tinsel which, when unwound on the floor in a bundle and pinned in bunches to the ceiling, gave off a sparkling effect. We put up the last piece and stood back admiring our handiwork, which looked like a glittering grotto from some pantomime. Suddenly the whole thing fused with little sparks all over the ceiling and we realised that someone, while pinning up the tinsel, had pushed a drawing pin into a live wire. The last piece hanging down had swung against a radiator and thereby completed the circuit and the whole ceiling was live-wired. We had plunged the pub into darkness. Merry Christmas, Tiny!

As exciting as the rhythm and blues revolution was, I refused to budge from my jazz-first policy. I recall that there was a thick, pea-souper of a fog the night Tony Coe played for us in 1963, and he managed to finish up in the wrong venue on the other side of town. He was an hour late by the time he followed our directions to the Concorde, but he was forgiven after playing some amazing jazz that explained why Humphrey Lyttelton described him as "a true musical genius with total mastery of all reed instruments."

Tony's fee that night – £10 10s.

I have kept copies of most contracts, and can tell you to the penny what musicians have earned when playing for their supper. I would not dream of revealing what I pay today's musicians, but am happy to talk about the sort of money we spent back in the Bassett days, because it is a reflection of our changing times.

Georgie Fame and the Blue Flames appeared for £45, John Mayall featuring Eric Clapton cost £85, and we got the Alex Welsh Band with guest trombonist Dickie Wells for £115.

The biggest fee I paid out in the 1960s was £180 to Humph when he visited the club with American jazz giants Buck Clayton and Big Joe Turner. I pluckily picked up the bill after the show when we went to eat at the Silhouette club in Southampton run by a colourful character called Brian 'Kiwi' Adamson. Big Joe, the 'Boss of the Blues', showed just how he had got to more than 20 stone by eating enough for a quartet. He was fascinating company, and told us between eating everything in sight how he had started singing for cents on street corners at the age of four after his father had died in a car crash.

One of my biggest shocks in those early days was when Coleman Hawkins came to play for us in 1967. I was a huge fan of 'The Hawk' and was as excited as a little boy at Christmas when I went to collect him from Southampton Central station. In my mind's eye I was going to meet a celebrated giant of American jazz, but when I found him standing on the pavement outside the station he looked a hunched, insignificant little man; more sparrow than hawk.

In one hand he held his tenor saxophone in a soft leather case, and in the other a brown paper bag, which I later found out contained a bottle of whisky.

By the time I poured him back on the train to Waterloo the bottle was empty, and the Hawk was as drunk as a lord. It was so sad to see him in this condition, and a little over a year later he was dead from pneumonia.

Ben Webster, one of the few players to rival Coleman Hawkins as King of the Tenor, was notorious for his wild and mean behaviour when drunk. He once cut up one of Duke Ellington's suits after a drunken argument that led to him leaving the Ellington orchestra.

I knew all about his tinderbox reputation, and treated him carefully and with the respect he deserved when he arrived to play with the Bruce Turner Jump Band in 1965. Everything was

Ben Webster looks in a good mood here with altoist Bruce Turner, but that was after Big Ben fell on me. You could say I had a crush on Webster, one of the all-time great jazz tenorists. Under his shirt, Ben wore a necklace of miniature brandy bottles.

fine, even though I could see him getting gradually loaded with pre-gig drinks. My friend Bob Champion saw him in the Bassett Hotel toilet adjusting a necklace of miniature brandy bottles that he wore under his shirt. This was not a fashion accessory, but vital fuel.

Hefty Ben was fairly unsteady on his feet when I helped him up on stage for the first session. He was at an angle and I had his full weight when suddenly he growled: "What the f***'s that?" He was glaring at one of our members, who had a tape recorder on the table in front of him. Suddenly Big Ben was tumbling back on to me, and it took several members of the band to haul him on to the stage. He refused to play a note until the tape recorder was removed from the room.

Ben gave a moody performance at first, but then revealed the passion and intensity that had made him admired and imitated by jazz tenorists the world over. In fairness to him, I should point out that many jazzmen were being ripped off at the time by secretly taped recordings that sounded as if they had been made in the lavatory.

I could hardly believe that I had managed to persuade the Hawk and Webster to play at my small club. They were true world-class jazz masters, and I was only able to book them because of a new agreement with the Musicians' Union. This allowed Americans to play in the UK in return for an equal number of British musicians getting the go-ahead to perform in the States. The first big temporary swap deal was the Count Basie Orchestra for Ted Heath's Band.

People often ask me what it was like having rock legends such as Elton John, Rod Stewart, Joe Cocker and Eric Clapton 'in the house.' My usual answer is that they were unknown when they played for me; in fact Elton John was still called by his real name Reg Dwight when he played the organ for Long John Baldry's Bluesology band in 1966. I paid them £50, so Reg probably pocketed a tenner that night.

By 1961 the club had 10,000 members, and I hardly had time to breathe as I chased bands to keep everybody entertained. It is a great compliment to the often-denigrated jazzmen (and women) that, in general, I found them more professional, more punctual and more polite than the so-called rock stars. They played longer sets, giving better value for money, and it was very rare for any of them to let me down. There were a lot of occasions when non-jazz bands pulled out at the last minute or arrived very late, and just occasionally didn't show at all. Their arrogance and shoddy behaviour really annoyed me.

I began to go off the R&B bands in the late Sixties as their amplification became more powerful. When they first started they would arrive with their little Marshall amps, and fill the domed ceiling nicely with their sounds. But bands like The Cream (with Eric Clapton and Ginger Baker) and Slade (with Noddy Holder) began to build a wall of loudspeakers at the back of the stage, and they produced enough ear-shattering volume to fill a stadium.

There was an extractor fan in the domed ceiling, but the heat became so intense that the walls ran with rivers of condensation. The water would drip on to the amps and wallpaper would start to peel. I used to wonder if we would all blow up one day.

Among other future legends of the rock world who played for me at fees of less than £50 were Rod Stewart, Alan Price, Shakin' Stevens, and Britain's 'Father of the Blues' Alexis Korner.

Many of them were jazzers at heart, particularly Mike Vickers, Georgie Fame, John Mayall, Mike Hugg, Ginger Baker and Eric Clapton, but they went with the flow of public taste.

It took me longer than I expected to book Alexis Korner for a residency. He was a true purist of the Blues who considered his music an art form. I sent off a letter inviting him to play at the club in the days when he lived in Moscow Court in London. Months later I received a letter with a United States stamp and a Russian stamp. I had apparently managed to leave 'Court' off the address, and the letter had gone to Moscow, then for some odd reason been forwarded to the United States before being finally sent back to me.

I tried to blame it on the fact that Tubby Hayes had trapped my hand in the door of the taxi, but nobody was buying it and I was on the end of a lot of mickey-taking jokes for ages after the story had been printed in the *Echo.*

I did not like the way the music scene was shifting in those early to mid-sixties. As much as I admired what The Beatles achieved, I personally think they did a lot of harm to the musical progress and taste of a lot of youngsters. Suddenly bands with a tenth of their talent were trying to ape them instead of aiming to improve their technique and become more proficient. It really disheartened me to see guitarists, who could barely play three chords, and one-beat drummers suddenly earning more for a single gig than some highly gifted jazz musicians were picking up in a month.

Ringo Starr, for example! I could name a score or more drummers who would play him under the table. But as Dave Brubeck's drum genius Joe Morello once said at a percussion clinic in London: "It is very difficult to tell somebody who has made so much money from playing the drums that he is doing it all wrong!" And John Lennon famously said: "Ringo is not even the best drummer in The Beatles."

One musician who bridged the worlds of jazz and R&B was Graham Bond, who along with John Mayall and Alexis Korner was one of the great catalytic figures of rhythm and blues in the 1960s. I was very fond of Graham, and marvelled at his ability to play the organ and alto saxophone – often at one and the same time. His Graham Bond Organisation, including the likes of Jack Bruce, Dick Heckstall-Smith, Ginger Baker and John McLaughlin, were huge favourites at the Concorde, and they had many enjoyable sessions on the stage and at the bar.

Graham sadly got involved in the drug scene, and started to have huge mood swings as his musical career started to unravel. In our final conversation he was in a manic-depressed state and nothing I could say got near to lifting him out of it. Not long afterwards, aged thirty-seven, he was killed when falling under a London tube train at Finsbury Park. It was generally considered that he had taken his own life. Graham left his alto saxophone at the club after his final gig for us, and it is still being kept in a safe place in respectful memory of a fantastic musician and thoroughly nice bloke who got sucked into the world of silly and dangerous substances.

A brief word here about drugs. I have never taken any and am totally against them. In the Sixties, I was naive enough to think that LSD meant pounds, shillings and pence. I have had reason to ask only one musician to leave the club because I caught him smoking pot on the premises. In all my years in and around the jazz world I have seen it as a problem with only a handful of musicians. It has been much more prevalent in the world of rock. I find good jazz gives me enough of a high without need of artificial assistance. Given the opportunity I would try to talk any of the musicians out of touching the life-destroying substances, but maybe they would come back at me and tell me I drink too much.

One jazz musician who never needed drugs to get high was the wonderful trombonist George Chisholm. He used to have the audience in fits of laughter when deliberately missing his mouth and getting the mouthpiece stuck on the end of his nose, or he would take the slide down so far that it would come off in his hand. George was a born comedian and made a good living as an all-round entertainer, but it was his beautiful trombone tone that set him apart and he could play jazz like an angel.

While we were serious about our jazz at the Concorde, there were many nights when we used to be reduced to helpless laughter. It was Mike Vickers and pianist Pete Gould who started the mad stuff in the early days of the club, trying to outdo each other with their crazy antics. Adrian Lightfoot, playing bass, used to join in, hiding behind the curtains on the stage and playing so that you could only see his hands. Then the whole band would follow him, also playing so that you could only see their hands on the instruments.

It became a competition between the lads to see which of them could come up with the best gag, and Pete Gould was the unofficial champion. He had a girlfriend who was a nurse, and for one gig he arrived in a wheelchair bound up like a mummy and he played the entire set while fully bandaged. Another time he came crawling into the club dressed in rags. Mike Vickers said: "Dr Livingstone, I presume." Pete shook his head, said "no" and crawled back out of the room, leaving us all laughing at his Goonish behaviour.

One Christmas they staged a mock pantomime, playing characters from Robin Hood. We carried a huge stump of a tree in from the garden, which acted as the forest. Some of the things they got up to on that stump would have made Maid Marian blush! It all triggered the idea for what was to become our hugely popular annual charity pantos that have raised lots of laughs and lots of money for deserving causes (see the separate Panto chapter in Part Two).

It was always pure mayhem whenever Gerry Brown and his Jazzmen were in the house. Gerry played a mean trumpet and a lot of crazy pranks. He and his wisecracking trombonist Bobby Fox were the main motivators of a sequence of games that at this distance sound very childish, but which had us all in fits.

To give you a flavour, I will describe just one of the games we used to play at impromptu late-night house parties following gigs at the club. It was called Stay On the Bus. We would arrange rows of chairs two by two as if they were bus seats. The driver, usually Gerry, would take the lone front seat, with a gaggle of 'passengers' behind. He would then mime driving the bus up and down hills, round sharp bends and roundabouts, suddenly stopping at lights or swerving to avoid stray cats, accelerating and then screeching to a halt to avoid crashing. Behind him we passengers, most of us well oiled, had to follow his mimes and commentary, and it would go on and on until everybody had fallen off their chairs. I did tell you it was childish, but great fun.

Here's a photograph bound to bring an instant thirst to original members of the Concorde. This was the bar at the Bassett Hotel-based club, when a pint cost two bob (20p) and there were no breathalysers and you could drink and smoke to your heart's content! Those were the days my friends.

I remember that Pat Masom and her then husband Stan Fry were at the hub of it all, and we used to go back to their home and continue the fun and games while polishing off bottles of cheap Spanish plonk. Pat later became my secretary, and all these years later we still have a laugh at the marvellous memories of what were generally happy times. Pat is rightly proud that her son, Adrian Fry, has developed into a top-flight jazz musician. I can remember him playing as a toddler in the club office. Now he comes to the Concorde and plays a mean trombone.

No doubt about the maddest night at the old Concorde during the Sixties. This involved the world premiere performance by Gutta Percha's Elastic Band. We feature a full report of one of the maddest concerts ever by the band's founder Mike Sadler (aka Gutta Percha) in Part Two.

Mike was a one-off and came up with all his off-the-wall comedy long before the Monty Python team had surfaced. His Elastic Band's appearance at Winchester Prison is part of Concorde legend. In response to a request from the prison chaplain, we took a huge ensemble, including Mike's innovative Elastic Band, to entertain the inmates. He had people like John Mann playing a milk bottle, his sister Christine on triangle and there were paper combs being played, along with kazoos, wooden blocks and shaken matchboxes. It was crazy but effective, and it had our captive audience roaring for more. Jock Lindsell, playing washboard, got one of the biggest cheers by managing to fall off stage during an encore.

I acted as compere, and battled on through muttered demands of, "Get off you big poofter."

As I recall, Shirley Morgan was pouring herself into a beautiful ballad when one of the prisoners in the first row said in a loud stage whisper: "Get your knickers off!"

Shirley disputes my version of the story, and says that the remark was made to another singer, Martine, who used to do a raunchy Eartha Kitt routine. When I reminded Shirley of the visit, she said: "It was a bit embarrassing because when I went out on stage I found that I knew many of the blokes in the audience."

At another prison gig we were well looked after by the trustees and got chatting to them after we had entertained them with light jazz and some standard songs.

While chatting to an inmate afterwards, I innocently asked: "What are you in for?"

"Oh," he said. "I thought you knew. We are all doing time for murder."

As I tried to digest this bit of chilling information, he added as an aside: "But don't worry. We're all harmless. We are all here for murdering our wives!"

We had another giant of jazz visit the Bassett in 1966 in the shape of Sonny Stitt, who played a dream of a saxophone in Charlie Parker style but with his own independent voice. He travelled the world all on his own to such an extent that he earned the nickname Lone Wolf, but he was hardly alone when he arrived at the Bassett. The liner *United States* had berthed in Southampton the night before, and dozens of the crew and passengers swelled the audience to bursting point to listen to one of the masters. Sonny was accompanied by piano/vibes virtuoso Bill Le Sage, who said: "That's the first time I've played in a British jazz club with more Americans in the audience than Brits!"

There was another of our mad nights when the extraordinary one-man American band Jesse Fuller was the star attraction. He played 12-string guitar, harmonica, drums, a self-manufactured foot-operated bass, kazoo, sang and tap-danced ... often all at once!

It was the winter of 1967 and there was a lot of snow about. Reggie Harris, my photographer pal who had generously given me wedding work in the early hard-up days, popped in for one Guinness which became several pints. He was a humorous man bordering on the eccentric, and he used to take off the Middle-East character Ali Oop, who was played on the Tommy Handley wireless show by Horace Percival. His catchphrase was "I go ... I come back," which he always used to say when leaving the room.

Reggie would say this when leaving the club, going out of the door and then immediately returning: "I go ... I come back." People of a certain age will know what I am talking about and are guaranteed to smile.

On this particular evening, Reggie – by now very, very merry, and with his ever-present trilby hat perched on his head – suddenly realised he should be home. He went to leave with his "I go, I come back" routine when he discovered he couldn't open the door. There had been a huge fall of snow and heavy drifts had come down the hill on which the Bassett Hotel stood and blocked the club door. We used muscle power to get it open, and Reggie disappeared into the wild night.

We went back to being mesmerised by the versatile Jesse Fuller, and about an hour had gone by when Reggie's wife, Joy, phoned to ask if her husband had been in. This rang alarm bells because they lived only ten minutes from the club. Jim Budd and I went out to search for Reggie and after a couple of minutes found the outline of a human body in a snow drift. It looked like one of those chalked shapes police make when they find a murdered body.

Jim and I were just about to panic when off in the distance we saw Reggie jumping up and down laughing and then staggering back on his journey home. He had tumbled face first in the snow and had fallen asleep!

Reggie, about twenty years my senior, was one of my favourite of all characters. I was once helping him at a church wedding, where he had been given permission to take photographs during the ceremony. "Whatever you do, don't make a noise while the service is in progress," he ordered. We crept upstairs to a wooden gallery directly above the altar. He left me looking after the tripod camera while he went to the other side to get shots from another angle. Reggie was so noisy as he clumped around the wooden floor that he was drowning out the vicar, who looked up in annoyance as the floorboards creaked under his heavy tread. Just as it was coming to the "if there is any person here who knows of any lawful impediment" bit Reggie looked down on the ceremony, and his trilby hat fell off and floated down in front of the bride.

He even topped this when he was commissioned to photograph an anniversary gathering of an Army regiment out near Middle Wallop in the heart of Hampshire. Reggie, adorned in a velvet smoking jacket and matching hat like you see upper-crust gentlemen wearing in the old silent movies, picked me up in his classic Riley Pathfinder. He was running late and drove so fast round the twisting country lanes that I thought I was going to bring up my breakfast.

I did not realise just what was involved in the photo shoot until we arrived in a clearing at the bottom of a valley where at least 300 soldiers in dress uniform stood on parade, flanked each side by helicopters, jeeps and small tanks. The Commanding Officer, a stereotype Colonel, had obviously spent weeks planning the set up for the photographs.

In a clipped military tone he said: "You only have a short time to take this photo Mr. Harris because at precisely 12 noon three Harriers will come over the rise and that's when I want the photograph to be taken."

There was a hoist which Reggie climbed into with his expensive Rolleiflex camera. As he was lifted into the air for the shoot, the Colonel gave orders into the walkie talkie, the helicopters started to hover, all the men came to attention, the tanks raised their guns and the Colonel barked, "Now, Mr Harris!"

Next came the question: "Did you get that old chap?"

"Uh, not quite' Reggie replied. "I forgot to put the film in the camera."

There were now two more attempts before the arrival of the Harriers over the rise, but both were aborted. First the hoist took Reggie up only for him to discover he had forgotten his release mechanism. Then, the third time, he took the wrong camera up in the hoist. Colonel Blimp's face was going from red to purple.

Finally, as the Harriers approached from over the top of the hill, Reggie got his shot but we were not asked back to the officers' mess for tea as expected.

One of the most amusing and engaging of the jazz musicians who used to play at the

Ronnie Scott was one of the early major stars to appear at the original Concorde, and here he is in 1959 playing at the Bassett Hotel shortly before he opened his own club in London. It was humorist Ronnie who said to me: "We have found an enjoyable way of losing money."

'Jim'll Fix-It' Budd and I are flanking one of the great cornetists 'Wild Bill' Davison, who was never wild with us provided we kept him well supplied with his favourite tipple. He could drink us all under the table. That was until his wife started coming on tour with him, and she made sure he stayed off the hooch. But drunk or sober, he could still play the cornet with the gusto and aggression that lit up those early recordings with Eddie Condon and which earned him the 'Wild' nickname rather than anything to do with his behaviour. He was a regular and much-loved visitor to the Concorde from 1965 right through to the 1980s. That's my old sparring partner Bob Champion with the beard.

Concorde in the early days was Eddie Thompson, a Londoner who was blind at birth and studied piano at the same Wandsworth school as George Shearing. He was an incredible bloke who used to travel the London underground with just his faithful guide dog, Max, and the pair of them would manage to find houses and hotels where Eddie was booked for piano-tuning sessions. When I collected him from Southampton station for his many gigs at the Concorde he would have me in fits of laughter with his latest one-liners. Just a few that I remember ...

"Did you hear about the dead blues singer who didn't wake up this morning?"

"What d'you call the guy who always hangs out with a bunch of jazz musicians? A drummer."

"You are trapped in a lift with the Big Ben Banjo Band and have only one bullet in your gun. What d'you do? Shoot yourself."

Eddie, guided by Max, used to walk on stage and deliberately miss the piano as he pretended to reach for the keys. "Nobody leave the building ... somebody's stolen the piano!" he'd say.

But once the joking was over he could play like a dream. He often used to out-shear Shearing. The fact that he could perfectly imitate so many other pianists such as Art Tatum, Oscar Peterson and Fats Waller, meant that he did not really have a standout style of his own. I would describe him as one of the best all-round jazz pianists I ever heard.

The man who could match Eddie for jokes was, of course, Ronnie Scott, who just before opening his famous Gerard Street (later Frith Street) London club in October 1959 appeared at the Concorde for £25. Ronnie not only played at his club but also acted as a deadpan master of ceremonies, with a joke or pun for every occasion. "While listening to the jazz please order our food," he would say, with a straight face. "You will find it very healthy, untouched by human hand ... the chef's a gorilla. Pygmies travel all the way from Africa just to dip their arrows in the soup. Let's be honest, a million flies can't be wrong."

There were several times when the club almost went bankrupt, and he once told me: "We have hired bouncers to throw customers IN!"

He was a master at word play on the titles of songs. Here is a cross section:

"I'll Be Loving you Sideways ..."

"The Cole Porter classic, Everytime We Say Good Riddance ..."

"Now for my bank manager because he owns both of mine, Body and Soul ..."

"This is sponsored by the curry house next door, Gone With the Wind ..."

"From My Fair Lady, I've Thrown A Custard at Her Face."

I will always have fond memories of a very funny, affable man with whom I had a close affinity because of our clubland adventures. He told me that he got more requests for his old jokes than for any tunes.

Ronnie was a unique entertainer who could easily have made a good living as a stand-up comedian, but most of all he was a superb tenor saxophonist. And he knew how to run a club, which – believe me – is not easy.

Another great personality and a regular visitor to the Concorde for more than forty years is Cuff Billett, a magnificent lead trumpeter with a procession of bands including his latest ensemble, the New Europa Jazz Band, which has been going – or blowing – for the little matter of 37 years without any change in personnel.

For the record, the line-up that has given loads of pleasure on New Orleans nights at the Concorde: Cuff Billett, trumpet and vocals; John Wiseman, trombone; Loz Garfield, clarinet/sax; Cliff Harper, bass; Pete Jackson, drums and Chris Tilley, banjo.

When I told Cuff I was putting this book together, he came up with the following memory of a crazy night at the club back in those Swingin' Sixties:

•I was touring with the Barry Martyn Band in 1964 when featuring two veteran New Orleans legends – Kid Thomas on trumpet and Emmanuel Paul on tenor sax.

One Friday you had booked us for the Bassett Hotel, which incidentally was once owned

This picture was taken the night Dr Ross, 'The Harmonica Boss,' played at the Concorde with the Bob Pearce Blues Band. That's Bob on the left, and I'm the one with the shoulder-length hair on the right! The chap standing at the back with the moustache is Tiny Smith's son, David, and alongside him holding a glass (as always) is Hugh 'Ugh' Collyns, one of my most unforgettable characters who could have been a P.G. Wodehouse creation. The legendary Fergie just gets into the shot.

or managed by my great grandmother in the early part of the century.

Included in Barry's band were Graham Paterson, a somewhat bristly person on piano, and on trombone Pete Dyer, ex-public school and congenitally never wrong.

After we had played a few numbers as a band, our drumming leader Barry Martyn called up the two veteran guests and asked Graham to play the piano in the background as he introduced them. Pete – always right – thought Barry had said *don't* play, and he pulled Graham's hands off the piano keyboard while he was attempting some introduction music.

With his hands being held in the air, Graham lost his rag and he and Pete started struggling, then wrestling and finally rolling around on the bandstand fighting like kids in a playground.

Both well into their sixties, Kid Thomas and Emmanuel Paul came calmly on stage and acknowledged the applause, much of which was aimed at the battling rhythm men!

Kid Thomas, who was pretty eccentric himself, actually stepped over the fighting musicians, seeming to think he was taking part in some sort of vaudeville act.

All this, I might say, taking place with us all done up in dinner jackets. To this day I still laugh at the memory of the faces of the audience, the reaction of our two guests and the fact that we then carried on as if nothing had happened.'

While I am talking great characters, it seems an appropriate place to mention an old friendly rival Bob Champion, who promoted jazz nights at the Dolphin Hotel in Botley and later at the Great Harry pub in Warsash. I had many happy hours with Bob and his charming wife, Andy. Bob was an entertaining, larger than life guy, who was always coming up with money-making schemes. We spent most of our time together swapping bantering insults and anybody hearing us must have thought we hated each other. But most of it was tongue-in-cheek stuff.

He and I got together promoting riverboat shuffles to the Isle of Wight, several of which I played on. Because of a mix-up we once sold 400 tickets for a boat that took a maximum 300 passengers, including the bands. Bob was unperturbed and hurriedly hired a smaller boat that followed on close behind the heaving shuffleboat, with the overflow of passengers straining to hear the music. When we got to Ryde we moved *en masse* into the Castle Hotel, bands as well as passengers. We just about drank the place dry, and I remember little of the homeward trip.

Bob was bankrolled in many of his ventures by an intriguing ex-public schoolboy called Hugh Collyns, known to his many friends on the Southampton jazz circuit as 'Ugh'. He was delightful company, with scores of anecdotes told in an awfully posh voice and with a thesaurus of a vocabulary. He could have stepped out of the pages of a P.G. Wodehouse book, and called everybody either 'Old Chap,' 'Old Bean' or 'My dear old thing.'

I was often in the same jazz haunts as Ugh, Bob Champion and two excellent local musicians, Cliff Harper and John Beirne, who together ran a music shop in Southampton. Cliff was a top-notch bass player, and drummer John was one of the finest tennis coach's in the county. Janie Harper, Cliff's wife, was a fine singer. They were close friends of mine and we used to knock around together. One time I remember going with them all to Ugh's house in Bitterne, where he had my old percussionist pal Kenny Harrison staying as a houseguest. Kenny, now domiciled in Australia, had drummed his way around the world and was always picking up recipes wherever he played. This particular night he challenged us to eat what he described as the hottest curry in the land.

I accepted the challenge, which lasted all of one mouthful. My mouth on fire, I dashed to the kitchen and drank a jug of water. For days afterwards I felt as if I had eaten hot coals. Ugh was the only one who finished his curry, washing it down with lashings of beer.

Ugh was an instantly likeable man who charmed everybody he met on his many visits to the old Concorde, and it was tragic to see him sinking into a depression. Eventually, this fascinating man of many moods took his own life.

As a complete contrast to the jazz and rhythm and blues that were the main attractions of the Concorde, imaginative *Daily Echo* reporter John Mann (known to everybody by his initials JEM) suggested in 1961 that we should have a night for folk music. I handed the responsibility for setting it up to John and his guitarist friend Dave Williams.

In no time at all The Balladeer was an exceptionally popular magnet for folk bands and singers, and it drew good attendances every Wednesday. John ran it in tandem with what was to become one of the most famous of all folk clubs, the Fo'c'sle at the Bay Tree Inn in Southampton. For all his love and knowledge of jazz, John was even more drawn to the folk scene and he booked some of the finest artists in the world, including The Spinners, Pepe Y Dorita, Ewan McColl, Peggy Seeger, Martin Carthy, Bob Davenport and Shirley Collins. He also featured Long John Baldry, who could comfortably cross between folk singing and blues.

There is one Balladeer night of which I have hazy but very happy memories. A lady called Joy Plummer acted as go-between in bringing to the club the crews of two Soviet training ships docked at Southampton. It was supposed to be an educational visit, with them learning about our folk music. They turned up in the back of a lorry, twenty young sailors and the only two among them who spoke English were their Curt Jurgens look-alike captain, and a black-suited commissar representative of the Russian government who could have stepped out of a KGB manual. You have to remember that the Cold War was at zero temperature at this time, with the Cuban crisis on the horizon.

The commissar told me very gravely: "On no account are you to serve any of these young men strong alcoholic drinks."

Our Concorde members had no idea about this restriction and, with good British hospitality, started plying the sailors with pints of best Watneys Red Barrel.

Within an hour of arriving the sailors were performing Cossack dances, and singing traditional Russian songs. They were encouraged by some wonderful British folk music from The Balladeers Dave Williams (guitar), Christine Sadler and Pete Mills (vocals), Vic Wilton (banjo), John Moxham (mandolin) and Gerald Young (accordion).

It was Gerald Young, world champion accordionist, who inspired the Cossack dancing with a highly individual version of the sabre dance. To add to the party atmosphere Dave Williams announced that he and Christine Sadler – sister of Mike Sadler, aka Gutta Percha -– were getting married. The Captain got on stage and toasted them before introducing his singing, dancing sailors, who accompanied themselves on two accordions, a guitar and a trumpet. By club closing time the cadets – including a by now very merry captain – insisted that a few members and I join them back at their main ship. Even the commissar had relaxed sufficiently to have a few drinks, but his all-seeing eye continued to view everything with suspicion.

The jolly cadets danced Cossack style along the middle of the main Southampton roads, and

The Balladeers, left to right: Vic Wilton (banjo), Pete Mills (vocals), John Moxham (mandolin) and Dave Williams (guitar). This picture was provided by Christine Williams, Dave's wife who often sang with the group and is the sister of Mike Slater (aka Gutta Percha). Dave ran the Ballader Club in partnership with Echo *columnist John Mann.*

when we got to their ship they laid out tables on the quayside and treated us to slices of Russian bread and tomatoes, washed down with lashings of vodka. By the time I left the quayside I didn't know whether I was in Southampton or St Petersburg. I have not drunk vodka since.

We all had a great giggle at John Mann's expense when he politely turned down an American artist who asked to appear at The Balladeer singing a selection of his own songs. John felt he could not warrant risking ten pounds of Concorde money on the little-known singer, who went by the name of Paul Simon!

Hands up, I have to admit I am not a great fan of folk music. I was happy to go along with it in the early days, but then the songs became far too political for my taste. I was not the only one who considered they were over-cooking the left wing message.

I started to take Wednesday – Balladeer night – as my one day off a week, and handed the management reins to good old faithful Jim Budd. I needed to take a break from what had become a hectic seven-days-a-week schedule. One afternoon two secret service officers paid me a visit. As it is now more than forty years ago I think I can talk about it without being sent to the Tower. But even at this distance I will not name names. They said they had received reports about the propaganda coming from the mouths of several performers at The Balladeer, and wanted my slant on it. I told them in all honesty that nobody connected with the Concorde had, to my knowledge, deliberately stirred up any anti-Government feelings.

You have to remember the background against which this was all happening. It was not long after the Cuban crisis, and 'Super Spy' Kim Philby had just defected to the Soviet Union. There was quite a bit of 'Reds under the Beds' anxiety, and I have to say that some of the lyrics I heard on the Balladeer nights were more Lenin and Marx than Lennon and McCartney.

I had complete faith in Jim to manage the Balladeer sessions. He had been at my side during the Yellow Dog Club days, and had come back into the family fold after his national service. A very shrewd chap, Jim, as well as being one of the most practical people I have ever known. When he was called up he was desperate to join the Signals, as it suited his engineering mind. So at his interview he told them he wanted to be a cook. He had cracked the Army logic, because he was assigned to the Signals, and spent most of his time in Cyprus learning all the tricks of the trade that were to eventually prove so useful to the Concorde.

He was (and remains) our Jim'll Fixit. No matter what needed doing he would turn his hand to it, and over the years he has developed into a top-flight sound engineer who has the confidence of all the musicians who play at the Concorde. He has retired several times, but makes more comebacks than Frank Sinatra and we are always grateful to have him on call.

A typical example of his ingenuity came when two outstanding disc jockeys, Simon Peterson (aka Foderingham) and Jon Ferris, persuaded me that it would be a good idea to have 'disco nights' at the Concorde. I fought hard against it because I wanted only live music, but again public demand and pure economics forced me to concede.

At first we started on Wednesday nights in place of the Balladeer Club, and it soon became so popular that we added Saturday evening shows, too. It hurt the jazz lover in me, but I had to be realistic and accept that well-presented recorded music was what the large majority of young people in Southampton wanted. Jazz was becoming more and more for the older generation.

To accompany the disco music we needed flashing, revolving lights, something we never thought of organising for the early Concorde jazz nights. Enter Jim, with a cleverly rigged lights system. By using a gramophone table mounted with a light tower that he had built, we quickly had a temporary solution to our problem until we were able to install the real thing.

As disco nights became established, we needed extra help with the DJ-ing and found a young enthusiast in Joe Craen, who told us that he had quite a good collection of 45s he could introduce at the club. I could not believe it when I went to his home to find wall-to-wall records. Never in my life have I seen so many LPs, 45s and 78s in one household. It was like walking into an HMV store. Joe was soon a popular member of the Concorde DJ-ing team.

Meantime, I had gone down the romantic road again and had fallen for Pauline Le Bas, a Concorde member who first helped in the cloakroom and then ran the ticket desk. She took no nonsense on the desk, and once famously ran the local gravedigger out of the club for trying to get in without paying. The gravedigger later became rather well known as Rod Stewart!

Eventually Pauline would become my wife, business partner and mother to Kirstie and Jamie, and she was at my side as we went into the 1970s with a revolutionary and top-secret plan that was frightening the life out of me.

AS the Sixties bridged into the Seventies I was secretly planning the boldest move of my life, and I was feeling petrified! When I first started out as a jazz club promoter I had no long-term visions, and thought I would be in the business for a handful of years at most. It took a long time to dawn on me that what had started out as a hobby was now developing into a way of life.

It was quite chilling when I realised early in 1969 that I had no security of tenure at the Bassett Hotel. I spent lots of time and money developing the old restaurant into the Concorde Club, but had no rights whatsoever and could be tossed out at short notice. I was at the mercy of the brewers Watneys, who owned the hotel.

There was a revolution going on among the major breweries as they started to launch pub/restaurant chains, such as Berni Inns and Schooner Inns. I knew the Concorde would not survive if they decided to convert the Bassett Hotel.

When I confided my fears to my good friend Roland Tucker, he quietly took on the job of finding an alternative venue just in case the Concorde was made homeless. That spring he came back to me very excited by details of a derelict Victorian village school in North Stoneham, Eastleigh. In those days Eastleigh was famous as an old railway workers' town, considered by some Southampton people to be, so to speak, on the wrong side of the tracks.

Roland and I went to see the old school together, and my immediate concern was that it was too remote a location. The building had been standing empty for years and was in a terrible state. It was positioned down a narrow, snaking lane on which two cars could not pass each other, the grounds were overgrown with weeds and tangled plants and it backed on to Monks Brook that flowed into the nearby River Itchen. The prospect of making it work as a jazz club seemed, to my amateur eyes, pretty hopeless. To me, it looked like Miss Haversham's decrepit old mansion in *Great Expectations*.

But while I was seeing all the worst things, Roland – by then developing a reputation as an international design consultant – had the vision for what it could become. He made little sketches and did a quick budget on the back of a matchbox.

The school and the couple of acres of land it stood in was up for sale at £7,250. Where the hell was I going to get my hands on that sort of money? Reading that in the 21st Century it seems laughable, but back in the early 1970s it represented a massive investment and much too rich for my pocket.

All this money for a place that was ramshackle and dilapidated. Back to the drawing board, Roland! I had no great expectations about the place whatsoever.

The Old School House at Eastleigh before the troops moved in. An army of helpers cleared the weeds and the jungle of twisted plants, plus mountains of broken bottles and glasses.

I pushed the thought of the old school from my mind, put Roland's rough plans into a drawer and went back to the Concorde with my fingers crossed that the Bassett would be left untouched by the brewery modernization.

My worst fears were realised late in 1969 when the landlord 'Tiny' Smith was offered a new pub by the brewers because they were going to develop the site as a Schooner Inn. I was given six months' notice.

Now where did I put those old school plans?

Roland and I returned to the school in Stoneham Lane, this time with serious intent. He drew up proper plans, and we decided the minimum we could spend to transform the school into a habitable club was £4,000. Now I had to try to raise a mortgage for £12,000.

Pauline and I went to see a procession of bank managers who looked at the plans, studied photos of the run-down buildings, considered the location and then bluntly told me: "You must be joking." Or words to that effect. The phrase "jazz club" did not exactly fill them with confidence. I recall that the NatWest was the first bank I approached, and their manager told me: "There is no way that a club will work down that obscure country lane." They were words that many years later would cause some amusement at NatWest.

I was feeling disheartened when 'Tiny' Smith threw an obvious suggestion at me: "Why not try your own bank?"

I had been reluctant to go down this route because my branch manager, a Welshman called John Morgan, lived just around the corner to the Bassett Hotel in Butterfield Road. In a mood of pessimism, I convinced myself that he would have opposed any idea of helping to fund a jazz club because of the early complaints we received about the noise levels.

As a last resort I went and saw Mr. Morgan at my local Lloyds branch and gave him my by now well-rehearsed pitch. I was astonished when he agreed to give me the money, repayable over 20 years. He said that as he lived close to the Bassett Hotel he knew just how popular the Concorde was, and that he saw it as a project with very good prospects.

We stayed with Lloyds bank for many many years, but by the time we had come to start some further alterations at the Club John Morgan had left and we moved our account to Williams & Glynn bank, which was taken over by the Royal Bank of Scotland. This was the beginning of a long relationship with the manager Wilf Barton, who was not only our bank manager but became a club member and good friend. He was always there to give me sound advice on money matters.

The early euphoria of getting what I wanted from the bank slowly gave way to a nagging fear about how I was going to repay all that money. In those days, many people went along with the old saying that "mortgages are a millstone around the neck."

We had to keep the project completely secret, because if the news leaked out rival buyers would come rushing for the old school and push up the price. When Roland and I approached Eastleigh Planning Department there had been a queue of potential purchasers for the Old School, but most of them fell by the wayside as they were talking of taking the roof off, knocking down some of the outside walls and generally changing the appearance of the place. But we liked the idea of having it look like an Old School, and we had another piece of luck that the previous occupiers, Prices Bakery, had used it as their Sports and Social Club, so we wouldn't have the problem of 'change of use' as it already had existing use as a club.

Among the potential buyers for the Old School was Ralph Hallett, who lived in a neighbouring house and wanted it to expand his tree surgeon business. He has become a friend as well as a good neighbour over the years, and always jokingly reminds me that I bought the school from under his nose.

While we were negotiating everything in secret, news leaked in an exclusive *Daily Echo* story by Charles Leonard that the brewers were ending the Concorde's life at the Bassett Hotel. All hell broke loose, and our angry members started a lively 'Save the Concorde' campaign. It was *Echo* reporter John Bennett who really got behind the campaign, and hundreds of people joined the protest. Like his colleague John Edgar Mann, John Bennett was a fine show business writer and a great friend and supporter of the club. It would be remiss of me not to mention the debt I owed him in those early days when we were living a day-to-day existence.

I could not let on to all our supporters that we were planning the move to Eastleigh, which

Acker Bilk is dwarfed by 'Tiny' Smith, the Bassett Hotel landlord whose encouragement and advice was so vital to me in the early days. It was Tiny who steered me towards my own bank branch manager when I was struggling to finance the purchase of the new club. Acker has played the old and new Concorde.

in those days would have been considered almost foreign parts by some Southampton people. But I sensed from their reaction to the pending closure of the Bassett-based Concorde that they would be in the mood to follow me to pastures new. The club I was planning – inspired by Roland's imagination – was going to be a huge improvement; or so I hoped!

When I finally revealed the big scheme there was general approval, although some grumbled about the new venue being too far away. Even my close confidant Adrian Lightfoot wondered if I was making a mistake because of the club's distant location. But what pessimists and critics of the move had not taken into account was that there was a bus stop right outside the school, and they had not seemed to realise there had been a quiet revolution on the roads. More and more young men and quite a lot of girls had taken to driving. For disco nights, I planned for ladies to be allowed in free. Where the girls went, the boys were sure to follow.

Watneys helped me with a small loan when they heard my plans. I had no part of the receipts from all the alcohol consumed at the Bassett, but at the new Concorde I could earn from the bar proceeds. That would be vital in my fight to survive.

Now the only problem was to obtain a liquor licence for the premises. Once again the loyal members got behind us and signed a petition to support an application for a new club licence. This gave Adrian Lightfoot perfect fuel when he made an eloquent case for a club licence, and he was able to use the petition to support the argument that there was an army of young people in need of the type of venue we were proposing. You need to know that to get a club licence in those days was tantamount to asking for the keys to debauchery. The traditionalists would shudder and think: "Club? Jazz? Drinking? Dancing? What is the world coming to?" But Adrian saw off all the arguments with his spell-binding delivery, and the case for a licence was won.

I continued to run the Concorde at the Bassett while preparing the old school house for the transfer of the club. Let me go on record and say that I would never have done it without the help of scores of members, who gave up their spare time to work on basic decorations.

The hardest job was clearing up the horrendous mess that had been left behind by the previous tenants. There was an ugly litter of thousands of empty beer and wine bottles and glasses that had been tossed carelessly into the river and were also blocking the toilet areas and carpeting the garden. It seemed like everywhere you looked there were mountains of glass, and we filled dozens of skips in a clearing operation that took weeks. It was dangerous to walk around the place because there was so much broken glass, and my poor old dog Fergie cut his paws many times.

Every day and night we had voluntary workers scurrying around the old school buildings painting, cleaning, polishing, wallpapering, and clearing the jungle-like overgrown grounds. There had been such a slapdash job done previously that we found a dartboard that had been papered over. The final professional paint work became the responsibility of decorator Les Light, who is my cousin, and his colleague Jim Tarrant, and an excellent job they made of it.

We all worked to Roland's plans, and Jim Budd was the main technician while I organised the troops. My younger brother Derek, known to one and all as 'Ginge,' was a dynamo and my

The Old School site (above) before the redevelopment work started, and here I am (right) ready for action. All right, I own up. It was a posed photograph. They would not have been silly enough to let me anywhere near the machine for real. It was claimed that it was specially named just for me. Yes, 'Burke.'

sister Jan pitched in willingly before marrying Derek Jones and moving to Devon.

One day after clearing up the mountains of glass Ginge and I sat in the club garden having a glass of beer. It was then I noticed, looking at the back roof of the school building, some new tiling. I said to my brother: "It looks as though there has been a problem with the roof."

He replied: "No, that was where the old bell tower was."

I asked how he knew, and Ginge said he had watched it being taken down years ago because it was unsafe and that he still had a lot of the bell tower wood in his shed at home. All the time we had been working on the Old School and he never thought of mentioning it!

I am not going down the road of naming names of all those people who so willingly helped because I know I am bound to forget to mention somebody, but suffice to say an army of people were responsible for getting the new Concorde up and running. I probably did least of all, but won praise for keeping everybody supplied with a conveyor belt of beer and sandwiches from the nearby Cricketers Arms.

During our digging and restructuring we came across some out of the ordinary items. Hidden behind a coalbunker we found a vast safe that had belonged to the school. That is still being used to keep club records. Later, we came across large seven-foot-square concrete blocks buried in the grounds that each had a big, rusting iron ring on top. We could not make out what they were for, until a World War Two buff pointed out that they would have been used to tether barrage balloons. They continually gave us huge problems when it came to laying pipes and electrical leads. It was like trying to drill through a mountainside.

Eastleigh, of course, is famous for being the location where R.J. Mitchell first designed and developed the Spitfire, and the original test flights were made from what is now Southampton International Airport, a short hop from the Concorde Club. This could explain why so many people think we named the club after the supersonic jet. We once had a cleaning lady apply for a job, and she was most disappointed to find that we were not looking for somebody to clean the plane!

Another thing we found in the far corner of the overgrown garden was a pair of shoes nailed high on the trunk of a tree. For many years an old traditional gypsy caravan had sat in this area of the grounds. I have been told that it is a gypsy custom to nail a pair of shoes in the same way as a horseshoe, for luck, usually by newly married couples. I decided I would not move them, just in case. I'm not superstitious, of course – touch wood. They were eventually bulldozed away by the M27 link construction men. It wasn't me, honest.

The major building work to the old school involved putting up a mezzanine floor, on which we had the staff offices and the DJ sound system that was linked to a small portable control unit in front of the dance floor. To save space, Roland had designed a narrow, upright spiral staircase, which over the years has had three different locations in the club. Only a handful of approved people were allowed up the staircase, and it began to gather an aura of mystery as to exactly what went on at the top. Members concocted stories about it having a hidden harem for me, and all sorts of crazy notions when in fact it just led to a very cramped working area.

The School as it was originally used. This remarkable photograph was taken from a 1902 postcard when the school was 27 years old. Members study the original in the Moldy Fig, wondering which one of the pupils is me. A couple of staff have seen (imagined?) a ghost of one of the children dressed in Edwardian clothes running through the Moldy Fig, which used to be the headmaster's house. Pauline and I lived there early in our marriage, and were never aware of any uninvited guests.

A true, hilarious story about the staircase. In the spring of 1972 I got a telephone call from a very plummy-voiced woman in Southampton who opened the conversation by saying: "I have a Mr. Charles Mingus booked for a liner cruise, and I need him to earn some money to help us pay for his accommodation the night before the liner sails on its maiden voyage."

"Mr. Charles Mingus?" I said. "I'm afraid I've never heard of him."

"But Mr. Ronnie Scott told me you would be delighted to book him when I rang his Soho office." she said.

It suddenly clicked. "Oh, you mean Charlie Mingus," I said. "He just happens to be the world's greatest jazz bassist."

"Yes, well he will be staying at the Southampton Park Hotel and a fee for playing at your club would pay for his hotel accommodation on the eve of the voyage."

It was a huge honour for the club, and I immediately agreed. It is not every day that somebody comes on the phone offering the services of one of the world's great jazzmen, even though the lady obviously did not have a clue as to his standing in the music world.

On the evening he was due to come to the club I was rushed off my feet, and so Pauline volunteered to collect him in her Ford Prefect. The only instructions I gave her were to look for a huge black man.

She got off to a bad start by going up to a black gentleman in the Park Hotel lounge and saying, "Charles Mingus?"

"No, that ain't him," came a deep voice behind her. "*I'm* Charles Mingus."

Both Charlie and his son were somewhere up around eighteen stone, and what with the bass you could say the two-door Prefect was fairly crowded on the drive to the Concorde.

So now we had Charlie Mingus in our midst and he was smouldering with restrained anger because the gig had been pushed on him. On top of that, he had been kept awake by the banging of construction workers carrying out alterations at the hotel. Just in case you don't know, Mingus was a tortured genius, notorious as the Wild Man of Jazz. He had once crushed his pianist's fingers by dropping the lid on his hands because he did not like what he was playing; and another time he had been charged with assault after punching his trombonist in the mouth.

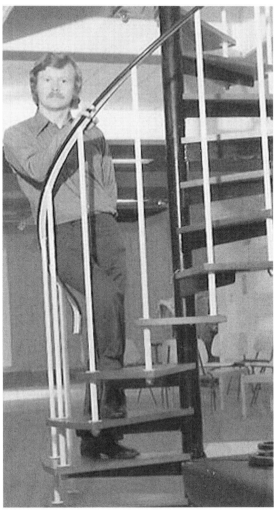

I am at the bottom of the famous spiral staircase on which Charlie Mingus got stuck. Legend had it that I had a harem at the top.

I found him a comfortable man to talk to when he first arrived at the club, but I had lots of aggravation from his son. In his managerial capacity, he talked to me as if I were the enemy rather than somebody in awe of his father and privileged to be showcasing him at my club.

While Charlie was playing the first set with pianist John Foster the plummy-voiced woman appeared at the reception desk saying she had to speak privately to Mingus. I told her the only privacy she would get was in my office at the top of the spiral staircase.

She went up there and waited while Charlie finished the set. I then explained that the woman who had hired him for the cruise was waiting upstairs to speak to him.

When I pointed to the spiral staircase big old Charlie gave a double take and said: "You gotta be joking me, man. There's no way I can get this body up them there stairs."

Foolishly, I persuaded him to try after his son – almost his size, but much more agile – had gone up ahead of him without too much trouble. The next few minutes provided priceless, unintentional comedy.

As he attempted to follow his son, Charlie got stuck halfway up the staircase. In a scene that could have come from a Laurel and Hardy film, he was so jammed that he could not move in either direction. Like the Grand Old Duke of York, he was neither halfway up nor halfway down. Finally, with me pushing from below and his son pulling from above he suddenly popped out, and we got the world's greatest bass player to the mezzanine landing.

I was soon wishing we had failed to get him unstuck. The woman had booked Charlie to play with a tea-dance band aboard the liner, and when it dawned on the shipping company just who Charlie was they told her there was no way he was right for that job. When she informed him that the shipping company was cancelling the cruise gig, Charlie lost his infamous temper. There was a crashing and bashing of things being thrown around my office accompanied by a barrage of shouted insults from Charlie and his obnoxious son. The woman then re-appeared in a distressed state, and left for the comfort and safety of what was no doubt a stately home.

We carefully manoeuvred Charlie down the staircase after he had regained his self-control, but he refused to go back on stage. Fortunately pianist John Foster was able to keep the audience entertained with some fantastic keyboard work.

Finally, a still-sulking Charlie Mingus appeared almost reluctantly alongside John Foster and started to accompany him on a small set of handbells that he carried around with him wrapped in tissue in a cardboard box. It sounded just beautiful and the audience was completely captivated by the mountain of a man who an hour earlier had erupted like a volcano. As music started to soothe the savage breast, Charlie got back into the mood for jazz and for an hour knocked us out with the finest bass playing I have ever heard. It was magical.

Not too long after returning to the States Charlie was confined to a wheelchair by a crippling brain-associated disease and at last doctors were able to fathom why he was a man of such contrasting moods. He had always been subject to huge depressions, and it was all a symptom of his illness. He was unable to play his bass any more but switched full-time to composing and arranging, and there are many who rate him in the Duke Ellington class for writing jazz scores.

I often think of Charlie when I look at our spiral staircase, which now resides in the garden alongside our pond and leading nowhere like a modern sculpture. It stands near a beautiful willow tree that, at the suggestion of my PA Lynne, was planted in memory of one of our most popular staff members, Jo Pearce, who among other things had been responsible for many of our wonderful pantomime costumes. A cancer victim, she was taken from us far too early.

We had bid a very noisy and somewhat emotional farewell to the Bassett on the evening

Alex Welsh (trumpet) plays us in on the opening night at the new Concorde. He is flanked by Roy Williams (trombone) and John Barnes (saxophone). Lennie 'The Loon' Hastings is on the drums.

of July 29 1970, which just happened to co-incide with my 33rd birthday. On what was a memorable and very boozy night we had a free-for-all jam session. Almost every local jazz musician dropped in, and there was a glorious reunion of The Balladeers, who had been such big favourites in the John Mann-run folk club.

Just twenty-one days later, on August 18 1970, the new Concorde Club opened. The Alex Welsh Band blew us in, and members were hanging from the rafters in what were pre-health and safety days when we would often shoehorn people in to give the place atmosphere.

For the record, the line-up of the Alex Welsh band on that historic first night was Alex (trumpet), John Barnes (clarinet and sax), Roy Williams (trombone), Fred Hunt (piano), Jim Douglas (guitar/banjo), Harvey Weston (bass) and that great personality percussionist Lennie Hastings (drums). 'Lennie the Loon' used to often sing his drum breaks.

A week later we had the Maynard Ferguson Big Band in the house, and they nearly lifted the refurbished roof! There was a hilarious incident as the gig was about to start. All the sax and brass section, including Maynard, placed pints of beer beneath their chairs because they knew, as the place was so crowded, they would not be able to get to the bar for re-fills. What none of them realised is that my 'wonder dog' Fergie – named after Maynard – happily lapped away at their drinks while they were pre-occupied getting ready to come on stage. They could not understand why, when they returned to their chairs, they were several mouthfuls short. The musicians were looking at each other accusingly, wondering which of them had been drinking their pints.

Fergie, the dog that is, has gone down in local folklore. A beautiful golden retriever, he was a present to me from Pauline as a sort of four-legged bodyguard. She thought he would be protection when I was closing up late at night. But as he did not have a vicious bone in his body, Fergie was about as threatening as a pussycat. Loved by everybody, he would wander off into the village and invariably come back by bus, getting off at the stop outside.Other times he would come back on board the local fire engine or ambulance, because he got himself adopted at the fire and ambulance stations.

When we started our cabaret nights there was a fine comedian called Ron Martin, who on this particular night was dying a death. He could not raise a titter. Suddenly Fergie came strolling on to the stage and sat down staring at him, as if to say: "Go on, make me laugh." Ron, as a good pro, seized the opportunity to play off him and the audience were soon roaring because Fergie seemed to be deliberately playing the straight man. "Fergie saved my act tonight," Ron told me later. "It was almost as if he knew I needed help."

Fergie was the most intelligent dog I have ever known. He became so popular that on the occasion of one of his birthdays we got an extra-time extension so that we could give him a party. He took his usual position sitting in the middle of the dance floor while everybody danced around him. At midnight they formed a big circle and sang 'Happy Birthday Fergie.' He thought it was time for his cabaret act, and so lay on his back and peed in the air! It reduced his audience to helpless laughter.

He was the first of a long line of Mathieson dogs who have become loved at the Club. Most have been named after jazz legends – Tubby (Hayes), Woody (Herman), Teddy (Wilson) and, the latest addition, Buddy (Rich ... or Holly, according to who tells the story!). We also have Yoshi, Pauline's dog, known to me as Boris (after Boris Karloff). Teddy had been abandoned as a puppy, and it was our membership secretary Jackie Baker who tipped me off that he was looking for a home. Without telling Jackie, I quietly went and collected him. The first Jackie knew of it was when I asked whether she knew where there was a spare lead.

Teddy has replaced Fergie in the hearts of members and musicians. The real Teddy Wilson gave an amazing display of his talent at the club in 1977. He was all elegance at the keyboard and seemed to just glide over the keys.

It was in his honour that we named our dog Teddy, and it has reached the point where that master of stride piano, Neville Dickie, refuses to accept payment from me and waits until Teddy has waddled on stage with his cheque clasped in his soft mouth. Crafty old Teddy knows he will be rewarded with a biscuit from Neville.

Among all the jazzmen Teddy is known as the Chip Inspector, because he gets his nose to their chips. When trumpeter Guy Barker and singer Ian Shaw headlined at the club in the spring of 2008, both were on diets and asked us not to provide chips. Teddy was almost mournful when he wandered into the dressing-room to find them eating salad!

I enjoy an opening night drink with Alex Welsh, who had been a favourite at the old club at the Bassett and gave us a great send off to our new life at Eastleigh in the summer of 1970. Alex toured with some of the greatest jazz musicians in the world, and played at the Concorde with Dickie Wells, Bud Freeman, Rex Stewart and Henry 'Red' Allen. I thought his band got nearest to the tight, controlled rhythm of the top Americans. Alex played in the USA with Earl 'Fatha' Hines and Ruby Braff, and his band boldly crossed the bridge from Dixieland to mainstream, taking a huge following with them.

While we were getting ourselves established in our new home, the manager who had taken over at the Bassett Hotel was convinced he could hang on to many of the members of the old club, but there was a sudden lack of control and discipline. One night the police raided the place and drugs were found.

This really annoyed me because it reflected on my club and all those members whose behaviour over the previous dozen years had been close to impeccable.

One problem we faced when first opening the new Concorde was a lack of proper cooking facilities. We came up with the novel gimmick of serving what we called school dinners, with my Billy Bunter rolls the house speciality. The menu read like this ...

BUNTER SPLITS 14p
(A giant French roll filled with a choice of cold meats)
SCHOOL GARDENER'S LUNCH 12p
(A ploughman's)
HEADMASTER'S DOORSTEP 9p
(Scotch egg)
PREFECT'S DELIGHT 4p
(Sausage on a stick)
PLAYTIME SNACK 9p
(A pork pie)

We served red and white wine at £1 a bottle, by the glass 16p, and a bottle of champagne would set you back £2.

None of us had experience of catering, and Pauline was a self-confessed novice in the kitchen. But she learned quickly and developed into an excellent chef. Our facilities were Neanderthal at the start and the only hot dish we could manage was chips. We craftily got customers queuing for the chips by pouring vinegar into our old boiler, which gave off an aroma that made everybody feel hungry.

Our hungriest customers were the members and guests dancing the night away on our DJ nights, which became enormously popular thanks to the excellent programmes put together by Simon Peterson (aka Foderingham) and Joe Craen. They presented from what were then state of the art facilities including double turntables, a TV monitor and twin microphones.

Between them they ran the very popular Monday night 'Revived 45' night and the Thursday night disco, both of which became huge in the town with queues out through the door and overwhelming our car park, which meant members had to park on the various verges right up to the end of the lane; this didn't please everybody. We gradually extended our car parking to get rid of this problem.

We have since had a procession of DJs, including Jess Pain, Dave Walker, Geoff Bartlett, John Clarke, Stuart Bennett, Gary Evans, Rob Paston, Paul Mico, Steve Phillips, Malcolm Williams, Dave Carson, Chris Golden, Mike Christie and Ian James.

Those early times at the Old School were enormous fun, but there was a lot of worry mixed in with the pleasure. We had to ride lots of storms with all the motorway and road changes that were being planned during our formative years at Stoneham Lane. The M27 from Cadnam down to Portsmouth had been cited on a road originally meant for a trunk road back in 1936. Suddenly there was a petition to move this, and to our consternation we found they were planning a dog-leg in the M27 which would have carried it virtually over the top of the club. This was known as the Lilley Line after Professor Lilley who promoted it. We thought of it as the Silly Line. There was a public enquiry with many objectors including ourselves, and we eventually won our case.

During the various inspections that followed our objections the enquiry inspector visited the club and came to the conclusion that we would lose some of our car park to the upgraded Stoneham Lane, connecting to the original line of the M27. He made the suggestion it might be wise to purchase some land on the other side of Monks Brook. It was some of the best advice I ever received, and I acted on it.

We had a bridge built across the Brook strong enough to take a tank, but only after beating another crisis that almost forced me to give up and get out of the business. This followed a nonsensical legal ruling that could have terminally damaged our club and also nightclubs, bars and entertainment outlets throughout the land.

We were going to be stopped from selling liquor beyond the pub licensing hours unless we had waitress service, and drinks had to be carried to customers sitting at tables. Back in those days pubs closed at 10.30pm, a time when nightclubs were just getting into their stride. This stupid law would have meant an overall loss of more than 200,000 staff and part-time jobs, not including those of musicians who would have struggled to find places to play and earn.

What made it all so maddening was that some police forces were enforcing the new law to the letter, while others were turning a blind eye. Down the road at Southampton they were not taking it seriously, while at Eastleigh the police were insisting on me following the new law. This meant roping off the bar at 10.30pm and instructing thirsty customers to wait at their tables until waitresses had taken their orders and then brought them their drinks. It got to the point where I very nearly threw in the towel after – and this is rare for me – having arguments with my staff over the enforcing of the law. It had all made me very irritable and for one of the few times in my life I wanted to get out of the club world.

The potty plan was finally shelved after the club and entertainment industry turned all their guns on the Establishment. The argument started to swing our way after the Northern clubs pointed out to Harold Wilson's Labour government that members at lots of working men's clubs would go thirsty if the law was allowed to stand. I complained to our local MP David (later Sir David) Price, who added his voice to our protests in a battle we finally won after proving that the Law was an ass.

It reached crisis point when I decided for the one and only time in my life to defy the law. I told my staff to abandon the roping-off process and let customers buy drinks from the bar as usual. I was fully prepared to be prosecuted over it, accepting that it could have meant losing my licence. If it had gone to court, I was ready to make the point that other police forces were disregarding the law.

I took myself off for a holiday, knowing that my club career was in the balance. All these years on I recall the relief I felt when, sunning myself on a beach in Portugal, I read that the ruling had been reversed. I was in the good company of Concorde member Andy Butcher, a loyal old friend and local copper who later became an inspector. The irony was that we learned the idea had been dumped from reading Andy's *Police Gazette*. Also on that trip with Pauline and I were Jill Parker, Richard and Sue Buswell and Mike Bagley. We celebrated heavily that night – with drinks brought to us by a waitress!

Just to add to all the pressures in those early Seventies, we also had a flooding crisis after weeks of heavy rain similar to that hitting the country in 2007. The old car park was under water and for a while it was touch and go whether it would reach the club, but thank goodness the water subsided before any major damage could be caused.

Meantime there was also a huge restructuring of my personal life. After seven years together, I finally got round to asking Pauline to marry me. Her brother, the esteemed solicitor Malcolm Le Bas (who really knows his jazz), gave her away, and my ten-year-old daughter, Fiona, was bridesmaid. For my best man I chose Roland Tucker, who has been such an influential force in the progress of the Concorde Club. As a special wedding gift for Pauline I presented her with a gift-wrapped mangle, one of the large old-fashioned iron jobs – and for some reason she never used it once! It now has pride of place in the Moldy Fig wine bar.

I have to confess to not always being the best behaved of husbands, and there have been times when Pauline has wanted to put me through the mangle. But we have somehow managed to come through the trials and tribulations in one piece. We have survived by generally going our own ways, and finding a balance to our lives that works for both of us. Take it from me, if you want a conventional marriage you should steer clear of the demands and disciplines of running a club.

It is fair to say that a charge of chauvinism against me might just well stick. When our children, first Kirstie and then Jamie, were due, I wanted the date of their arrivals to be dictated by the club calendar. I pointed out that it would make life difficult if they were born on the same day as our jazz nights. Pauline was not best pleased, and gives her version of events in the Family Affairs section in Part Two.

By the mid-seventies Pauline was my partner in both marriage and the club business, and in the early days we lived in what used to be the headmaster's house – now the Moldy Fig. This was not as convenient and as comfortable as it sounds because it meant the club was with us twenty-four hours a day. Despite all the strains and stresses, Pauline has managed to keep the books and (much of the time) me in a well-ordered state.

It was during the 1970s that we started getting involved in charity work. We staged country fairs in the field opposite the club (including an annual Grand Nurdling contest), magical mystery tour walks through the Forest and, of course, our annual pantomime, to which we dedicate a chapter later in the book. Everything was designed to having fun while helping

It is just registering with Pauline and I that we are married, for better or worse. Pauline could produce evidence that sometimes I've made it for the worse. My advice if you want a conventional marriage is don't take on the responsibility of running a club like the Concorde.

others less fortunate. I never cease to be amazed at the generosity of our members, who time and again stump up money for worthy causes. The club has raised thousands of pounds to improve the lives of old folk, to purchase mini-buses for the handicapped and to help generate money to buy guide dogs for the blind, for cancer research, and boost other local and national charities. But, mostly, we have concentrated on raising money for children's charities. I am so proud of the big heart that beats at The Concorde.

I am letting others give you their pantomime memories, but two stick out in my memory for contrasting reasons. When Jamie was a youngster in short trousers I used to take him along to our panto rehearsals, not realising that he was absorbing what was some comical but crude adult humour. Pauline and I recognised that we needed to have a quiet word with him when one morrning – after watching a *Snow White and the Seven Dwarfs* rehearsal – he skipped happily off to school singing: "Hi Ho Hi Ho - it's off to work we go ... Just you and me and a packet of three ... Hi Ho Hi Ho!"

The other memory I have to record was when we used to make it exclusive for local old folk rather than a pay-to-watch charity show. We used to send a coach to collect the senior citizens, then feed them and entertain them before putting them back on their coaches.

There was one particular year when we found we were one short in a coach preparing to leave the Concorde. When we looked for the elderly lady we found her, so we thought, fast asleep in her seat facing the stage. Sadly, we found she was not asleep but had passed away.

Quickly moving on ... This was a typical week's entertainment at The Concorde during the early 1970s:

SUNDAY
Shakin' Stevens and the Sunsets
MONDAY
Sweet Sounds, disco with Simon Peterson and Joe Craen
TUESDAY
Jazz workshop, with Bill Le Sage
WEDNESDAY
Jess Pain, DJ presenting progressive disco
THURSDAY
Country and Western
FRIDAY
George Melly, with John Chilton's Feetwarmers
SATURDAY
The Simon and Joe Show, disco

That Thursday date – Country and Western – jumps out and hits me in the eye like a hot flame. I can remember only two times having my defences down sufficiently to allow Country and Western music under the door and into the club. When I went to the doctor's recently I

What the Concorde ladies were wearing in the 70s. Left to right: Pat Fry (now Masom, who was my secretary), with her sister, Margaret, 'Baby Jill' Waters and her best friend Lynette.

used the old Buddy Rich line when asked if I was allergic to anything: "Only Country and Western music." I dislike it, and am almost ashamed that I actually booked Country and Western bands. This followed the request from a member whom I will not name and shame, but just a clue for regulars at the club: He is fond of wearing white shoes!

There was one Country and Western singer I remember interviewing when he came down from London for an audition. He told me in a strong Cockney accent: "I give the audience wot they want, mate, plenty of hey diddle diddle (fiddle) and the old banjo."

Alan Ball was a popular visitor to the Concorde over many years, and he had his own corner of the bar where he used to hold court. He was always ready to help us with any of our charity projects. Here he is handing over the keys of one of our mini-buses, accompanied by Gill Jeffery, fresh from her triumph as Fanny in Dick Whittington.

A few minutes later he went on stage and started talking into the microphone with a deep Yankee accent and shouting 'Yee-haaa.' It wasn't long before I told him to yee-haaa off.

Jazz remained my personal first love along with a growing appreciation of opera and the classics (I am very proud of my daughter Kirstie, a trained opera singer with the voice of an angel ... but occasionally the bite of a Rotweiler!). It was with reluctance that I allowed jazz to take something of a back seat to the music that the younger generation wanted. The young boy who had started out blindly on a jazz journey in 1957 had grown up as reality of the real world struck home. With so many pressing overheads, I needed to make The Concorde a serious business venture and I no longer looked on 'commercial' as being a dirty word.

For instance, I never in my life thought I would ever book a band called Screaming Lord Sutch and the Savages. Sutch, of course, was not a real Lord but a master at self-publicity, as he proved with the fame of his Monster Raving Looney political party. He started his act by rising out of a coffin, and when I heard him sing I thought that if there were many more about like him he could use the coffin to bury music. Talking to him later, I found him a charming bloke but lost in a world of fantasy. One of his electioneering ideas that appealed to me was that he would have a Wurlitzer organ installed in the House of Commons to liven things up a bit. As you will learn from Andy Butcher in Part Two, that was the night Screaming Lord Sutch nearly gave me a heart attack. Let's just say as a tease that I felt the club was being stripped of its dignity.

I hired out the club for a David Essex record launch, and Mud used it to release their 'Dynamite' disc in 1973. I was particularly impressed by David Essex, who was not only a nice guy but a singer who could easily have adapted to the jazz world.

One worrying time I remember came in the winter of 1974 when the Government were battling with the miners, and a three-day week was introduced. We tried to get by using candlelight, which a lot of the members thought nicely romantic but love did not power the amplifiers. It was good old Jim'll Fix-It Budd who came up with an inventive solution to the problem as the power cuts started to bring the country to a standstill.

He brought in a DC/AC converter, and lined up the cars of staff and members facing the club. He had rows of wires running off car batteries, and at the moment we got hit by a power cut he would give the signal for everybody to rev up their engines. This fed energy into a generator he had installed, which in turn switched on pigmy lights that he had set up around the club, and his ingenious system kept the vital PA system working. Don't ask me for fine detail how he made it work. Only Jim could answer that. When the energy crisis turned into a long-term problem, Jim set up a proper generator. He is a miracle man in moments of crisis.

There was an occasion I almost caused Jim a serious injury, which at one and the same time was a scary yet hilarious moment. He was trying to set up a structure so that we could lower the lighting on a frame that hung down from the ceiling by chains. I was doing my bit by holding the ladder on which he was precariously perched. He asked from way above my head how it looked, and I dozily walked away from the ladder to get a panoramic view. This left the ladder unattended and Jim swayed back and forth as he reached for what was suddenly a moving, tilting frame. He threw a few panic-filled curses in my direction as I dashed back and controlled the ladder. Moments later and he would have crashed heavily to the ground.

We surpassed this a few years later when we both finished in the pond while trying to do bridge repairs. I will leave it to a grassing member of staff to tell the story in Part Two.

It was the early 70s when we launched a Christmas idea that grew hugely popular. We started out calling it the Christmas Eve Lunchtime Jazz Event, and the first band featured was 'Some like it Hot' led by Dave Davis. The line-up was made up mostly of locals, such as Tony Hurst, Dave Arlot, Chris Walker, Dave Meggeson, John Whatmough and many others. Gradually, this ensemble morphed into 'Santa's Jazzband,' still led by Dave and including in recent years several members of Chris Barber's band.

Musicians used to just descend on us, and others I recall sitting in included Pete Newton, Mike Blakesey, Colin Collins, Ray and Alvern Ember, Roy White, Butch Holden, Tony

Carter, Bob Hunt, Adrian Fry, Brian Barker, Tony Day and, of course, Shirley Morgan.

Every year it became busier, and I used to take our then kids Kirstie and Jamie along. This led to members asking if they could bring their children, and I said they were perfectly welcome. It had now blossomed into a full-scale Christmas party, mostly with the kids in mind, and our then meeter-and-seater John Bonnet used to dress up as Santa Claus, with a goodies-filled sack that he carried across the lawn to the Musicians Bar set up as a grotto. Club members Johnny Johnson and his wife Maisie, who had a chalk and crayon factory, provided packs of crayon and other members pitched in with small gifts for the children.

It had now grown into something of a monster, and I was not sure if it was legal under our licence. It reached the point where we had what seemed like hundreds of children running everywhere, including over the stage and scrambling around the piano. Members not only brought their kids but the neighbours' kids too! I became almost frantic with worry in case one of them fell into the brook. Health and Safety now rules, and you need to be careful at every turn or they come down on you like a ton of bricks. In the end I had to become Scrooge-like (bah humbug) and banned children from the event.

It is still as good a Christmas Party as you could ever wish for … even though it's now just for the grown-ups.

In 1976 I took the decision to switch the main jazz night from Friday to Wednesday. This, I knew, suited the audience I was after, and there were better chances of getting the top players who were usually booked for weekend gigs in London. It was the start of me putting the club back in business as a major attraction for the top jazzmen.

There was an aggravation that we all had to get used to in 1973 when Value Added Tax was introduced, first at a rate of 10%. Thank goodness I had good accountants to guide me through the minefield of VAT, but a lot of musicians got in a terrible tangle with it. Acker Bilk was the first musician who had to give me a VAT invoice. His fee was £125, plus the new ten per cent tax. Acker was not best pleased, and if he could have got his hands on the Chancellor he could have become a Strangler on the Shore. Sorry.

The biggest fee I handed out in the 1970s was £900 for the 'World's Greatest Jazz Band.' It was an over-the-top title but the music the veterans produced was almost as good as it gets. This was the line-up of the band that gave the Concorde one of its most memorable nights in October 1974 (and again with a return show a year later): Bud Freeman (tenor), Bob Wilber (clarinet, soprano), Yank Lawson (trumpet), Billy Butterfield (trumpet), Bennie Morton (trombone), Sonny Russo (trombone), Dick Wellstood (piano), Bobby Haggart (bass), Gus Johnson Jnr (drums), Maxine Sullivan (vocalist). They produced some sensational sounds. This was the night Yank Lawson threatened to walk out on the band mid-gig, a dramatic story that I will let my good friend and music agent Brian Peerless tell in Part Two.

We staged regular jazz workshops on Tuesday nights, a magnet for local musicians wanting to learn from the masters. Joe Harriott, one of the first major players to appear at the old Concorde, later settled down to live in Southampton and came to Stoneham Lane in 1971 to give an insight into his ground-breaking 'free, abstract' jazz, much of which – I have

The Concorde football team, 1978-79: Back row: Mike Ward, Clive Butcher, Ian Waight, Mick Cass, Mike Goddard, Chris Biddlecombe, Pete Gurd; Front row: Steve Colmer, Tosh Goddard, Peter Campbell, Derek Manser, Barry Driscoll, Colin Masters.

to be honest – went right over my head. I remember being shocked by Joe's appearance. He had been the epitome of 'cool' when playing for us a few years earlier, but was now looking drawn and emaciated. A little over a year later he died of cancer, and is buried in Bitterne churchyard in Southampton. On his gravestone, his own much-quoted words provide his epitaph: "Charlie Parker? There's them over here can play a few aces too." Joe was just 44.

When he moved down to Southampton Jamaica-born Joe was befriended by one of the Concorde's greatest musical servants, Teddy Layton. I know for a fact that big-hearted Teddy and his wife, Marilyn, helped Joe out in his last years when he was near penniless and unable to get much-needed work because his jazz was too far out for most ears.

While on his deathbed, Joe presented his alto to Teddy. It was the last thing of any value that he had left. Teddy, who knew a thing or three about playing the saxophone, could never tell me the story without getting choked up. Pete King, Ronnie Scott's partner, took the alto from Teddy and he thought he was never going to see it again. But a few weeks later it was presented back to him completely refurbished. It was Pete King's personal gesture to keep alive the memory of a one-off talent.

As I put these recollections down on paper more then thirty years later the music of Joe Harriott is being re-discovered, and he is being given long overdue recognition for having been light-years ahead of his time with his pioneering jazz.

I visited Joe's grave in spring 2008 and found it carpeted with bluebells. It looked beautiful, and I got the sense that Joe was getting the rest he deserved.

The biggest day for the people of Southampton in the Seventies was May 1 1976. That was when the Saints beat Manchester United 1-0 at Wembley to win the FA Cup. The celebrations at the Concorde went on for days, and for long after that we welcomed any players at our club like the heroes they were.

Manager Lawrie McMenemy (occasionally with his wife, Anne) and many players were regular visitors, including Peter Shilton, Alan Ball, Kevin Keegan, Hughie Fisher, Peter Osgood and Mick Channon.

Kevin Keegan famously turned up one night only to find himself barred from entering until he showed his honorary membership card to our receptionist Joan Tucker. Good girl, she was doing her job. I could hardly tick her off because as anybody who knows me well will confirm, I don't know one side of a football from the other. A true story about me is that Peter Shilton once arrived at the club with the then England and Manchester United captain Bryan Robson in tow. I was standing next to Robson at the bar, and asked: "So what do you do for a living?"

I suppose it's what you would call a spectacular own goal.

Our procession of receptionists have done a great job, and are always the friendly welcoming face of the club. But don't mess with them! I remember one of our early 'desk dollies' was Jan White, a quite short lady who could become a big barrier if anybody tried to trick their way past her. She was a real Tartar and earned the nickname Poisoned Dwarf. But she was brilliant at her job.

It was Pat Sparling who set the highest standards. She was really formidable if there was a problem with an improperly dressed or inebriated visitor, and could put people in their place with just a look. You did not need bouncers (sorry, door supervisors) when Pat was around. She had a photographic memory, and knew every face and every name of all the regulars. This was long before the television comedy *Cheers* made the claim of being 'the place where everyone knows your name.'

Trouble is that I – the proprietor – am the worst person in the world for names, but the receptionists never let me down. Rushing across my memory screen are the likes of Elaine Tanner, Pat Masom, Jo Pearce, Joan Tucker, Nicky Marsh, Lyn Marsh, Gail Jenkins, Kari Roberts, Gill Jeffery, Jill Butcher, Jackie Baker and the two Lesleys, who are fondly remembered in an imaginative contribution from Lesley Bridson in Part Two. My present PA and right hand, Lynne Wicks, also did a tour of duty at the desk.

Our receptionists were on first-name terms with many of the Southampton footballers who used to regularly drop in after matches. Lawrie McMenemy, who has become a firm friend, told me while Saints manager in the days of The Dell: "I don't mind the lads coming here for a drink, but don't encourage them if it's the day before a match! If they ever step out of line, just tell me. I'll sort it."

At every opportunity Lawrie reminds me that it was he who put me back in touch with Georgie Fame after we had lost contact. They had got talking at a party and found themselves discussing jazz. My name came up, and Georgie gave Lawrie his phone number for me to call him to arrange a gig at the Concorde. He then got back to playing a regular date with us.

There were several occasions when I had to pour Lawrie's Saints players into taxis, but nothing that we could not handle. There were only rare times when I had to ask Lawrie to have a quiet word with a couple of his players about their boisterous behaviour. Dropping trousers on the dance floor is not the done thing at the Concorde, unless you are in the panto!

We used to have what we called Alan Ball's corner, where the little man would hold court. His big love away from football was horse racing, and he and top trainer Mick Channon offered me a leg of a syndicate horse, but to my lasting regret I turned it down.

Peter Osgood was one of my favourites. He was such a likeable man, and during one of his many visits to the Concorde he confirmed a story that is almost impossible to believe.

After the banquet in London that followed their sensational 1976 victory, the club some-how managed to put the treasured trophy in the keeping of the old King of the King's Road (Ossie's title when he starred at Stamford Bridge).

He had plenty of partying experience at Chelsea to call on, and was leading the celebra-tions when suddenly entrusted with the job of making sure the FA Cup got back safely to Southampton. It was like putting the Titanic entertainments officer in charge of the QEII.

So it was that at three o'clock on the morning after the final a seriously sozzled Ossie was showing off the FA Cup to astonished Saints supporters having a coffee at a mobile snackbar on the A3. Then, as you do, Ossie took the Cup home and slept with it! "It was the best way of looking after it and keeping it safe," Ossie later told me with the sort of logic that made sense only to him. What a character.

The activities of the club took off in all directions, with members forming football teams (having great success in the Southampton Inter-Office League), and the ladies started a netball team. There had been football teams associated with the club from back in 1968, but it was 1979-80 when it was generally agreed the Concorde Football Club came of age. A new ground was secured opposite the club in Stoneham Lane, and Brian Kingsnorth, Barry Driscoll and Mike Ward were the early motivating forces, with me – famously not knowing an overlap from an underpass – voted in as President, and Pauline as treasurer.

There were now clubs within the club and as we entered the 1980s the Concorde was well established as a leading social centre as well as one of the finest jazz clubs outside London.

IT was a real coming of age for us as we bounced into the 1980s with a modern new look to mark 21 years of the Concorde Club. I now had confidence in myself as a businessman, with clear targets for what I wanted to achieve. Goodness knows how it happened, but I had morphed into an energetic entrepreneur and unrecognisable from the shy lad who had started out at the Bassett Hotel all those years before.

There is no way I can take all the credit. As we became established, I got an excellent management team around me. Pauline was brilliant at bookkeeping, Jackie Baker an astute and industrious membership secretary, David Ophaus an executive chef second to none and, a real key to the success, the arrival of Lynne Wicks as my PA.

We had been soldiering on with a part-time staff stretched almost to breaking point. The workload was enormous, but as the club grew so I realized that I had to get a professional and efficient team together. Simon Foderingham brought his energy and inventive mind to the project, and Lynne got to work dragging the office set-up into the twentieth century. When she took the job as my right-hand woman we were toiling on typewriters, had an almost non-existent records department and were poorly organized. But she gradually helped turn us into a highly efficient unit fit for the big plans we had for the future.

Her predecessor Pat Masom, formerly Fry, had done a magnificent job, but was always part-time in a post that required total commitment. You could almost see the sparks flying as Lynne took the controls.

It was this team that laid the foundations to the Concorde becoming much more than just a jazz club, and I know that Fiona, Kirstie and Jamie appreciated all that they had done by the time they eventually joined the company in their various roles.

Full of confidence as we moved through the Eighties, we carried out refurbishments that cost more than £100,000. We doubled the size of the dining area, improved the dance floor and stage, installed air conditioning throughout and a central heating system. Roland Tucker's imaginative designs also gave us a third drinking area in what we called the Musicians Bar, and which – after more changes later in the decade – became the Moldy Fig. Roland's design work so impressed Ronnie Scott that he was commissioned to install a near replica of our main bar in Ronnie's famous London jazz club.

We added a new sound system. masterminded by Jim Budd, that had a mix of up to twelve microphones in perfect high-fidelity that would please any listener's ear, and which made our visiting musicians purr with pleasure at the vastly improved acoustics.

There were also extensions to the completely refitted kitchen, and we had plans for a larger car parking area. For extra atmosphere we added railway station and platform signs as a mark

The Waiter, the Porter and the Upstairs Maid, featuring the one and only Teddy Layton, me and the delightful Anne Latham during one of our pre-Christmas parties. Anne was a popular singer in the Moldy Fig. The picture comes from the collection of her husband Phil, a regular Wednesday night jazz disciple at the Concorde.

of the history of Eastleigh as a traditional railway workers' town.

The Musicians Bar has always, fittingly, had the best resident musicians playing in it, starting in 1981 with the Teddy Layton Quartet, later adding the delicious Anne Latham as vocalist.

There have been a procession of players who became part of the fixtures and fittings in the Bar. They include the Alan Duddington Trio, Dave Lewin Trio, Chris Walker and Dave Shepherd, the loyal and lovely Shirley Morgan with Tony Day on the keyboard, and, of course, solo performances from Roger on the piano.

Teddy Layton was a treasured friend of mine as well as being a top-flight reedman, and he often used to invite me to play along with him. We were both fans of the Nicholas Brothers, and even took tap-dancing lessons to try to emulate them. No chance! We had some fun trios with Anne Latham in the Moldy Fig, featuring among other songs the Bing Crosby numbers *The Waiter, the Porter and the Upstairs Maid* and *Busy Doin' Nothin'*.

I have tried hard not to turn this into a list-of-names book, but in honour of Teddy I want to nod in the direction of the guest players and singers who appeared with his regular quartet of himself, Ray Ember, Arthur Ward, Alan Duddington, and Anne Latham on vocals. This list of just some of the musicians who guested might light up a memory for you of those marvellous sessions with Teddy:

Ron Andrews, Ray Baugh, Jim Byrne, Cuff Billett, Mike Blakesley, Derek Butterworth, Al Casey, Terry Cole, Colin Collins, Tony Carter, Andy Cooper, John Coverdale, Dave Cutler, Andy Daniels, Claire Davis, Dave Davis, Tony Day, Andy Dickens, Rick Foot, Adrian Fry, Nat Gonella, Stan Greig, Don Hardiman, Kenny Harrison, Spike Heatley, Butch Holden, Ronnie Horler, Mike Hutton, Gill Langford, Rick Laughlin, Cole Mathieson (!), John Marshall, Peter Maxfield, Alan Melly, Paul Morgan, Shirley Morgan, Dave Newton, Brett Nevill, Ken Nutley, Keith Papworth, Butch Pearce, Ron Poole, Bill Pritchard, Sarah Pritchard, Malcolm Saul, John Seaman, Ray Shay, Tam Smart, Don Speitch, Paul Styles, Dennis Taylor, Mike Treend, Bill Mudge, Bobby Wellins, Monty Worlock. And, of course, Paul Francis and Andy Stansfield are pianists who have followed the unique Ray Ember. Dave Lewin's Trio with Colin Bryant, Rex Dorman and regular guest Alan Melly are also established as 'Fig' favourites.

You may wonder how I can conjure up so many names from the past when there are times I cannot even remember my own name. It's all thanks to Maureen Chapman and her incredible archives. Without her research work, I would be lost. Please give her all the credit for the correct facts in this book, and blame me for the wrong ones! Maureen used to work for the Inland Revenue and pays enormous attention to detail. She has produced two vast volumes of the names of most musicians who have played at the Concorde. These are cross referenced to dates that they appeared; plus she has collated every major (and often minor) fact about the club into large year-by-year, decade-by-decade files that threaten you with a hernia whenever you try to lift them. There is just a taste of her collection at the back end of the book. It is a remarkable work of research by a good friend who knows and loves her jazz. Thank you Maureen.

Right from the earliest days of the Stoneham Lane club I have had to take a lot of jocular stick for insisting on a strict dress code that bars the wearing of jeans, trainers, earrings (by gentlemen) and casual clothes that belong on the beach. It has all been about standards, and I have always wanted our members to be as proud as me to walk into a club that hugs them like an old friend and gives them a feeling of comfort and yet at the same time is smart and elegant. So I will continue to ignore all those jokes about me being like Basil Fawlty, with his "no riff-raff" policy. I could, I suppose, be persuaded to change the no-earrings policy. But when I introduced the rule it was during an era when men wearing earrings were invariably the trouble-making sort.

The Mayor and Mayoress of Eastleigh, Councillor and Mrs Pat Halifax, were guests of honour at our opening of the modernised club on February 19 1980, when we celebrated both our tenth anniversary at Stoneham Lane and 21 years of the Concorde. Humphrey Lyttelton played us into the new era and reminded the audience that I had first booked him in 1964 for what he called "a pub gig for pennies." Back in those days I had paid him £165, much of which went into the pocket of his guest trumpeter Buck Clayton. By 1980 the fee had gone up, and Humph was worth every penny.

With my new confidence and the full support of the wonderfully organised Pauline, I was determined to go back to my original plan of attracting the top jazz musicians to the club. I don't think I am going over the top with my opinion that during the Eighties we matched any jazz club in the country – possibly the world – with our line-up of international stars.

I have been warned by family and friends not to make this a book just about jazz, but it is my first love and the subject that I know most about. If I am boring you, I apologise. To be able to sign up so many heroes of mine to play at the club has been the most satisfying thing of all about running a business that has become bigger than I ever imagined.

Among the most eagerly awaited sessions of the 80s was the appearance of Benny Carter, one of the unquestioned kings of jazz who was a multi-instrumentalist and respected composer and arranger. Naturally we were completely sold out well in advance, and there was an excited air of anticipation about his visit. As with Ben Webster, some musicians had a phobia about being unofficially recorded at clubs but, of course, now that had long gone, to be replaced by a fear of being filmed by video camera.

I don't think Benny Carter himself had a problem with this, but my friend, John Beirne, turned up with a very early black and white video camera to record his visit just for posterity. It was not as if the quality of those early videos could ever have been used for commercial purposes. The music on the night was absolutely sensational, but I fell out with the featured singer Elaine Delmar who – spotting John using his camera – took me to task in the middle of one of Benny's fantastic solos. I was really annoyed by her interference and the manner in which she voiced her opinion. It was a major falling out and I didn't book Elaine for another eleven years. We have kissed and made up, but it spoiled that great Benny Carter night for me.

One of the best of a myriad of memories is of the night the Preservation Hall Jazz Band from New Orleans paraded at the Concorde. They came through the audience playing as if marching down South Rampart Street, and they blew us all away despite an average age of 70-plus. The band was led by the two Humphrey brothers, Percy, aged 75, on trumpet, and older brother Willie on clarinet, and still able to kick up a storm at the age of 80.

The seven members of the band had nearly 500 years playing experience between them, and they rekindled my original love for the New Orleans jazz sounds that first captured my heart as a thirteen-year-old schoolboy. On a visit some years later to the birthplace of jazz they were kind enough to make me an Honorary Citizen of New Orleans because of the small part I had played in keeping the flame alight on our side of the pond. That was something really special to me.

Adrian Lightfoot, my close buddy and a brilliant solicitor, who followed his father in always giving me the best possible advice. He was made to feel like Perry Mason in New Orleans.

I was accompanied on the trip by Adrian Lightfoot, not only my solicitor but a life-long friend. He was a trombonist and bassist of note, but in New Orleans he was given the red carpet treatment for his role as a solicitor. My dear friend Ronnie Kole, the magnificent pianist-entertainer who has often charmed us at the Concorde with his artistry and anecdotes, opened the doors for us. He is an influential force in the government of Louisiana, and he made sure that Adrian and I got the full VIP treatment.

Adrian had mentioned he would like to see some of how the legal system worked in Louisiana and Ronnie arranged for us to look around the Louisiana Appeal Court. Having shown us all their state-of-the-art computers we were then ushered into the main courtroom where a case was just about to be introduced by the lawyer who had defended Jack Ruby (the man who shot Lee

Harvey Oswald). Then the chief judge held up his hand and said: "I would like to interrupt you for one moment to introduce two important visitors – one who runs a jazz club and is keeping New Orleans music alive in Europe, and the other a top solicitor in the UK." The judge, talking in that inimitable Louisiana drawl, told the court: "Now gen'lemen, when I say he's a solicitor it has nothing to do with what we would call soliciting here in the US of A. No, he is a noted lawyer and we are proud to have him watching United States justice at work. Please welcome from England Mr. Cole Mathieson, and the esteemed Mr. Adrian Lightfoot."

I told you in the 1950s chapter how Adrian's father resembled Rumpole of the Bailey. Suddenly, Adrian had a look about him of Perry Mason.

Can you imagine this happening at the Old Bailey? Only in America.

We are accustomed to legends coming through the doors of the Concorde, and they did not come any more famous, more fabulous or more fastidious than French violin virtuoso Stephane Grappelli.

He was a really temperamental genius, who could explode into boiling temper one minute and then be charming and very chummy the next. Stephane was openly bi-sexual and could be irritatingly effeminate at times; much of it an act.

I saw him in full flow once when his brilliant British accompanist Diz Disley bullied him into crossing the Channel for a gig at the Concorde that Stephane claimed was not in his diary.

Diz, a guitarist out of the Django Reinhardt school, insisted: "Get your French arse over here immediately. We can't let Cole down."

Stephane, who hated flying, reluctantly decided to come over by ferry and had a really rough crossing on a heaving sea. The driver we sent to pick him up at Portsmouth could not find him, mainly because the ship had docked at Poole! Stephane finished up getting a cab that got lost. He finally arrived with minutes to spare before the first set.

He tore into Diz with a stream of invective that proved he had a command of the Anglo Saxon language. Leaving out the expletives, he said something to Diz to the effect: "You piece of s**t, do you know what you 'ave put me through. I 'ave come charging 'ere from Lyons, crossing on water on which fish would be sea-sick. There is no driver to meet me. I 'ave an imbecile taxi driver who thinks ze Concorde is some plane and so takes me to ze airport. I 'ave never been so angry and upset before going out to make ze music."

Diz listened quite casually to all this with his feet up on a chair. He had obviously heard it all before, and when Stephane had finally quietened down he said: "All right, old cock, let's get the show on the road."

Stephane was still smouldering as he followed Diz on to the stage, and then proceeded to play like an angel, with swinging support from Diz, Denny Wright and the doyen of bassists Len Skeat.

On a return visit to the Concorde Stephane arrived when the musicians' dressing room was still being refurbished. He came through the door looking absolutely immaculate in a beautifully tailored camel-haired overcoat that he wore casually yet stylishly slung over his shoulders.

He summoned me, kissed me on each cheek and then said: "Dear Cole, I want you to do

Stephane Grappelli, the French violin virtuoso who was a talented if temperamental visitor to the Concorde. He made the fiddle acceptable in the world of jazz. Dutchman Tim Kliphuis is carrying on the Grapelli tradition and is a popular performer at the club.

me a favour. I want zis overcoot of mine hung up separate from any other clothes. It is most expensive, and I want nothing to brush against it."

Stephane took a panoramic view of the bare, yet-to-be-decorated room, turned up his nose and said: "Zis is not good, Cole. Ze room looks a mess. Where do I 'ang my coot, mm?"

We had no wardrobe facility at that time, and I said: "Not to worry, Stephane. I will get our man Jim to come and organise a special place to hang your coat."

Jim did not quite grasp just how pedantic Stephane was about his coat, and arrived with a six-inch nail that he proceeded to bang into a wall.

Stephane looked aghast. "Cole," he said, his eyes wide, "I cannot possibly 'ang my coot on zat! A nialle. You want me to 'ang my coot on a nialle?"

He then took his coat off, folded it as if it were as precious as the Turin shroud and laid it on the sofa. "On no account, Cole," he said, wagging a finger at me, "is anybody to sit on zat sofa. Please put it out of bounds. I put you personally in charge of my coot."

Stephane then took his beloved Stradivarius out of its case and started to warm up ready for the concert, breaking off to say: "Cole, ze coot ..."

He signalled with his eyes towards the sofa: "Don't let anybody sit on ze coot."

Stephane then went out and set the stage on fire with a fantastic session with the Diz Disley trio. As he came off to tumultuous applause he said to me out of the side of his mouth: "Ze coot, Cole. Is ze coot all right?"

I assured him it was, not adding that Fergie had found it a very comfortable resting place. That would have caused an earthquake of a breakdown by Stephane.

Later, as he left the club with the coat back on his shoulders, he said as a parting shot: "Next time I come back 'ere to ze Concorde, Cole, you must 'ave somewhere to 'ang my coot."

Another Frenchman who won the hearts of the Concorde audience was singing idol Sacha Distel – and he did not warble a single note. He had it written into the contract that he would not sing, and was only there to play the guitar. He had been drawn into doing it by the prospect of playing with one of his guitarist idols, Barney Kessel.

Sacha was shaking like a leaf in the dressing room before the gig started. "I 'ave never been so nervous in all my life," he told me. "Barney Kessel was one of my big 'eroes when I was playing the guitar in my jazz days, and now I am about to go and play alongside 'im. I 'ave not played the guitar seriously for twenty-five years, but this is too good an opportunity to miss."

With Peter Appleyard on vibes, Brian Dee on piano, Paul Morgan on bass and Kenny Clare on drums giving superb backing, Barney and Sacha produced some magical guitar work. The only disappointed people in the audience were the flock of women who had come hoping to persuade Sacha to sing. But I think they were just happy looking at him.

A surprising jazz session during these Eighties came with a return visit of British-born, Canadian-based Peter Appleyard. He teamed up on vibes with Alan Randall. Yes, that's right, the George Formby impersonator who was famous for his prowess on the ukulele. Alan arrived late because his car had broken down, and he and Peter only met each other for the first time that night. They went on stage and played four handed on the vibes and were just sensational. Alan later told me: "The vibraphone is my favourite instrument, but the ukulele is easier to carry around, and it's a bit difficult to sing *When I'm Cleaning Windows* while accompanying myself on the vibes."

The most flummoxed arrival I ever saw of a star musician was when Eddie 'Lockjaw' Davis, ex-Count Basie saxophonist, came legging it through the car park trying to escape the attentions of the two geese who used to roam around as though they owned the place. The most aggressive one, we called him Gonzo, at one time had Eddie's foot almost in his mouth. Lockjaw Gonzo! As he threw himself through the entrance door just ahead of the honking geese he found Fergie lying in his path in his favourite position, all four legs up in the air. "This is like a mad zoo," Eddie said as he clambered past the immoveable Fergie.

Daily Echo reporter John Mann, known to us all as JEM, was surprised by a special tribute evening for all he had done to help put the Concorde on the map. On the right is Dave Williams, who was a Balladeer and John's partner in spreading the sounds of folk music.

That night he gave an incredible performance, supported by the Best of British in Teddy Layton (tenor, clarinet), Mike Blakesley (trombone), Ray Ember (piano), Paul Morgan (bass) and the old Ted Heath drum master Ronnie Verrell.

Davis could not believe his ears when he heard Ray Ember's piano. "Where have you been hiding this guy?" he asked. "He looks like a bank manager and plays like a dream."

From then on Ray was known throughout the business as 'The Bank Manager' because of his elegant appearance (and also because he had a safe pair of hands!). He could have been one of the world's most acclaimed jazz pianists but lacked any real ambition and was happy to be the supporting man in the background.

Trumpeter Billy Butterfield was another visiting American knocked over by Ray's piano playing. "Where the hell did he come from?" he asked aloud to nobody in particular.

Back came the classic response from Teddy Layton: "Woolston."

We threw a surprise sort of *This Is Your Life* party for Ray, whose drum-playing brother Alvern was also a regular at the Concorde. Musicians from all over the place called in or telephoned with their tributes. He was the pianist's pianist, and we wanted him to know just how much he was appreciated. The same went for our inveterate reporter John Edgar Mann, good old JEM who had done so much not only to publicise the Concorde but to bring the best folk music in the world to our little corner of Hampshire. We threw him a surprise party just like the one he had helped us plan for Ray Ember. It was just a small token of our gratitude for helping to give the right acceptable image to jazz in general and the Concorde in particular.

One of the most interesting characters I encountered during those Eighties adventures was trumpet and flugelhorn maestro Clark Terry, who ripped through amazing solo work with the Basie, Ellington and Quincy Jones orchestras. He told me that his dream as a kid was to "be the two Louis's – play the trumpet like Louis Armstrong and box like Joe Louis."

He failed on the boxing front after an opponent busted his lip, which meant he could not practise trumpet for a week. Then he switched full-time to blowing the horn, with many good judges rating him as good a player as there has ever been.

Clark treated the Concorde audience to a memorable session, including fascinating anecdotes on his life and times. He revealed that he had started out as a tenor saxophonist, calling himself Henry Sausage, and he named his backing group the Pork Chops.

He played one tune using just the mouthpiece of his flugelhorn, and accompanied himself with muted scat singing that was his trademark and earned him the nickname "Mumbles."

But Clark was beaten for eccentricity by pianist/guitarist/bongos player Slim Gaillard, who showed off a unique style in which he played the piano with his palms facing upwards! He had huge hands, each of which could comfortably reach a 12-note stretch.

Slim was the man who invented jazz jive talk, and among his compositions were *Flat Foot Floogie With a Floy-Floy* that was a hit for Fats Waller. He described his new language as "Vout oreenee," and when I asked him how he had come to first use the style of talk he said: "I talks like I play. If you ain't got rhythm when you talk then, man, you sure as hell ain't gonna swing."

He had a popular double act in the thirties with bassist Slam Stewart, who was equally inventive and introduced the method of playing the bass with a cello while humming along simultaneously an octave higher. I used to be enthralled by Slim and Slam in those old black and white Hollywood musicals when they would be featured in nightclub scenes, and the tap-dancing Nicholas Brothers would often appear in a similar sumptuous setting. My all-time favourite film is *Casablanca*, again with a nightclub setting. Subconsciously, I wonder if the ambience of those swish nightclubs on the big screen gave me the ambition to one day run a nightclub of my own. I have so far resisted saying to any woman coming into the club: "Of all the gin joints in all the towns in all the world, you have to walk into mine" And saying, "Play it again, Roger" does not quite have the same ring as, "Play it again, Sam."

We had Slam Stewart in the house in 1984 for the Benny Goodman tribute concert. I just wish I had been able to get Slim and Slam back together one more time. The line-up that night was right out of the top drawer: Peter Appleyard, Hank Jones, Abe Most, Don Lamond, Slam Stewart, Urbie Green, Jack Brymer, Billy Butterfield. They were magical together.

One reunion I did manage was King of Skiffle Lonnie Donegan with clarinettist Monty Sunshine. They had started out together back in the 1950s with the Ken Colyer and then

Lonnie Donegan was very happy to hand over a £3,000 Concorde pantomime charity cheque for the purchase of Phonic Ears for Deaf Children. Pauline supervised the hand-over.

Chris Barber Bands. Their gig set me back £1,500. Fifteen years earlier Monty had played the Concorde for a fee of £65!

Lonnie told us the hilarious story of how he inadvertently almost caused the world money market to collapse. A dyslexic messenger in a Tokyo stockbroker's office read a ticker tape message revealing that Lonnie Donegan had suffered a heart attack. He called across the office that Ronald Reagan had had a heart attack. One of the money merchants was on the phone to New York at the time and repeated it, so that now both the Tokyo and Wall Street offices were suddenly in a selling panic, until it was confirmed that Reagan was happily and healthily at home in the White House.

Another returning musician was Alan Price. He had appeared at the original Concorde club in 1965 for £40, but cost quite a bit more twenty-two years later! He and Georgie Fame were good pals, and during one of Georgie's gigs at the Concorde Alan dropped in to listen. It ended with the pair of them having a long reunion natter hours after the members had left for bed.

The least likeable artist that I booked in the Eighties was blues singer (or shouter) Jimmy

Witherspoon. He had a brusque manner and arrogant attitude that threatened to alienate his temporary supporting musicians Ray Ember, Arthur Ward and Paul Morgan.

The hostility between them got to a peak when Witherspoon announced that "in the second set I plays me a bit of bass." Paul Morgan, usually a proper gentleman and one of our finest rhythm players, said: "Not on this bass you f****** don't."

There was a reunion of sorts for me in 1985 when I welcomed to the club clarinettist Cy Laurie, who along with Ken Colyer made a guest appearance with Aussie trombonist Max Collie. I told Cy that as a teenager I had been a regular visitor to his famous Great Windmill Street club until he suddenly dropped off the radar screen. When I asked where he had been, Cy told me: "I decided in 1960 that life was too stressful and took myself off to study meditation and philosophy." Suddenly, that seems like a good idea!

American classic jazz lover Bob Wilber gave us two memorable big band nights, first of all with a recreation of the historic Benny Goodman concert at Carnegie Hall in 1938. Just for the record, this was the line-up of the band that night including Bob's English wife Joanne Horton as vocalist: Saxes/clarinets: Bob Wilber, Spike Robinson, Henry McKenzie, Alan Barnes, Danny Moss, Olaf Vass, Dave Clift, Bill Skeat; Trumpets: Kenny Baker, Paul Eshelby, Ronnie Hughes, Colin Smith; Trombones: Richard Edwards, Roy Williams, Maurice Pratt. The rhythm section: Brian Dee piano, Len Skeat bass, Bobby Orr drums.

Two years later Bob was back with a debut performance of a piece written exclusively for Her Majesty the Queen by Duke Ellington. Called *The Queen's Suite*, the Duke made only one pressing of the record, which he presented to the Queen. This was the first time it had been heard by an audience outside the Palace, and Bob was giving it a trial run before its world premiere at the Royal Festival Hall.

Bob always gave the warmest of greetings to Fergie, and told me: "I've been a dog lover since back in the days when I first met Sidney Bechet. He used to play with a Great Dane called Butch curled at his feet. Sidney took me under his wing, and I moved into his house with Sidney, his lady called Laura and Butch, who ruled the place. I think that Butch and Fergie between them must have heard some of the greatest jazz ever played."

The memories continue to crowd in on me, and I have to admit they are nearly all jazz-driven. I recall Chris Barber once apologising for keeping me waiting when ringing me back about a booking for his enormously popular band. "Sorry, Cole," he said, "but I've been tinkering with Julia and Emma." These were his pride and joy, two six-cylinder, four-and-a-half litre vintage Lagondas. Something else you may not know about Chris is that he trained to be an actuary, and is the fastest of any of our bandleaders at checking a bill or an invoice. You can count on Chris.

When top cornetist Nat Adderley – brother of altoist Cannonball Adderley – played for us in the summer of August 1985 he could have kicked off with *Strangers in the Night*. Apart from pianist John Horler, he had never met his supporting group before – John Marshall (alto), Paul Morgan (bass) and Arthur Ward (drums). He told the audience: "I would now like to introduce the boys in the band – and I am meeting them for the first time, too!"

But being outstanding pros, they quickly got it together and produced a great session full of innovative, top-of-the-head jazz, the way it should be.

It was pleasing to hear Nat confirm my view that John Horler is one of the finest jazz pianists in the world. I like to think of the Concorde as a family club, and John has followed his trumpet-playing Dad, Ronnie, on to our stage. Other father and son connections have been John and Alec Dankworth (and, of course, Dame Cleo and daughter Jacqui), Jimmy and Alan Skidmore, Danny Moss and Danny Jnr, Georgie Fame, with Tristan and James, Stan and Clark Tracey. And, keeping it all in the family, there have also been the wonderful Skeat brothers, Bill (clarinet) and Len (bass), Ray and Alvern Ember, Charlie and Joe Byrd, and Terry and Paddy Lightfoot, no relation to my solicitor friend Adrian; and, of course, the Mathiesons!

One of the few times I have seen a standing ovation from the entire audience was when Peanuts Hucko and his Pied Piper Quintet featured at the club in the early Eighties. The man who had played clarinet and alto with the Glenn Miller, Louis Armstrong and Benny Goodman bands touched perfection as he was driven on by his gifted colleagues Ralph Sutton (piano), Pete Appleyard (vibes), Jack Lesberg (bass) and Woody Herman's ex-drummer Jake Hanna.

Peanuts – a nickname given to him when he was a kid because he ate so many of them – became a regular at the Concorde, including playing for his singer wife Louise Tobin, who had been the first Mrs Harry James. Peanuts (first name Michael) told me he had originally started out as a tenor player, but switched to clarinet when he joined the Glenn Miller Army Air Force Band in Europe during the war – "because it was easier when marching in the sand."

In what was our most expensive jazz project to date, we had Peanuts and his All Stars playing back-to-back concerts with Yank Lawson's Fats Waller tribute band. The two shows in two days in the autumn of 1987 set us back £4,250. We lost money but won many new members, who appreciated our efforts to showcase the best possible jazz.

I continued to make many trips to London to catch the jazz giants, with a view to booking them for the Concorde. One evening in the Eighties I took up Allan Ganley's invitation to hear him supporting former Count Basie saxophonist Benny Waters at the Pizza Express in Dean Street. When I got to the restaurant at the interval following the first set Allan was nowhere to be seen. I went backstage to the dressing-room to find him bent double in agony. "I've done my back in," he told me. "There's no way I can go out for the second set. Do me a favour, Cole, and fill in for me."

So it was that a nervous but privileged Cole Mathieson took the drummer's chair behind the awesome Benny Waters, who told me in a slow-drawl of a voice: "You just paddle those brushes, man, and leave the rest to me."

I spent the next forty-five minutes paddling in paradise. I thought back on this with a smile and a tear in March 2008, with the sad news of Allan's passing. He had a near-50 year association with the Concorde and he and I had a special rapport.

Talking to Benny Waters after the session, I told him that I had just been to Ronnie Scott's where I saw Pharoah Sanders playing sax. At the end of a couple of numbers he had taken the sax out of his mouth and it went on honking for a few seconds. I asked Benny if he knew

Chris Barber brought his band to the Concorde in 1983 to support guest trombonist/guitarist Eddie Durham. Chris has been attracting capacity crowds to the club since back in the 60s.

how it was done. Benny, who was out of the old cool-cat school of jazz and prefaced every sentence with "matta fac, matta fac", replied off the cuff: "Well man, matta fac, matta fac I do remember a saxophone player who used to send his saxophone to do de gig by itself. Matta fac, matta fac, I remember I was de cat who sent his saxophone all de way from New York to LA to do a session and boy it played well – but I turned up at de end of de gig for de cheque." He then rolled around laughing like a big cuddly clown.

Some time later Benny was back at the Concorde shortly after celebrating his eightieth birthday, and I asked if he was still in touch with his old playing partner Bill Coleman. "Don't mention that cat to me," the octogenarian spat. "Last year he stole my chick from me."

We had a mad night to mark our twenty-fifth anniversary in 1983. Ex-Goon Michael Bentine was the guest speaker, and had everybody falling about at his lunacy. He included a rubber tyre that did impersonations and a vulture as a ventriloquist's dummy. Our regular ball of fun, MC Bob Kemp, set the mood. He talked as if he was Benny Hill and then Professor Stanley Unwin, and he just may have had something to do with a giant, man-size chicken making a speech.

The Mayor of Eastleigh, Councillor Cliff Simpkins, got in on the act by recalling that he had been a Concorde regular back in the days when he was a Manfred Mann fan. He had members in fits by continually referring to me as Carl.

Pauline and I were sitting with our close pals Richard and Sue Buswell and Andy and Jill Butcher, not knowing that they were all in on the gag that was about to be played on me.

Hats off from the T-shirt teasers. It was a triumph for Jill Butcher and Gerry Seymour. I have to hand it to them. The teasers pictured above are Richard Martin, Eric Harmsworth, Dereck Robson (behind the hat), Trevor Carley, Gerry Seymour, Jim Woodward, George Martin. Flanking Pauline and me: Andy Butcher, Bob Kemp and Howard Barker. Richard Buswell is, quite rightly, at my knees, and Simon Foderingham is on the floor with a glass in his hand. So what's new? Guest speaker Michael Bentine was in on the joke, and also wore one of the incriminating T-shirts.

At a given signal, twelve of the male diners – the Dirty Dozen – suddenly removed their dress shirts to reveal T-shirts emblazoned with a rude picture of me apparently showing off my private parts. It was in actual fact my hand, but the photograph had been taken at such an angle to suggest it was another part of my anatomy.

Long-time member Gerry Seymour, who instigated the prank with Jill Butcher as his co-

conspirator, gave me this version of the affair, which was all cooked up in secret:

*The story behind the joke started when a group of close friends were on a short holiday break in Ibiza. Jill wanted to capture some moments of our group with a new camera she had just purchased. When the time approached for Jill to retire after a rather heavy drinking evening she also had at the ready, fully loaded with film, her new camera, hoping to catch everybody the morning after the night before.

To her joy, at the crack of dawn, Cole was the first to rise. Opening the curtain with his right hand he had his left arm rested at his side. One of his fingers on his left hand was outstretched, leaving a lovely picture on Jill's camera that gave the impression that his wee winkle was exposed to all and sundry.

Jill, thrilled with her capture, came to my office with the negative, mischievously suggesting something could and should be made of this.

With the forthcoming dinner approaching fast, I – aided and abetted by most of my female staff – hurriedly made two sets of place and wine mats with the said photograph prominently placed in the centre. Then I dashed around to purchase a number of white T-shirts on to which I got printed a large blown up picture of Cole apparently relieving himself after the heavy night of drinking the night before.

We had a confidential word with Michael Bentine, the guest speaker at the anniversary dinner, and he was only too pleased to be part of the joke.

Everything went perfectly to plan. We took our places and enjoyed the food and wine plus all the usual banter that has become an accepted and important part of Concorde life.

When the time came for MC Bobby Kemp to introduce the speaker, everybody stood up, including Michael Bentine. We all started to remove our evening shirts to reveal for the first time the picture planted firmly on the front.

Only then did Pauline – not part of the plot – scream out loud at the shock of seeing this picture also on the place mats in front of her. Cole's face, well it was a picture!*

Thank you very much Gerry and Jill. One day, revenge will be mine!

It was a fantastically mad and memorable night. Local TV covered the dinner, with Concorde member Peter Hunt directing. It gave the club a great platform on television and there was a spurt of interest, which further established us as a premier club.

By the time we got round to our 30th anniversary the club had again taken on a new, modernised look. Many members were grateful for the fact that the reconstruction meant that we were able to get rid of the two large pillars that partly obscured the view of the stage.

Working as usual to Roland Tucker's designs, we added a fully glazed conservatory extension to the restaurant, and the refurbished Musicians' Bar now became the Moldy Fig, a name taken from a derogatory description that be-bop musicians used to make about traditionalists. The bill was a hefty quarter of a million pounds, but it was money well spent. I had come a long way from the days when I was petrified at the prospect of paying £7,250 for the Old School.

A slice of good fortune as Pauline and I cut the cake to mark thirty years of the Concorde.

The removal of the brick pillars was a very complicated procedure engineered by Jim Watkinson. It entailed holding the whole side of the building up whilst slim metal pillars were dropped in as replacements for the old-fashioned, view-blocking wide pillars. It was a major operation that I just couldn't face watching, so I took myself off to the USA for a much-needed holiday break with Richard and Sue Buswell and our respective families.

While in Las Vegas Richard talked Pauline and me into joining the Buswells at a Gladys Knight show. As it was scorching hot, I was wearing just very lightweight clothes. Aggressive comedian Frank Gorshin was doing the warm-up, and – jet-lagged – I found myself drifting off into a doze. Sue Buswell, sitting alongside me, knocked over a glass of iced water right into my lap, and I jumped up screaming. It felt as if I had been stabbed in the family jewels. Frank Gorshin stopped mid-joke, glared at us and said: "Everything all right down there? Let's keep this friendly."

If it had happened in the Concorde, I would have thrown me out.

We were well enough established to start attracting major corporate and conference events, and the local Round Table and Rotary Clubs became regular occupants. I had joined the Rotary back in the mid-70s, but found I was too busy to attend meetings even though they were under my roof. I have a tremendous respect for the work that the Rotarians do, and they know they can count on my support at any time. Many of the friendships I forged in my Rotary days thrive to this day.

The BBC considered our refurbished home suitable enough to stage one of their Jazz Score radio quiz shows, featuring Humphrey Lyttelton, Ronnie Scott, John Barnes, Benny Green and Campbell Burnap. John Barnes said it was like a homecoming for him, because he had played with the Alex Welsh Band on the opening evening..

Our 'Friday Night is Cabaret Night' addition was proving widely popular, particularly a young comedian called Bradley Walsh who was so good we invited him to entertain us at several of our staff outings aboard the Solent Blue Funnel boat. Wayne Dobson, Joe Pasquale, Dave Ismay, Paul McKenna and Shane Richie were among a procession of other bright young entertainers who brought fun and laughter into the Concorde throughout the Eighties.

Georgie Fame (or Clive Powell to give him his real name) could fit comfortably into a cabaret or jazz role. He always has an amusing tale to tell. One evening after a gig we sat talking into the early hours, George tinkling away on the piano while sharing stories and a bottle of scotch. We suddenly realised how late it was, and by then he'd had too much to drink to be able to drive. So I invited him to my home and he slipped into the bed where my mother-in-law usually slept on her visits to us. Next morning I was woken up by little Jamie, who said: "Dad, there's something odd going on here. I just got into bed to kiss Grandma and there's a strange man in there."

Thinking of Georgie tinkling at the keyboard reminds me how advisable it is to have a good piano. Our piano actually had two or three notes missing at the end, and not the full 88. A sensational pianist called Bobby Enriquez, who was very energetic when playing our piano, pointed it out. He used his elbows as well as his fingers when flying up and down the keyboard. As a gag, he finished one dazzling run by falling off the end of the keyboard and tumbling on the floor and then announcing to the audience there were not enough keys to complete the run.

I had already realised that it was imperative that we purchased a new piano. I approached Stan Greig, who knows a thing or three about piano playing, having appeared with many of the top bands since the 1950s and starring in his own right as a leading exponent of boogie-woogie. He became my tester. We visited one of the biggest piano showrooms in the country and Stan tried out more than a dozen pianos before telling me: "This is the one, Cole."

It was a Yamaha C3 that cost around £6,000, a lot of money back in the 1980s. It has three pedals and the full run of 88 keys. We get nothing but praise for the piano from our visiting musicians, who always tell me how much they look forward to playing at the Concorde because they love the keyboard. Concorde member Graeme Bryant regularly keeps it tuned for us.

When the piano first arrived we had a devilish job getting it on and off the stage because of the different levels. Call in Jim'll Fix-it Budd. Using blocks of wood with grooves, he made a sort of miniature wooden railway on to which we could comfortably push the piano to the side of the stage between concerts.

While talking pianos, a quick jump ahead into the 1990s. Most pianists, when they arrive for a gig, make straight for the piano and practise a few runs to get the feel of the keyboard. But not Gene Harris, one of the most stunning players I have ever heard. When he arrived to play with sax/flute genius Frank Wess, he just took a look at the piano and nodded his approval.

"You're not going to try it out?" I asked.

"If it ain't right," he said, "nothing ain't gonna change it now!"

Frank Wess was actually depping for Stanley Turrentine, tenor sax, who at the last minute declined to fly to the UK. There were 24 hours of absolutely frantic activity to get a replacement, and we were so lucky to find that ex-Basie sideman Wess was prepared to jump on a 'plane and fly over at a moment's notice. We picked him up at Heathrow and he and Gene Harris proceeded to give us one of the most dazzling evenings we have ever had at the Club. One could feel everybody transfixed as Frank moved up through his solos to come to a sensational climax, and the intake and then outpouring of breath from the audience at the end of each solo proved we were all hanging on his every note.

An enormous cheer followed each solo as if the audience was greeting a winning goal at Wembley. It was dramatic stuff, and all of it captured for a BBC Radio 3 recording.

Live music continued to be my priority, but I recognised there was a call for non-jazz nights. Dave Walker, who also performed at Earls Court and Olympia and the Southampton Boat Show, was prominent among our DJs pulling in large attendances for our discotheque nights.

A major difference I have noted between our jazz and disco sessions is that the record-playing nights are socially more successful. It is a long-held tradition that nobody speaks while the jazz is being played, while the audience drawn by the DJs chat away to each other and firm, often romantic, friendships are struck up during the course of an evening.

Our lively Sunday night Trad jazz in the 80s was in the capable hands of Cuff Billett, Chris

For the record, a spin off of Concorde disc jockeys in the 1980s: Stuart Bennett, Dave Walker, Dave Carson, Joe Craen, Simon Foderingham, Geoff Bartlett. Simon was the pioneer DJ, who talked me into including recorded music when the disco craze started in the late 1960s. I was very reluctant because I am a lover of 'live' music, but I have to concede that the DJ nights have been an enormous success.

Walker and later John Maddocks, who has been entertaining Concorde members since back in 1973, both on the main stage and in the Moldy Fig wine bar. Chris goes back even further, making his club debut at the Bassett with the Mike Daniels Band in the early sixties. He is a regular broadcaster on local radio, and has been hugely influential in helping to promote and publicise jazz throughout the South. Moldy Fig regulars enjoyed many foot-tapping nights when he regularly shared the Monday residency with doyen of clarinettists, Dave Shepherd.

We were always trying to be imaginative and innovative, and among our attempts to entertain our members were murder mystery nights. One, I recall, went hilariously wrong when a member, Jessie Benfield, went to the toilet. She found a body with a knife sticking in its back, forgot what sort of night it was and let out a piercing scream! She had discovered our corpse.

There was an important day in October 1988 when our new executive chef David Ophaus, formerly of the Angry Trout restaurant in Romsey, joined us. He has been majestically in charge of our food ever since and runs one of the best club kitchens in the land. We get wide-ranging praise for our food, and David takes enormous pride in making sure everything is perfect. He took a two-week field residency at the top-rated Langan's restaurant in London and came back brimming with inventive ideas.

David not only brought us his wonderful culinary skills, but also a superb tenor voice that adds a touch of class to our panto nights. The Singing Chef has added much to our entertainment menu. And when you hear him singing beautifully in harmony with my daughter Kirstie, you will realise why jazz often takes a back seat to opera in my musical taste.

A lot of the so-called celebrity chefs are making a name for themselves by ranting and raving in the kitchen. You get none of that from David, who is always composed and collected, even when I am telling him that we have suddenly got twenty extra for dinner. He takes it all in his stride, and does not threaten to "Ramsay" me into the ground. I have known David since he was just a lad, as he will tell you in Part Two. I'll give you a clue: he's a 'chop' off the old block.

In the summer of 1987 I took a highly confidential call from our local Tory MP, Sir David Price, to tell me that Prime Minister Margaret Thatcher would be making her final pre-General Election speech in our local constituency. He wanted to know if they could use the Concorde grounds for the event.

How could I not agree? For the week leading up to her speech the club was crawling with undercover police keeping surveillance and making sure nothing more dangerous than flower bulbs were planted. The Brighton bomb outrage during the Tory Party conference was still fresh in the mind.

A few hundred local people were invited to the club grounds to give their support as Maggie climbed on to a banner-bedecked wagon and called on the nation to put her back in for a third term, which they did. As busy as she was, Maggie found time to send me a personal letter of thanks for my co-operation.

A little more history for the Concorde as we planned for the 1990s.

In the last week in 1989, one of our staff – a German girl called Heidi – returned from a holiday at home. She gave me a gift-wrapped piece of the Berlin Wall that had been hacked down the previous month.

It made me think of the lovely old boys in the Preservation Hall Band who had included *Joshua Fought the Battle of Jericho* in their storming programme.

And the Walls came tumbling down.

I had nothing but optimism as we moved into the new decade.

THE idea first came to me in the late 1970s. I was looking out of the window of the club and thought: "What a good location this would be for a hotel." As you do.

I ran it past design master Roland Tucker, and he immediately saw the merit of the concept. We made preliminary plans but shelved them when we were assured that there was no chance of planning permission because of the strict Green Belt laws.

Early in the 1980s I got round to thinking again of building a hotel, after reading that Southampton was seriously under-bedded for the number of visitors coming to the area each year. But a sudden recession made me run for cover. It was a time for tin hats rather than extravagant expansion.

The turning point came when IBM were given the go-ahead to build an office development close by, with the proviso that they refurbished the grand Old Rectory building. When NDS – the digital pay-TV company – took over from IBM, they got planning permission for a second large office block, so there was now a precedent for encroaching on the protected countryside between Eastleigh and Southampton. It made me think: "If they can, then I can."

I made the point that we would not be diminishing what was known as 'the strategic green gap', because the hotel building I had in mind was going to take up unused space that would be well screened.

Working to Roland Tucker's designs, I brought Gordon Rogers in as a planning consultant. We decided to have dormer windows and redbrick walls to complement the Old School House building. It was the ancient meeting the modern, a Victorian building married to one being built with the New Millennium in mind.

Roland's stunning plans allowed for 36 air-conditioned bedrooms, all en-suite, and landscaped gardens overlooking Monks Brook. There would be a Japanese-style pedestrian bridge, and an old walk-way that had once seen service on the *Queen Mary*. It looked great on paper and even the opponents of the idea were impressed as a series of committees pored over the plans during 1997.

One councillor forcibly made the point that the NDS offices were hidden from view, and were therefore not spoiling what was considered an area of natural beauty. Former Mayor of Eastleigh, Peter Madsen, a jazz musician who was arguing on our side, produced photographic evidence that the latest office block, still under construction, was a far-from-attractive concrete frame compared with the building of beauty designed by Roland.

Among the early objections was one from the Environment Agency on the grounds that the hotel's proposed location alongside Monks Brook meant it was liable to flood. Planning officers visited the club, and we were able to convince them that flooding was a remote possibility. We simply pointed out that the path of the motorway had removed the dogleg in

The Ellington Lodge Hotel, which was completed in time for a New Millennium opening. The superb design work was by Roland Tucker.

the stream that had caused earlier problems.

The original plan was for the hotel to butt on to the club, to make it one large complex. But the planning department told us that this would be unacceptable, and that they might reconsider if it was a stand-alone building on the south side of the Brook. I am sure they thought this would turn us off the idea and would, so to speak, be a bridge too far. Instead it made us more determined, and the plans were resubmitted. This time – because of laws relating to disabled guests – we had to lose one of the planned bedrooms in the two-storey building to make way for a lift,

At one stage we looked like getting beaten by the daft suggestion that their preference was for a hotel at the airport. We had to make the fairly obvious point that we wanted to accommodate visitors to the Concorde rather than transit passengers. Some time later they got their wish for an airport hotel, and I will make no comment other than to say – trying to keep a straight face – what a beautiful building that is!

Balancing the criticism of the plan for our hotel, Councillor Johnny Roche told his committee colleagues: "The Concorde is an internationally recognised venue. How many times can Eastleigh boast that an international event is being staged in this borough? This development will put Eastleigh on the map."

After a lot of in-fighting and intense arguments for and against, the various Council committees finally came down strongly in favour of giving the go ahead for the hotel to be built.

But the Policy Officer insisted that as it was against guidelines it would have to go to the Minister ('Two Jags' Prescott), and it was finally approved.

The Royal Bank of Scotland, our bankers for more than twenty years, and our then manager Nick Wright were behind the project, and we had agreed and signed the mortgage loan, but suddenly out of the blue the RBS head office asked us to change the type of building contract. We were well on the way to starting the work, and this would have caused a six month delay in getting on with the job. It would have made the project significantly more expensive, to the point where it was not viable.

Nick Wright took up the fight for us but it appeared the real reason was that they were – to use a money-market term – 'losing their appetite for hotels'. They dispatched their hotel expert from Manchester by rail to Southampton. He had never been to the area before and, to our astonishment, told us that this was not a good location for a hotel and there were not enough visitors to the area.

'Uh, but what about the international airport?' I asked, completely flabbergasted by his comment.

'Which airport is that?' he asked, 'Gatwick, Heathrow?'

He had done his homework so well that he did not even know of the existence of South-ampton Airport, an entire three minutes away from the Concorde. It was yet another example of a bank head office turning down a scheme and not taking sufficient note of the specialist knowledge of their local offices. Bear in mind that the project was well under way at that point and had cost the Club considerable sums in planning applications, designers and builders.

Graham Martin, who had followed Bill Elliott and, later, Peter Grinyer as my accountant, suggested that I went to Barclays. We found local manager Kevin Keiron full of enthusiasm for the project, and Barclays came up with the necessary money with no arguments because they could see the potential of the hotel business plan.

It was a triumph for the expert advice I had received from Graham, who has been an enormous help to me and the Club since he took over the accounts. He has dragged us into the 21st Century with his computer-driven accountancy that has eased the workload for Pauline, whose beautifully compiled – almost artistic – handwritten books are now archive exhibits.

We set our sights on a 2000 opening date, and Eastleigh mayor, Councillor Jane Welsh, joined me at the controls of a giant JCB digger to cut the first sod. The sight of me on the digger for the publicity photographs caused great merriment among our staff, because they knew that if I were to actually drive the thing there would have been total mayhem.

Even if I say it myself, it was astounding what we had achieved from that Bassett Hotel start forty years earlier.

As the old Duke Ellington classic goes, *I'm Just A Lucky So and So ...*

It was luck that John Fanner found the Bassett Hotel location for me ... it was luck that one of the early members of the club was a rising young designer called Roland Tucker ... it was luck that Roland pointed me in the direction of the Old School House ... it was luck that the School House had been a social club ... it was luck that Adrian Lightfoot was a young trombonist at the club with a legal mind as sharp as any I have come across ... it was luck that a sudden price boom meant the Old School trebled in value within two years of us moving in ... it was luck that Pauline Le Bas came into my life and used her book-keeping skills to help

Sacha Distel and Barney Kessel both have rooms named after them in the Ellington Lodge Hotel. Brian Dee on piano and bassist Paul Morgan are also in this photograph, taken the night Sacha went back to his jazz roots.

get the new Concorde up and running … and it was luck that the club attracted members who were willing to pitch in to help turn the Concorde into a thriving entertainment centre.

Yes I repeat, as Louis Armstrong sang to Duke's melody: *I'm just a lucky so and so*. And it was the Duke I was proud to honour by naming the hotel the Ellington Lodge Hotel. Keeping to the jazz theme, we named all but the Ellington room after jazz giants who had played the Concorde. What a band we could put together from the following, all with room numbers:

Ground Floor: 1. Adelaide Hall; 2. Slam Stewart; 3. Big Joe Turner; 4. Wild Bill Davison; 5. Billy Butterfield; 6. Clark Terry; 7. Kenny Baker; 8. Benny Carter; 9. Buddy Tate; 10. Gene Harris; 11. Ben Webster; 12. Maxine Sullivan; 14. Buck Clayton; 15. Dick Wellstood; 16. Jay McShann; 17. Henry 'Red' Allen; 18. Bob Haggert. First floor: 101. Hank Jones; 102. Gus Johnson; 103. Charlie Byrd; 104. Benny Waters; 105. Sacha Distel; 106. Nat Gonella; 107. Maynard Ferguson; 108. Coleman Hawkins; 109. Stephane Grappelli; 110. Ronnie Scott; 111. Duke Ellington; 112. Bud Freeman; 114. Barney Kessel; 115. Clark Terry; 116. Al Cohn; 117. Herb Ellis; 118. Nat Adderley; 119. Frank Wess.

You will notice there is no 13 or 113. This is more for the superstitious Americans than anything else, because they do not have thirteen in any of their hotels.

I selected the names out of respect for each player, and if we ever extend the hotel to take in more rooms the first five to be named will be John Dankworth, Humphrey Lyttelton, Kenny

Ball, Acker Bilk and Chris Barber, all of whom have been established in domestic jazz even longer than the Concorde. And there will be rooms named Rosemary Squires, Stacey Kent and Clare Teal. Come to think of it, I could build a skyscraper hotel and still not accommodate all my jazz idols.

Apart from the excitement of planning the addition of the hotel, the Nineties were a time of challenging changes at the club with an ambitious widening of our activities. We added a Wine Society, a Ladies Business Club started by function co-ordinator Lynne Wicks, Ladies Luncheons under the supervision of Gill Jeffery, a Summer Ball, a Beer Festival and we were kept busy with fashion shows, wedding receptions, funeral wakes, sporting testimonial evenings, conferences, nights at the opera (organised by Kirstie), plus, of course, our cabaret and DJ nights.

Our Summer Ball immediately took off in a big way and has become a major annual event. We have marquees in the grounds, strolling musicians, jazz and marching bands, a fun fair including dodgem cars and the big wheel, ladies in their beautiful ball gowns, the men in their DJs. Chef David and his team surpass themselves each year with their sumptuous buffets, and there is dancing, drinking and fun into the early hours. It is almost like our yearly cup final, with tickets snapped up months in advance.

Yes, it was all a long, long way from the Bassett Hotel days, but for me the Wednesday night jazz continued to be the highlight of each week.

I was glad to welcome back Simon Foderingham (aka Peterson) in a general manager capacity after his adventures running Simons Wine Bar and Pepper Joe's restaurant in Southampton. We had started the businesses together, and were pioneers in opening the first wine bar in Southampton. Simon, always entrepreneurial, had come a long way from his days as our first DJ at the Bassett. He was brimming with ideas and energy, and he played a big part in the cementing of the Concorde as an all-round place of entertainment. He also brought class and comedy to our pantomimes, revealing a natural gift for playing the lead man and never afraid to make a fool of himself for the sake of the popularity of the panto.

Reluctantly, I also have to add for the record that we introduced an annual Concorde Golf tournament at the picturesque Paultons Golf Centre at Ower, which we now run in conjunction with an old friend Peter Cooper of VW, and his son Darren. I have a duck trophy on my mantelpiece at home to remind me that I am one of the world's worst golfers. This was presented to me as a member of Graham Martin's team in the second year of the tournament, when – much to everybody's amusement – I visited virtually every part of the golf course except the fairway. I spent more time in the bunker than Adolf Hitler, and it was just as well that Graham was an accountant to help keep my score. He has developed into a very good golfer, but I remain King Rabbit.

The Wine Society was quite an eye-opener (and bottle opener) for me. For our very first session we had eighty people taking part, and each had eight glasses to taste red, white and rosé samples. That's a little matter of 640 glasses per sitting. I made the gag then that I have been using ever since: "Please take your glasses to the bar when you have finished, ready for me to wash up in the morning."

It has been exceptionally successful, and is without doubt one of the finest Wine Societies

We are celebrating the testimonial dinner night of Hampshire cricketer Bobby Parks with Richard Digance, Simon Foderingham and David Gower, with me at silly point.

in the South of England. We were encouraged to start the Society by one of our members, Mike Bagley, who had been in the wine industry. Simon and I did not need much persuasion, and the response of our members right from day one has been remarkable. Former Saints footballer Mike Judd is a strong motivating force within the Society, and as I write John Purkess is organising our first wine-tasting trip for the members to Bergerac. Vintage stuff.

Our Beaujolais Nouveau Day – now re-named the French Day – has become widely popular. It is worth visiting just for the experience of seeing our chef David Ophaus excelling himself. The food display has to be seen (and tasted) to be believed, fish always being a feature: a whole Tuna so big it took three chefs to lift it, and one year we had a complete Swordfish some seven foot long. There are huge joints of beef, miles of mussels, exotic fruits and, of course, the first tasting of the *Beaujolais Nouveau*. The fun commences at 11.00am, and lasts all day, with feasting and non-stop entertaining. We usually finish up in the Moldy Fig, drinking coffee at 1.00am the next morning. I almost ruined the show one year by having the floor polished before our can-can dancers came on with their dazzling act. You can read about that bit of idiocy by me in Part Two. You could say that I slipped up that year.

We have forged a good relationship with Hampshire County Cricket Club, and are delighted to host benefit dinners for their long-serving cricketers. I became particularly close to Adi and Marie Aymes, who met at our club; also England batting master Robin Smith and his wife, Kath, who did their courting at the Concorde. Most of the cricket dinners have the slightly maniacal touch of the larger-than-life Denis Bundy, whose MC-ing guarantees laughs and groans in equal measure. Hughie Fisher, a fine footballer with the Saints, was a regular visitor as a player, and later in his role as regional sales manager for Scottish and Newcastle Brewery. We once had a boozy trip together to Hamburg, where we explored the notorious *Reeperbahn* district. But the less said about that the better, not that I can recall very much!

Richard Digance, while based at Romsey, became extremely popular at the club with his uniquely clever entertainment performances. He is a good friend of both the club and myself, and he put in a lot of volunteer time and effort to help make our money-raising pantomimes more professional. I could never understand why the BBC dropped his regular television show that provided original material and was ten times more entertaining than the so-called reality rubbish that they put on these days.

The first time I met Richard I was dressed in lederhosen, with leather shorts that were embarrassingly short. I was appearing 'live' on the Tom O'Connor TV programme with my slapper of a partner Richard Buswell, performing our pantomime slap act. I had no idea in those days who Richard Digance was, and I said to him at the side of the stage before the show exactly what I once said to England football captain Bryan Robson: "And what do you do?" It just so happened he was topping the bill that day.

Richard is one of many celebrities who have helped enormously in our fund-raising ventures. He first got involved when presenting the *Cinders* sailing boat to the Youth Challenge Trust, which was paid for from monies raised by our pantomime *Cinderella*. The Concorde has over the years earned a reputation for charity work that fills me with pride, but the praise should not be aimed at me as much as at our members. And here I must mention local businessman Paul Murray. I have met few more energetic and imaginative fund-raisers than this human dynamo, who has been the powerhouse behind such club-night themes as the Oil Baron's Ball, the Cotton Club, D-Day Revisited and Cabaret. His idea to swamp the club with Swastikas when recreating the Kit Kat nightclub in Berlin caused controversy among some members, but I was happy to go along with it in the cause of charity.

The Nineties got off to a sad start with the death in February 1990 of Mick Erridge, the popular and likeable trumpet-leader of Southampton's Solent City Jazzmen for more than thirty years. He died of a heart problem, and journalist John Edgar Mann and cartoonist/bassist Toni Goffe put together a book of funny jazz anecdotes called *For the Love of Mick*, and designed to raise money for the British Heart Foundation in Mick's memory.

My favourite story from the book came from Jimmy Frost, leader of Southampton's Gateway Jazz Band, who first played for me in the original Concorde Club back in 1961. He recalled: "I was a bit confused when somebody came up to me during a gig and asked for the band to play *Sid James in Germany Blues*. We worked it out that what he meant was *St James Infirmary Blues*."

Mick Erridge and I went right back even farther than Jimmy Frost. I often played drums with him in the mid-1950s – with the Climax Jazz Band, the Yellow Dog Stompers and the Solent City Band, which he led for many years with his powerful trumpet playing. I warmly recall that Mick had a risqué Ronnie Scott style of introducing songs. "Ok, we're now going to play something with a medium rhythm and we would like a few couples on the floor," he would say. "Others among you may care to dance."

It was typical of Mick that in his will he left instructions for money to be deposited behind the bar for musicians to drink his health at his wake! We saw him off as he would have wanted with a fantastic New Orleans-style funeral that included the entire congregation of several hundred walking behind the horse drawn carriage, while Mick's band played their hearts out.

During that first year of the 1990s I made the decision to increase the minimum guest age from 21 to 25. I just instinctively knew that this was right for a club that had as its twin aims to be both tasteful and stylish. More 'Basil Fawlty' taunts came my way, but a large majority of members agreed with my autocratic ruling.

One of my closest friends in those days was Alan Connock, a long-time member of the club who, along with his wife, Liz, shared my passion for jazz. He invited me to one of his birthday parties at his home, where he had playing for him American jazz masters Buddy Tate and Al Grey, with Brian Lemon on piano, Len Skeat on bass and Jack Parnell on drums. Now that's what you call style. Since Alan passed on I can honestly say there is not a Wednesday jazz night goes by without my thinking of him, and other old regulars Brian Tubbs and trombonist Keith Samuels, who have also gone to what I euphemistcally call the great jazz club in the sky. Their widows, Jill Tubbs and Judy Samuels, continue to come to the club on Wednesday jazz nights, along with Derrick Holloway's widow, the lovely Dawn.

I was really excited at the prospect of bringing to the club Lionel Hampton, one of my all-time heroes who turned the vibraphone into a magical jazz instrument. The contracts were signed and a date arranged when Lionel made his Europe tour in 1991. The week before he was due he had a stroke while playing in Paris. It was a sad way to lose one of my best captures.

When the Original Jubilee Jazz Band were playing one Sunday evening in 1991 they had a player sitting in who looked familiar. It was none other than *Bullseye* presenter Jim Bowen, a jazz fanatic who told me he was playing a cornet that had once been owned by his idol, Jimmy McPartland. I showed him an autographed picture we had on the Moldy Fig wall of McPartland, who had appeared at the Concorde ten years earlier with Brian Dee and Jack Parnell. I couldn't resist asking Jim what was his funniest memory of presenting *Bullseye* and he told me: "I asked a contestant what he did for a living and he told me he had been unemployed for two years. Without thinking I said 'Smashing'. It was left in the show and, much to my embarrassment, ended up being broadcast."

Jim told me the jazzy *Bullseye* theme music was composed by John Patrick, Birmingham-based pianist who, with his trio, has supported jazz giants such as Art Farmer, Gerry Mulligan and Nat Adderley. As Michael Caine might say, not a lot of people know that.

There was a prestigious honour for the Concorde in 1992 when we were voted one of the top three national jazz venues in the land. The poll was organised by tenor player, raconteur, cricket and jazz historian Benny Green in his *Sunday Express* column. To mark the occasion Benny played at the club with guitar maestro Gary Potter and his Quartet, with the vocals provided by one of my all-time favourite songbirds Rosemary Squires.

In my opinion, not enough fuss is made about our small army of lady singers. I am thinking of the likes of Dame Cleo Laine (and daughter Jacqui Dankworth), Annie Ross, Carol Kidd, Maxine Daniels, Shirley Morgan, Val Wiseman, Elaine Delmar, Julie Driscoll, Tina May, Trudi Kerr, Barbara Jay, Elkie Brooks, Lee Gibson, and the stunning Clare Teal, all of whom have sung beautifully for their supper at the Concorde.

They, along with 'Our Rosemary', can look any of the female jazz singers in the world in the eye and claim to be as good, if not better, than most of them. And we can almost claim America's amazing Stacey Kent as one of ours. She and her British sax-playing husband Jim Tomlinson are always made to feel at home at the Concorde, where they have a huge

Stacey Kent, captured by the camera of club member Gordon Sapsed, was established as a favourite at the Concorde Club long before exploding on the international scene. She is accompanied here by piano maestro Dave Newton.

The Team, on our 35th anniversary in 1992: Function co-ordinator Lynne Wicks, Pauline, ideas man Simon Foderingham and our master chef David Ophaus. In support we had Jackie Baker and Jim Budd and dozens of superb back-up staff who helped make the machine work smoothly. The Concorde had long ago ceased to be 'just a jazz club.'

following of fans who appreciated her long before she took off to international stardom.

I remember the first time the wonderful Clare Teal came to the club she was accompanied by a BBCtv film crew. "They're doing a jazz documentary on you?" I asked.

"Not quite, love," she said in that Yorkshire accent of hers. "They're doing an investigative piece on a notorious con man and as I know something of what he's been up to they're including a contribution from me in the film."

There never seems to be a shortage of incidents when Clare is at the Concorde. On her second visit she was signing CDs in the foyer when a woman in the queue told her in slightly hysterical tones that she'd discovered just a few minutes earlier her husband was having an affair. "She promptly punished him," Clare told me, "by buying six CDs on his credit card!"

In all my years at the Concorde, only one musician has threatened me with physical violence. Back in the early days we controlled the drunken Don Byas before he could use his flick knife, and Charlie Mingus resorted only to verbal violence when he lost his temper in the Incident of the Spiral Staircase. But with cornet and trumpet genius Ruby Braff I was in danger of getting throttled.

Ruby was notorious throughout the jazz world for his touchpaper temper, but I found him a real pussycat on his numerous visits to the Concorde. On one trip he loaded praise on me from the stage, telling everybody that it was one of the greatest jazz clubs in the world, his favourite place to play in Europe, that the food was second to none and what a great host I was.

At the bar during the interval he continued to praise me to the hilt, and I had to interrupt him to take a telephone call. When I came back from the call I told him it was from a music agent who, to protect the innocent, let's call John Smith. I said: "He sends his regards."

At the mention of the agent's name Ruby's eyes almost popped out of his head. "John Smith? John f****** Smith!," he said, with rising anger in his voice. "Don't dare mention that ****'s name in my hearing."

With that, he came towards me and started shaking me by the shoulders and his hands were nearing my neck as I pulled away. He ranted on about the agent and used every swear word he could put his tongue to, and including me in the tirade simply because I had taken the phone call. Then he quietened down and became the same affable Ruby Braff of before the call. He did not give a word of apology, and just acted as if nothing had happened, while I was still shaking from what was a traumatic and totally unexpected experience.

Generally speaking, I found Ruby very likeable despite his abrasive manner. He played his last gig but one with us, which was the last thing he recorded. This was with John Barnes, Roy Williams, Kenny Baldock, Jon Wheatley and Allan Ganley. Then he travelled to Scotland for what proved to be his final appearance at the 2002 Nairn Jazz Festival. He was taken ill and cancelled the remainder of his British tour. Unable to play again, he died the following year and left behind memories of a brilliant, self-taught cornettist who had a unique sound.

Ruby loved the food at the Concorde, but somebody who enjoyed it even more was guitarist Charlie Byrd. His playing with Barney Kessel and Herb Ellis provided some of the most memorable moments in the history of the club. It was guitar heaven.

One evening Charlie was sitting in the restaurant and summoned me over. "Cole," he said, pointing to his near-empty plate, "I want you to tell the chef that there was nothing that could have been done to my Dover sole to make it taste any better. It was sheer perfection."

It was music to the ears of our master chef David Ophaus, because he knew that Charlie was a gourmet who had published books on recipes he had collected from around the world.

Bud Shank, that artist of the alto and flute, went on record with the opinion that "the Concorde Club is one of the nicest places to play in the world and with the finest food."

Another who said in his inimitable style that he "liked our nosh and noggins" was the flamboyant, matchless George Melly. He performed at the club over a stretch of more than thirty years, and was never less than entertaining and often in an over-the-top way that shocked as well as amused the audience. George played his last gig but one for us, despite having – and this was his description – "one foot in the grave."

I remember once sitting chatting to him after he had, as usual, arrived early for his gig. He said he liked to get to the club as early as possible to enjoy the ambience and the setting, and sometimes to get outdoors for his hobby of fly-fishing. "It does wonders for me to fill my lungs with good Hampshire air," he said. On this particular occasion he was nursing a hangover from the night before. "Went to a party with the Stones," he said. "Saw Jagger there and told him what a bloody mess he looked. I offered the unsolicited opinion that he had more lines on his face than British Rail. 'These are laughter lines,' Jagger said. I looked at him and replied with a straight face, 'Nothing's that bloody funny!'"

As I rolled over laughing, he came back with another hilarious Rolling Stones story. "Keith Richard called me over," he said, "and asked me, as an art expert, if I'd ever seen anything as beautiful as the picture he was studying. I looked at it and said, 'That's a bloody window, you stupid prat.'"

I would hate anybody to think there is some sort of curse on the Concorde, but quite a few top players have made their final or last but one appearance with us including Nat Gonella, Ruby Braff, Charlie Mingus, George Melly, Humph of course, and, the one fairly young man among them, Roy Budd. I was a massive Roy Budd fan from way back when he first appeared on the scene as a boy genius. He could pick out tunes on the piano from the age of two! He appeared at the Concorde three times in the 1990s, always with Dick Morrissey driving him along with his inspirational tenor playing.

After one gig in 1992 I drove Roy to Southampton Parkway to catch the Waterloo train. "When's your next gig?" I asked.

His reply was not in any way meant to be pretentious, because he did not have an arrogant bone in his body. This is how it went: "Well tomorrow I have to be at Heathrow for a flight to Moscow. I'm playing with the Moscow State Orchestra at the weekend ... then I fly on to LA to finish a film score ... and the following week I am at Carnegie Hall before going on to Rome, and I am back here in England to play with my trio at the Festival Hall in the second week of next month ..."

If you want to hear just how special Roy was as a film score composer and arranger, tune your ears to *Get Carter,* the Michael Caine version. Roy's music track is spell binding.

We recorded him at the Concorde in 1993 with his trio and top tenor player Dick Morrissey. They were in sensational form, Roy and Dick bringing the best out of each other. In all my time listening to jazz I never experienced two musicians pushing each other so hard as Roy and Dick that night. Every cascade of notes pouring from Dick would be equalled and then surpassed by Roy ... then Dick would improvise with dazzling runs, which were immediately matched by Roy. It was absolutely stunning and left everybody breathless.

Tragically, a few weeks later Roy died of a brain haemorrhage. He was just 46. We have been trying hard to get his final record released as a tribute to one of the UK's finest jazz pianists, and his family are kindly considering it as this book is prepared for publication. It would also stand as a fitting homage to the talent of Dick Morrissey, who was struck down by cancer not long after this astonishing Concorde performance with Roy Budd.

Roy made an equally excellent recording at the club with the splendid Spike Robinson, and this might be the one that gets the vote from the Budd family as representative of his genius.

Among the jazz enthusiasts who called into the club in the 90s was local Eastleigh Tory MP Stephen Milligan. He came to the official opening of the Moldy Fig in September 1992, and – living just down the road at Chandler's Ford – he used to pop in to listen to the jazz whenever he was free from his Westminster duties. I found him a real charmer of a man, and we talked at length about his hopes and ambitions. He even tried his hand at playing the drums under my tutelage. Some hope! Stephen was an intelligent and interesting Oxford University graduate, ex-Foreign Editor of the *Sunday Times* and BBC-tv reporter. He was regarded as the

The matchless Roy Budd, who made his last ever recording at the Concorde before dying suddenly at the age of 46. Listen to his film score for Get Carter to appreciate his genius.

brightest of the Tory backbenchers and a certainty for a future Cabinet post.

So I was as shocked and saddened as everybody else when in 1994 he was found dead in his London home in, to say the least, bizarre circumstances. The coroner recorded a verdict of death by misadventure.

Now how on earth do I follow that? Let's talk about the Ink Spots!

When I was a kid growing up I used to love listening to the Ink Spots singing on the radio. They were a superb close harmony group, and sang with a powerful rhythm that many consider provided the inspiration for rock 'n' roll. Somebody else who shared my love of the Ink Spots was television presenter Fred Dineage.

The producer of his Southern Television show rang to say that the Ink Spots were briefly in town, and could they use the Concorde stage on which to record a Fred Dineage interview with the group. Fred was so taken with them that he joined in singing *Whispering Grass*, and told me as he came off stage: "Now I can die happy … I've sung with the Ink Spots!"

In 1993 I at last succeeded in a long-held ambition to present one of the kings of British jazz at the Concorde, John (now Sir John) Dankworth. He broke into a USA tour to fly home for the gig, and during the second set told the audience: "Our drummer Allan Ganley has been nagging me for years to play here. Now I know why. I wish I had listened to him long ago."

It is now, I am proud to say, looked on as a regular venue for the entire Dankworth family, Sir John and Dame Cleo, son Alec and daughter Jacqui.

I remember when I was first getting interested in jazz in the mid-1950s Sir John – Johnny Dankworth as he was known then – once won no fewer than eight of the categories in the *Melody Maker* annual jazz awards: Best altoist, best soloist, best small band (the Dankworth Seven), best big band, best composer, best arranger, best British jazz musician and Jazz Personality of the Year! Around forty years later there he was playing for me at the Concorde. When I reminded him of the year he swept all the honours, he said with typical humour: "Ah yes, the *Melody Maker* lingers on …."

No doubt about the most unusually entertaining band that we featured during the 1990s, and come to think of it also in the Seventies, Eighties and right up into the Naughties – it's a runaway victory for 'Mad' Bob Kerr and his Whoopee Band, a cross between Monty Python, the Goons and Spike Jones and his City Slickers. Whenever they come to the club it is as if the place suddenly turns into a mad house. They are as potty off stage as on.

After arriving in their creaking old band bus, they take an hour unloading boxes of instruments and stage props, and they saunter in and out wearing pilot's headgear and weird masks. 'Professor' John Percival, the long-bearded Stephane Grappelli of the musical saw, invariably announces his arrival by honking a huge hand-held motor horn. He is the chief prop maker for the band, a graphic designer who has worked for Walt Disney and the Muppet Show.

An early member of the Bonzo Dog Doo Dah Band, Bob Kerr is a multi-instrumentalist who plays the cornet, bass, all the saxes, trombone, banjo, guitar, euphonium and "the hot teapot!" And he sometimes manages to play most of them during one tune. He also sings, and it is his voice – projected through a megaphone – that featured on the New Vaudeville Band hit song, *Winchester Cathedral*. If Bob had concentrated solely on his cornet playing I am convinced he would have established himself as one of the world's great jazz cornettists, but he elected to have fun instead. How bad's that?

Bob's band kick off *You Always Hurt the One You Love* by firing a starter's pistol. Our dog Fergie jumped a mile in the air the first time he heard it and ran off, and after that always made himself scarce whenever the band appeared.

Bob and the boys played a brilliant prank on me that has me laughing out loud whenever I think about it. I will let that old rascal Bob tell the story in Part Two.

From mad musicians to a deadly serious one, Scott Hamilton, who regularly brings his superb sounds to the Concorde. He has an uncanny ability to play mainstream in the style of my old idols Ben Webster and Coleman Hawkins, yet managing to retain his own identity. When you hear him playing with his regular British support of John Pearce (piano), Dave Green (bass) and Steve Brown (drums) you are hearing jazz at simply its best. As anybody will testify who heard Scott on stage at the club with clarinet genius Kenny Davern it was as

The pianist's view of the main club room after our 1990s refurbishments.

if we had been transported to mainstream heaven.

I have rarely seen flying keyboard fingers to match those of Dick Hyman, who has featured on more than one hundred albums in a career stretching back even farther than the history of the Concorde. During a 1995 visit to the club, he told me a true story about when he deputised for the regular pianist at a synagogue hall in his native New York. After giving a piano recital suited to the venue, he told the congregation: "This is not my usual thing. I'll now show you in just one number how I earn my living away from playing religious music."

He then let fly with a rattling jazz tune during which his fingers were a blur. As the applause died down, he overheard a woman in the audience say to her neighbour in a thick Bronx accent: "Did you see the way his hands moved, Sadie? D'you think he does windows?"

We had once organised the Eastleigh Jazz Festival in the adjacent Lakeside Country Park in conjunction with Eastleigh Borough Council, and so so it seemed particularly fitting when one of the lakes in the beautiful park was officially named Lake Concorde.

As the 1990s drew to a close, the Ellington Lodge Hotel was rising from its foundations and the New Millennium approached with the Concorde Club buoyant and looking forward to its half century. How *tempus fugits* when you're having fun.

Yet it was not long into the 21st century before I feared that the club was not going to make it to the fiftieth anniversary.

AS we approached the half century, they should have been the best of times. But, to paraphrase Dickens, they almost became the worst of times. I made the biggest mistake of my life when I decided to change bankers, and I came close to wrecking all that I had worked for since moving into the Old School House back in 1970.

Everything was running smoothly on all fronts before what became a monumental crisis. The Ellington Lodge Hotel was launched on schedule in 2000, under the conscientious management of Mark Pinn, Assistant Manager Sue Stanley and the team. It was a near-miraculous performance by the Winchester-based builders Wilding and Butler to meet the deadline after some of the wettest weather on record.

I used to worry and fret about the incessant rain, but John Clinton was an unflappable site manager who was Noah-like in his certainty that he could cope with the water. I also had the reassuring support of engineering masters Brian Hillman and Alan McLean, and in particular the great assistance of quantity surveyor Robert Jackson, in his role as project manager. Seeing them all working together was like listening to the Basie band, perfect in timing and precision.

Adrian Lightfoot was there for me at all times in his solicitor's role, and our accountant Graham Martin burned the midnight oil with me as we turned what had been a crazy dream into reality. They were the Freddie Green and Sonny Payne of the band, giving everything a strong, reliable rhythm. I was definitely Basie, doing very little but hitting the right notes when necessary. Pauline, bringing her vital book-keeping skills to the team, comes into this metaphor as one-time Basie singer Billie Holiday, and we were all in harmony and playing from the same sheet music along with Lynne, Jackie and Jim.

In 2002 the Disability Rights Commission published a statutory Code of Practice, agreed by Parliament. It meant we needed to make changes and improvements to our disabled facilities at the Concorde. First of all we looked into providing ramps, and then widening the entrance to the Moldy Fig. We realised this would mean changes to the toilets. While Graham Martin and I were discussing the necessary alterations I mentioned that the chairs in the club were looking tired. Before we knew it our planning had taken in a complete refurbishment of the club and reception area. We could have done it in phases, but decided to go for a total make-over, with new bars, restaurant area, stage and sound system, cloakrooms, wall-to-wall carpets, the installation of new air-conditioning throughout and, of course, the improvement to our disabled facilities. We also decided to include an extension to the Moldy Fig wine bar, with an al fresco dining area looking out on to the secluded, landscaped gardens and Monks Brook.

What had started out as minor changes costing a few thousand pounds had mushroomed to an overhaul that would set us back more than one million pounds. Just over thirty years earlier I had quaked in my shoes at the thought of repaying a £12,000 mortgage!

To borrow money on that scale you have to shop around for the best possible rates of interest. I curse the day that I discovered that an overseas bank was offering a rate at half a point under anybody else (I will refrain from naming them to avoid legal fisticuffs … they know who they are!). That half point, I knew, would make a major difference in the repayments.

We had first of all approached Barclays, but an anonymous executive in London refused to fund us despite our previous good relationships with the bank. Our local manager, the totally reliable Kevin Kerian, backed our modernization scheme, as did his boss and his boss's boss, but the men in London as usual ignored their advice and turned us down flat. Throughout my long experience of banks and bankers, I find the local staff generally have an excellent grasp of things and try to be co-operative and encouraging, but their hands are invariably tied by head office busybodies who – as soon as they hear 'club' – imagine a purple-painted warehouse with seedy clientele.

So it was that I went to a Scandinavian bank that had a Southampton branch staffed mainly by ex-Barclays employees. They seemed only too happy to give us the financial support we needed, and filled us with all the confidence in the world by stating quite categorically: "We are a bank that takes the long view."

There was no hint of problems on the horizon in the early stages. In discussion with our excellent building team Vear, led by John Davies, surveyor Nick Childs and Chief Executive Hugh Turner, along with the designers HPW, we worked out a plan for the reconstruction work to enable us to keep part of the club always open so there would be regular but drastically reduced income.

But as we got into the project we found that there was very difficult work from a health and safety point of view. It became obvious that we would have to close down everything with the exception of the Green Room area. This could be partitioned off and used for meals. Suddenly there was very little income and we had staff wages to pay and bank loan repayments to meet.

I asked the bank for their indulgence while we completed the work but found it had set off alarm bells. They started harassing me with a barrage of emails and telephone calls, so much so that if I were to put all their emails together it would be as long (but not as interesting!) as this book. It certainly took its toll on Pauline and myself, and we could never remember being so down in all the years we had been running the Club.

Finally the Bank came up with a deadline of December 31 2006 to repay their money in full. Happy New Year!

By now Adrian Lightfoot had retired and I certainly missed his guidance, but I was able to turn to Pauline's brother Malcolm Le Bas. He just happens to be one of the best known corporate solicitors in the south, and he gave me sound advice at a time of great stress. Malcolm is highly influential in Southampton and is involved in many organizations including The

Princes Trust, Business Southampton and for 25 years has been a trustee of the Wessex Cancer Trust, which we are hoping to help with the publication of this book. Malcolm is to say the least a useful ally to have on your side and an all-round splendid chap.

We hit brick walls when trying to tell the manager of the Scandinavian bank that they were being totally unreasonable. I could not get on the same wave-length as him and on his one social visit I left him in the more charming company of Pauline.

She realised that she might be struggling after telling him that Sir John Dankworth was due to play at the club. He looked at her blankly. "You know," she said, "Dame Cleo Laine's husband." Pauline might as well have been talking about Martians.

For a bank "that takes the long view" they were remarkably short on endurance. They were not ready to accept that it was going to take a little time for members to get back into the routine of coming to the club and settling to the new surroundings and a slightly different atmosphere.

Malcolm got us a three-month stay of execution on the loan being recalled, and -– with the help of our accountant Graham Martin – I went to NatWest and local manager Mike Harrison. He had experience of the Concorde and was immediately enthusiastic and co-operative because he knew all about the exciting potential of the new-look club. He advised his bank to get behind me and just after Christmas 2006 I got the news that the club was back on track and the overseas bank could have their money back.

What made it even more galling was that the shenanigans with the bank had taken our concentration off our vital Golden Jubilee Year, and we did not have the time to plan the celebrations as we would have liked.

It was the nearest I had come to losing everything, and it was not a pleasant experience. It has taken me just a few hundred words to tell the story, but I can assure you it cost me many sleepless hours.

As we cracked open a bottle of Champagne to toast our new deal, I took great delight in reminding our new bankers that some forty years earlier NatWest had turned down my first approach for a mortgage because they said "a club will never work down that obscure country lane."

In retrospect, I can say the foreign bank gave us a new desire and determination to succeed. We wanted to prove that they had made a big mistake.

After a slow start immediately after the refurbishments everything started to pick up and the club has really flourished, and as we approach the conclusion of my part in this book I can start thinking again with that *Over the Rainbow* optimism. We have expanded on all fronts, and are busy night and day. Things are booming as never before, and my son Jamie – in his role as manager – has had to grow up much faster in the business than I ever had to. He and the team are doing a fantastic job.

When I first thought of writing a book I was going to call it *What Do You Do During the Day?* People always seem to think I only work at night, not realising that by the time they

Side by side with Sir John Dankworth, arguably the most gifted all-round British jazzman of my life time. The Dankworth family are great favourites at the Concorde.

arrive at the club I will have worked with our staff on, for example, a networking business breakfast, a Rotary Club Lunch or a product launch.

The bank loan experience brought home to me the fact that I am no longer a spring chicken; more an old cock. But I am not yet ready to bow out. Down in a remote region of France a canal boat – *Fusilier II* – awaits me, along with chilled bottles of my favourite *Menetou-Salon* wine. The boat motors at an average speed of 5mph and the temptation to take the foot off life's accelerator is tempting.

But first I want to cement the future of the Concorde. My son Jamie has developed impressively since taking over the club manager reins from Simon Foderingham. My daughters Fiona and Kirstie handle their duties expertly, and Pauline is still a significant force and will take some following when it comes to organising the books. She is an amazing lady. We were in danger of losing her in 2003 when she suffered an aneurysm on the brain. Pauline battled back after three operations, and these days is full of vitality and with a much sharper brain than mine; it was ever thus. At the peak (or depths) of her crisis, I was standing in the hospital ward when she had to be wheeled off for some treatment. As the porter pushed her off in the wheelchair, she looked at me with a very straight face and said: "That's another fine mess you've got me into ..."

I stood there feeling like Stan Laurel, and roared with laughter. Pauline was so brave, and I cannot praise her (and her medical team) highly enough for the way she pulled through.

The Concorde remains very much a family business, with a strong supporting team of fantastically loyal people whom I look on as mates rather than employees. I am the first to admit that I am only as good as the staff around me, and I pay what I hope is a fitting tribute when I have the Last Word in the book in Part Two.

Two staff members I wish to pick out for special mention – Val Anderson and Marlene Slant, who came with us from the Bassett, and gave us great service before their retirements.

There is one one staff member I have to single out – and all her colleagues will know why. Our greeter-seater Pammi Fernandes is a fascinating, multi-lingual lady who – and she admits it – can be as daffy as a doughnut. While waiting tables she once managed to spill gravy down the Mayor's back, and surpassed herself in the Moldy Fig one night.

Long-time member Jerry Gillen ordered a bottle of *Chablis Premier Cru* which was opened at his table, and he then went to the loo. On his return, he could not find his wine. He was convinced somebody had filched it. The mystery was soon solved. Pammi had gone round putting atmospheric candles into bottle candle-holders, and had plonked one into the neck of Jerry's full bottle and then ceremoniously lit it.

Cameos like this help to make life at the Concorde so richly entertaining, and it sure as hell beats working nine-to-five in an office. Where else could I wander up to a gas fitter laying a pipe – this was during the last major refurbishment – and say: "Any chance of doing the job a bit quicker, mate?" Back came his classic response: "I could do it much quicker if you would give me back my membership that was taken away last year."

Only at the Concorde!

Will there be a SECOND Fifty Years of the Club? That is a question others will have to answer rather than me. I will eventually hand over the baton, and I hope it will be Jamie, Fiona and Kirstie who will run with it. I have had several approaches from companies interested in buying me out, but the future is in the hands of 'the kids'.

I very nearly threw in the towel early in the New Millennium when there was a new licencing act that nightclubs had to employ licensed 'door supervisors' – a bouncer in old money. I got clearance from the Council to carry on as usual when I was able to show that I had never had problems in more than thirty years at the Stoneham Lane venue. There is no way that I want any part of a world where the law of bouncers, sorry, door supervisors, reigns. In my opinion they tend to cause more problems than they solve. I have stood up to several drunks in my time and always managed to control them by using commonsense rather than strong-arm tactics. Like I say, my Army training as a psychiatric orderly has helped.

What really annoyed me about the way I was messed about by the foreign bank is that it

Concorde team photograph 2000: Front row – Lynne Wicks, Ellington Lodge Hotel manager Mark Pinn, me (looking like Don Corleone), Simon Foderingham, Pauline. Back row – Gill Jeffery, Jackie Baker, David Ophaus, Jim Budd.

took my focus off the 50th anniversary of the Club. I had so many plans to celebrate the year, but just could not put my mind to implementing them because of grave concerns about the future.

But it all came right in the end. Fiona, Kirstie and Jamie secretly organised a wonderful 50th anniversary night, with Elkie Brooks topping the bill. It was a great gesture by 'the kids', and Pauline and I were really moved by the evening. Richard Cartridge, that fine broadcaster and an excellent musician, MC'd the show, and embarrassed the life out of me by introducing a procession of people paying tributes, including messages from the likes of Humphrey Lyttelton and Sir John Dankworth. My good friend Lawrie McMenemy and his wife Anne sat alongside me and were in on the secret. I was particularly touched by Rosemary Squires putting herself out to come and make a personal statement about Pauline, the Club and me. She was a star when I was first starting out at the original Concorde, and has been a wonderful advertisement for the music profession. She is, in my view, long overdue being made a Dame.

Elkie Brooks was a knockout, and Alan Barnes matched the show-closing comedian Adger Brown with his hilarious tribute. It was so well organised that it proved to me that Fiona, Kirstie and Jamie have got what it takes to keep the Concorde going over the next 50 years!

Is jazz likely to stay at the heart of the club? I would like to think so, but I accept that the jazz bug has not spread throughout the family. There is also some evidence that jazz lovers are getting fewer as my generation slowly dies off.

But there is hope on the horizon, because there is a procession of brilliant young jazz musicians coming through, particularly from the colleges where the students are well grounded in not only jazz but also the classics. Somehow they have to find a way of appealing to their own generation, rather than old listeners like me. Youngsters have to be taught to appreciate jazz. They need to learn to listen to it and to understand the finer points, such as harmony, phrasing and improvisation. But where will they find a Cy Laurie's, a Flamingo or even a Yellow Dog Jazz Club to serve their apprenticeship? And where can they hear regular jazz on radio and television? I would like to see the magnificent National Youth Jazz Orchestra – often featured at the club over the years – given a regular platform on television and radio, so they can reach youngsters of their age and open their eyes and ears to the superb sounds that they make.

My apprenticeship was served listening to, first, Louis Armstrong and then taking in as many New Orleans bands as I could find on '78' records before moving on to mainstream and modern jazz. This transition was thanks to radio stations like AFN and the BBC Light programme, when they used to feature Kenny Baker's Dozen every Monday night.

You can imagine what a thrill it was for me to stage three reunions of the Kenny Baker Dozen during the Nineties when the great man was still blowing strong. And it was a pleasure to have his widow, Sue, as the first guest to stay in the Kenny Baker suite after Eastleigh Mayor Peter Humphreys officially opened the Ellington Lodge Hotel in May 2000.

Kenny was always a huge source of encouragement and inspiration to young jazz musicians, and I know he would approve of our policy of giving a platform to as many young, up-and-coming jazz prodigies as possible. A standout one, of course, is Jamie Cullum, who was making an impact at the Concorde long before he became an overnight star thanks to his projection on the Parkinson show. At 5ft 4in, he is just a tiny Dudley Moorish figure at the keyboard, but what a sound he can get out of a piano. Jazz purists tend to wince when they hear his name because he has entered what they consider the commercial world. But I think it is good for both him and jazz that he is spreading his great talent and the sounds of jazz as far and as wide as possible. The more young ears he reaches the better.

Bandleader Digby Fairweather was preparing to play a gig with Paul Jones at the club in 2008 when my son Jamie introduced himself. "Hi," he said, "I'm Jamie, Cole's son."

"Jamie Cullum!" said jazz historian Digby. "Wow, you've grown since we last met."

I am privileged to sit on the nominations panels for both the British Jazz Awards and BBC Jazz Awards, and I feel qualified to say that the young jazz scene, as far as the musicians go,

Arthur Ward, Teddy Layton and Alan Duddington, exceptional musicians who gave Moldy Fig regulars hours of pleasure. I hired them as musicians and loved them as mates.

is as strong and as exciting as for many decades. If you close your eyes and listen to Simon Spillett, for instance, you will be convinced you are back in the company of tenor master Tubby Hayes. Simon has already collected the 2007 Rising Star award and is destined to make a long and lasting impact.

And to bring back memories of the likes of Kathy Stobart and Betty Smith there are wonderfully gifted young lady saxophonists such as Karen Sharp and Jo Fooks, proving that jazz is not, like many think, a male preserve. The Concorde bookings quickly mount up when news gets around that super songbirds like Stacey Kent or Clare Teal are going to be in the house. And trumpeting big band leader Georgina Bromilow is great music to the ears.

The future of jazz is in good, talented hands. Male and female. All they need is to find a young audience that will stay loyal to them as so many of the Concorde members have stayed loyal to the club.

Sadly but inevitably, as the New Millennium dawned more and more of my contemporaries started to fall off the tree. I was particularly saddened to lose within a short space of time two of my dearest old friends, Teddy Layton and Arthur Ward, both of them exceptional musicians who had a long affinity with the Concorde.

Teddy led the resident band in the Musicians Bar (and then the Moldy Fig) for more than twenty years, and was as good a reedman as anywhere in the land. Whether playing New Orleans or mainstream, Teddy could kick up a storm. He often used to invite me to join him on the drums, and it was always a pleasure to listen to him while trying to keep the beat.

There were so many stories told about Teddy that he became a walking, talking legend. One I shall try to relate here is fairly sensitive, but he used to tell it about himself: "I got home the worse for wear in the early hours and for some reason, don't ask how, I had a Durex hanging from my fly. As I was trying to silently undress my wife woke up and saw the French Letter dangling, and I came out with the classic line: 'It's not what it seems …'"

I got the permission of his widow, Marilyn, to tell that story. It was just one of a thousand tales that Teddy used to tell about himself.

Arthur Ward, Teddy's faithful drummer, was a regular at the Concorde for a stretch of more then 45 years, going right back to the early days of the original club. His widow, Anne, and son, Simon, asked me if his ashes could be scattered into the stream running through the grounds of the Concorde Club. It had been Arthur's request because he enjoyed his times at the Concorde so much. I had no hesitation in agreeing, and – with his pals Bill Harvey on trumpet and Chris Waters on sousaphone playing appropriate music – dear Arthur's ashes were tossed from the bridge. It was as moving a moment as you can get … and then became almost amusing as a sudden gust of wind caught Arthur's ashes and blew them back into our faces. Anne and Simon laughed, convinced it was Arthur having the last word. It was a real ashes to ashes affair.

The unmatchable Don Lusher was the next of my great favourites to depart. He and I had a special bond because we both grew up as Salvationists, and it was while playing with the Salvation Army in his native Peterborough that Don first perfected that unique trombone sound that was as lush as his name.

Don was the perfect gentleman and always immaculately turned out, and rightly proud of a unique tone that was almost romantic in its delivery. A trombonist from the fortissimo school of playing once asked him: "Can't you play loud?"

"Of course I can," said Don, quietly. "But not all the time."

Whenever Frank Sinatra came over he always insisted on having three specific Brits in his band … trumpet king Kenny Baker, clarinet and sax master Vic Ash and, of course, Don. I understand Sinatra called him: "The Don of trombonists." A good title, but a little too sinister for a God-fearing man who treated everybody with respect.

Don was full of fascinating anecdotes about his illustrious career, and I recall him telling me how he was playing with the Ted Heath Band in Alabama backing the one and only Nat King Cole. Suddenly two members of the Ku Klux Klan ran on to the stage and punched the singer in the face before members of the Heath Band rescued him. A true Salvationist, Don said: "It made me wonder about man's inhumanity to man."

I knew Don was in trouble on his last visit to the Concorde with the Great British Jazz Band in 2005. Three times in a short period he asked me the same question, and for a man who was always so well organised he seemed a little confused and just not his usual relaxed self.

Don was dead within six months. I felt enormously privileged to attend his memorial service in London for what was an emotional mix of Salvation Army music, swing and jazz

Alan Barnes, a British saxophonist who rates with the best in the world and is a naturally funny man who could comfortably make a living as a stand-up comedian. Born in Altrincham, Manchester, Alan studied at Leeds College of Music at the same time as another Concorde regular, Dave Newton.

and there was also an appearance from the Royal Marines band to mark the fact that Don was a professor of music at their Portsmouth headquarters. A few months later we staged in conjunction with the Musicians Union a memorable Don Lusher Benefit night at the Concorde when we raised a considerable amount of money for his Memorial Fund.

Another great jazzer laid to rest was Mick Mulligan, a legendary bon viveur who was as famous for his outrageous behaviour as his trumpet playing. I have never known a congregation so convulsed with laughter as at Mick's funeral in a beautiful ancient church in Pagham, Sussex. We held our breath when self-confessed atheist George Melly, Mick's life-long friend and old drinking partner, hobbled to the front of the church to deliver his eulogy. He stood behind the coffin, almost leaning on it, and told one story in which he quoted Mick as calling a pub a shit hole because they didn't serve his type of beer. That caused an intake of breath. Then, looking around the magnificent building, George said: "This is a wonderful church, but the Mick Mulligan I knew wouldn't be seen dead in it."

The congregation, including the vicar, roared. George, who followed Mick into the great bandstand in the sky soon after, said: "I am willing to reconsider my views on atheism if someone can convince me that there's a bar in heaven. I just hope Mick gets served, and that the place is not another shit hole."

Mick Mulligan, George Melly. They don't make them like that any more.

As I write, the 21st Century is into its eighth year, the Concorde Club is buoyant and great jazz continues to please my ears from regular visitors such as Alan Barnes (the Altrincham Sax maniac, who is not only multi talented but also as funny as any stand-up comedian) … sax virtuosos Derek Nash, Simon Spillett, Bobby Wellins, Jimmy Hastings, and the grand old masters Tommy Whittle and Don Weller … Roy Williams (veteran trombonist sounding as good as ever) … Mark Nightingale, Adrian Fry, Ray Wordsworth (superb trombonists) … Enrico Tomasso, Bruce Adams and Mark Armstrong (red hot trumpeters) … sax/clarinet maestro Vic Ash (who shares with Tommy Whittle the record of playing the Concorde over a longer stretch than any other musicians) … bassist Dave Green (who has made most appearances at the club apart from resident band members, with another fine bassist, Paul Morgan, not far behind him) … Dave Chamberlain, Andy Cleyndert, Len Skeat, John Rees-Jones (more great bass players) … Bobby Worth, Steve Brown, Martin Drew, Clark Tracey, Matt Skelton, Richard Pite, Adrian Macintosh (all as good as any of the much-vaunted American drummers, although Butch Miles takes some beating!) … Ray Gelato (who always has the place rocking) … Georgie Fame, with Guy Barker and Alan Skidmore (they never fail to ignite) … Dave Newton, Neville Dickie, Robin Aspland, John Horler, Keith Nichols, John Critchinson, Brian Lemon, Stan Greig, John Pearce, Martin Litton, Brian Dee, Craig Milverton, Nick Dawson, Ted Beament (all of them piano maestros) … Pete Long (always humorous with his numerous bands) … Humph (who played his last session with us) … the Dankworth Family … unstoppable Kenny Ball … the Big Chris Barber band … and illustrious overseas visitors of the calibre of Ken Peplowski, Scott Hamilton, Rossano Sportiello, John Colianni, Dutch

A proud day as I am presented with my Eastleigh Citizen of Honour medal by 2003 Mayor Councillor Gillian Connell. We like to think that the Concorde has played a small part in putting Eastleigh on the map and this honour was for the entire Club.

violin artiste Tim Kliphuis, Bud Shank and the unique-sounding Marlene VerPlanck.

I had better shut up because I am bound to forget somebody obvious, but they have all been literally music to my ears. These names have come off the top of my head without reference to Maureen Chapman's archives. They nestle in my memory like old friends, and for me it is pure pleasure to welcome them to the Concorde and to pay the piper.

There have been even more famous names at the Concorde, such as Buddy Holly, David Bowie, Robbie Williams, Michael Jackson, Phil Collins and Kylie Minogue, to name but a few of the superstars who have entertained at the club.

These, of course, have all been impersonated on our Tribute Nights -- suggested and superbly organised by Jamie – that have become a regular part of the Concorde menu as we move with the times.

Rod Stewart, Eric Clapton and Elton John appeared for real at the original Concorde, and their clones have performed at the Stoneham Lane venue.

Me, I only like the real thing but there is a large following for tribute acts and so, somewhat reluctantly, I gave them a stage at the Concorde following the success of a couple of charity-boosting Stars in their Eyes specials early in the new century. We now have a Tribute Night every week, and I have to admit the standard is improving all the time as talented artists wake up to the fact that there is good money to be earned being somebody else.

It is the authentic Laurie Holloway whom we are always glad to see and hear at the Concorde for his rare solo appearances away from his intensive work on television. A sublime pianist, Laurie first came to the club as accompanist to his late wife Marion Montgomery in 1997. She had made her club debut on an exciting night in 1984, supported by guitar giants Herb Ellis and Barney Kessel.

I remember the adorable Marion telling me an amusing story about the start of her romance with Laurie. She was singing at the Cool Elephant, a club in London where John Dankworth was the musical director. Laurie, meeting her for the first time, accompanied her on the piano and was immediately smitten. The Dudley Moore trio had played the opening session.

Laurie plucked up the courage to ask if he could take Marion home after the show, but she told him: "I have already agreed for Dudley Moore to take me, sorry."

Marion said: "I was wearing a fur coat and got into Dudley's cute Austin Healey, which had the hood down. As he whisked me through the London streets the heavens opened and I got soaked. I was like a drowned rat by the time he got me to my apartment, and I didn't invite him in for coffee! The next night Laurie took me home, and we've been together ever since."

Shortly after Laurie had appeared at the club in 2007, with the brilliant Alan Barnes helping to drive him along, we had something of a scare when, on St Patrick's Day, a fire started in a duct in our Moldy Fig kitchen. The flames quickly leapt up to the roof and the Moldy Fig was suddenly in danger of being engulfed. What could have been a desperately serious situation was quickly brought under control by the magnificent fire brigade. They arrived with three engines following our alarm call and, using three powerful jets, they had the flames beaten within fifteen minutes of their arrival.

One of the first things I would have rescued had the fire spread to the Moldy Fig restaurant is the sculpture of Roland, the striking, life-size skeletal figure of a jazz saxophonist that has become a popular fixture at the club. It is an imaginative piece of art by Baz Durrant, who first of all let us have it on a temporary basis as an example of his work. We called it Roland because of the surreal resemblance to our design master Roland Tucker, and we grew so fond of it that I finally convinced the sculptor that he should sell it to us.

With Kirstie as our motivating force, we are very keen to strengthen our association with the Arts (and I will always argue that jazz belongs in that bracket). Since 2006 we have sponsored The Point Dance & Arts centre in Eastleigh to form a partnership to promote the Arts at two venues within the area. Because of this sponsorship we were awarded funds by Arts & Business to commission local textile artist Terrie Hitchcock to prepare a work of art

This is Roland (on the right!), the sculpture that has become something of a trademark figure in the Moldy Fig. It is the imaginative work of Baz Durrant, and we call it Roland because of its uncanny resemblance to my life-long friend Roland Tucker

to mark our fiftieth anniversary, and in March 2007 we were proud to unveil – in the Green Room – her stunning combination of fabric and stitch with paint, showing off the human figure in a unique and striking way.

The Arts – with jazz at the heart – are alive and well at the Concorde.

It will not have gone unnoticed that I've had few stories to tell about non-jazz music nights. I have wanted this to be an honest account of my fifty-plus years in the club business, and I admit to having a blank memory if the topic is away from jazz (or, more recently, opera and the light classics). I was therefore delighted in the summer of 2007 when versatile entertainer and former R&B musician David St John came to me with an idea for a reunion of R&B musicians and DJs who used to feature in the Southampton area in the Sixties, several of them in the original Concorde at the Bassett Hotel.

With David as the driving force, we set the reunion date for February 8, 2008, with no idea of what sort of response the idea would get. We quickly found out that forty years on there was still a huge appetite for the rocking music of that era, and we had a complete sell out.

David gives a note-by-note account of the 'Back to the Sixties' reunion on his splendid website at www.davidstjohn.co.uk. What made it all so worthwhile is that the evening raised more than £4,600 for the Liberty Child charity supported by Mayor of Eastleigh, Councillor Roger Smith, who used to be a regular at the first Concorde Club forty-five years earlier.

It was good to see Bob Pearce back leading one of the six bands featured on the night. He often played at the Bassett, and later featured with his Blues Band when we moved to Stoneham Lane. Known as Southampton's "King of the Blues," Bob showed he had lost none of his ability to kick up a storm. He reminded me that he often played the 'graveyard' spot at the Concorde, following the top-line acts and giving solo performances with his guitar and neck-rack harmonica. "You were paying me ten pounds plus a meal," he told me. "But I would have paid for the experience because it was such good grounding."

Musicians had travelled from as far and wide as Australia and the United States for the reunion, and one of our early DJs – Chris Golden – arrived from Canada. Joe Craen was another former Concorde DJ who was there to share memories of "the good old days".

Several of the overseas visitors stayed at the Ellington Lodge Hotel, which is where I seek refuge on the Wednesday jazz nights when I sometimes over-indulge with my wine intake. So where do they put me when it is fully booked? In the 'Wendy House,' a wooden cabin used as the linen store. What a way to treat the Boss!

In the summer of 2006 my life in jazz came to something of a full circle. I received an invitation from Lord Montagu to join him for the 50th anniversary of the Beaulieu Jazz Festival. I told him that I played in that Festival with the Climax Jazz Band, and in the programme I was described as Col. Mathieson. In truth, I hardly ranked as a drummer. I was more private than Colonel.

I reminded Lord Montagu that in the following year of 1957 I helped organise the Festival as secretary of the then Yellow Dog Jazz Club, when Stephane Grappelli topped the bill … and moaned many years later to me because his name on the posters had been spelt Grappelly!

Slim Newton's Band was the main attraction at the second Festival because they were playing for us at the Yellow Dog. Slim later played many times at the old and new Concorde clubs. Two of his original band went on to find fame in contrasting careers. Bob Fuest became a leading film and TV director, including *The Avengers* among his works, and Peter Beasley was a constable who worked his way up to the rank of Chief Police Inspector.

For me, personally, there was the privilege of being presented with a Citizen of Honour award by Eastleigh Council. That fills me with pride, because when I opened the Club back in 1970 people tended to consider Eastleigh as something of a backwater. Well now it is a thriving place, and I like to think the Concorde has helped in a small way to put it on the map.

As I prepare to pass the book over to the more reliable memories of others, I think of my favourite film *Casablanca*. Thanks for dropping in. Here's looking at you, kid.

Or, as the great sax master Spike Robinson always used to say: *Keep swinging.*

Part Two

Pantomime fun and games, family, staff, musicians and members' memories

Strictly speaking, Pauline has been a dominant presence in the Concorde pantomimes.

126 The Concorde Club: The First 50 Years

THE CONCORDE CLUB: The First 50 Years
Pantotime: He's Behind You ... Oh Yes He Is!

THE Great Concorde Pantomime grew out of the annual Christmas party given by the Concorde Sports and Social Club for local senior citizens. It started with a sing-along and then a cabaret, eventually building into a full-scale pantomime with *Snow White and the Seven Dwarfs* in 1975.

With Simon Foderingham as a huge driving force, the panto developed into a fantastic money-raising source for a variety of charities. It has the fairly novel twist of usually being staged closer to Easter than Christmas.

When director/writer/leading man Simon took his considerable talents elsewhere – running and co-owning the highly regarded Oxfords restaurant in Southampton – no less a person than Richard Digance took over for a while as the main motivator.

The unique entertainer scripted (with some additional material from zany comedian Joe Pasquale) the classic *Adventures of Peter Pun*, then followed with *Alice in Blunderland.* and *Yellow Brick Road.*

The pantos are a laugh-a-minute – certainly for the cast, and sometimes for the audience too! It has been strictly adults-only humour; nothing offensive, but plenty that lands below the belt and drives the PC brigade towards apoplexy. Some mild examples …

> From *Robin Hood*: "Who's Maid Marian?" Male chorus: "We all have."
> From *Aladdin*: "Have you had Aladdin there?" Widow Wankey: "Plenty of old men, but no lads."
> From *Snow White*: "Are you feeling sleepy, Snow White?" Response: "No, but he's having a good grope of me."
> From *Jack and the Beanstalk:* "That's a big stalk you have there, Jack. Is that down to those magic beans?" Jack: "No, it's down to my Viagra pills."
> From *Dick Whittington:* "That's a nice pussy you have there, Dick." Response: "And you have a nice dick, Dick."

You get the drift. All good harmless adult fun and with local charities having the last laugh. These were the observations for our book from the redoubtable Richard Digance:

•My connections with the Concorde began when I first moved to Hampshire fifteen years ago. I first went to the Club with Hants cricketer Mark Nicholas and soon became friends with many people there, particularly my good mate Cole, a tremendously nice man and totally crap actor. Which brings me onto the panto!

I was invited to get involved with the charity pantomime production as they'd lost their long-serving director Simon, and the whole thing seemed to be in jeopardy, so for a few years I found myself at the Concorde on many Sunday morning rehearsals putting the staff through their paces. I was amazed to discover exactly what the panto meant to them all. Within the staff ranks were highly talented performers and singers who wanted to get it right as well as enjoy themselves, the perfect blend.

I did my best to get the full potential from the willing team, despite protests from the odd one or two who thought I was pushing them too hard. Most of them agreed that a professional approach would make for a better production and was well worth the effort.

Nobody ever dropped out despite the pressure upon them to rehearse regularly and learn their lines in a very short space of time.

I wrote three pantos in all, and thoroughly enjoyed acting as warm-up for the audience on production nights too as part of my contribution. I don't really know how much money we made but I felt very proud to have been part of a continuing tradition of the Concorde by keeping the panto going.

The team, I think, thought three years of me was well and truly enough, because I was never asked back after that, something I seem to find a regular occurrence around the theatres of Britain!

I missed my involvement with the productions and the ensuing fun very much, but I have great memories of watching nervous actors becoming great actors on the night, reluctant dancers becoming superb dancers through Gilly Jeffery's hard work on the choreography front, and audiences praising a bunch of willing performers who acted far beyond a normal amateur production. I watched from the wings, so proud of each and every one of them.

I hope the tradition continues and goes from strength to strength.'

Brian Kingsnorth always made a big impact as the giant in a procession of pantos before going off to live and work in the United States with his lovely wife, Beth, who was also a popular member of the panto chorus.

Contacting us from his new home in Louisiana, Brian recalled: 'Pantomimes were always fun times and several memories come to mind. One year, in its early days when performing for the local old folks, we eliminated a complete scene because the audience was falling asleep. No one noticed and they all thought the show was wonderful!

Another year, one of the performers came on stage soaking wet and covered in mud. He had gone to relieve himself outside the Portakabin before going on stage, and fell down the bank and into Monks Brook. He was a real trouper with the traditional 'the show must go on' spirit.

Oh yes, and ask Cole about the burning tights episode!'

Over to Cole: "I was part of a trio of dancing, singing chickens with Howard Barker and Howard Carstairs in Jack and the Beanstalk. As Brian – in his role as the giant – came on stage his appearance was to be greeted with a clap of thunder and a sheet of flame. Jim Budd, as usual, was in charge of the pyrotechnics. He let the flame off too close to me and I

Bring on the dancing girls, the Concorde crackers Sue Smith, Jane MacKinnon, Kari Roberts, Gill Jeffery and the PA who leads me a dance, Lynne Wicks.

jumped a mile in the air as my, uh, under-carriage was scalded. It brought the biggest laugh of the night. Nobody showed me any sympathy as my bright yellow and now singed tights – moulded to my legs – were dragged off me in the dressing-room. Our act had really set the place alight!"

Cole recalled from the early senior-citizen pantomime days: "The reason we cut an entire act from the show was because half the audience had dozed off and the other half were complaining that they would miss *Coronation Street*. Yes, we really held them spellbound."

Another priceless memory of a wonderfully embarrassing moment for Cole comes from regular panto dancer and choreographer Gill Jeffery: "It was the Dick Whittington panto in 1994, about the time political correctness was rearing its ugly head. Cole and our chef David Ophaus performed a comedy dance as Zulu tribesmen with their faces blackened and dressed in black lycra body suits – not a pretty sight.

There ain't nothin' like this Dame – Concorde pantomime favourite, Bernie Thomason

"To shield their embarrassment they wore multicoloured grass skirts and with trick bones through their noses, curly black wigs and beads they really looked the part."

"The dance was quite energetic, and they threw themselves into it like a couple of professionals. At a very crucial point in the performance Cole's skirt dropped to the floor leaving him looking like a rather nasty oil slick. The audience thought this was the best bit and the ladies were very impressed that Cole had such a good handle on it – the dance that is, of course. They left the stage to tremendous applause and cries for more!"

It is typical of the imaginative Dereck 'Robbo' Robson, a popular and regular cast member, that when we asked for his recollections he came back with his memories in panto-style form:

> I first went to the Concorde
> With Rotary at One
> We had lunch and often speakers
> And generally lots of fun.
>
> I then progressed to evenings
> And often late at night
> When the girls were wearing dresses
> That were really rather tight.
>
> New Year's was just a knockout
> With Beaujolais in the Fall
> Being Silly at the Fun Fair
> Whilst at The Summer Ball.
>
> Along then came the Pantos
> And what I liked the most
> Was playing the idiot
> Alongside mine Host.
>
> We thought we'd learned our lines O.K.
> Til we got out on the stage
> Then realised we'd lost it
> By the end of the first page.
>
> Too late to go back now said Cole
> It was sink or it was swim
> So it's a "Thank You from Me"
> And a "Thank You from Him."

Brian Kingsnorth has his long johns in a twist as he becomes the crutch for the jokes of the suitably gay Simon Foderingham, who (acting, of course) minced through dozens of pantos.

No question that Simon Foderingham was a major influence in establishing the charity panto-mimes as an important part of the Concorde calendar. Simon put action where his mouth was, often directing and writing the scripts as well as playing the leading (loosely speaking) man. He took time off from running the smart Oxfords restaurant in Southampton, that he co-owns, to share these memories:

•We used to hold parties for the senior citizens of Eastleigh. They arrived for tea and cakes followed by a show. The funniest was when we played the Older Generation Game based on 'Brucie's' famous show. Eating jelly and blancmange with hands tied behind their backs was good for a laugh – often the participants would return to their seats leaving their dentures in the jelly. To this day I'm sure several people went home with the wrong set.

The parties came to an end when on the last old folks' show that we did, one old lady, sit-ting in the front row, missed the bus home. We thought she had fallen asleep but in fact the poor dear had quietly passed away with, I might add, a smile on her face. I didn't think the jokes were that bad!

We then decided to replace the parties with what became the Concorde Pantomime. There are many funny stories but a couple come to mind. I was playing the part of Sir Gaylord – what a surprise – in our version of *Sleeping Beauty*. I had on a full set of armour and before the curtain went up, was lowered rather carefully onto our panto horse.

On I came to *Tiptoe Through the Tulips* – what else – when suddenly as I rode my fearless stallion around the stage it collapsed, leaving me lying on my back on the floor. The crowd were hysterical with laughter, but I couldn't move. Eventually the front end of the horse lowered its head.

'What's going on?' I said from my prone position.

'Sorry about that,' the horse 's head replied. 'The back end got caught short and was last seen running through the audience to go for a pee!'

There were also a few disasters and I will never forget the sight of Cole dressed as a funky chicken – leaping across the stage with his tights on fire. The audience were shrieking with laughter not realising that this was not part of the act, but that one of the pyrotechnics had gone off and set fire to his tights.

Luckily Cole only received minor burns and could be heard saying the show must go on – what a trouper!

Then there was the occasion when we did the longest panto ever, over five hours – should be in *The Guinness Book of Records*. I had persuaded a snake charmer to take part in the show and she patiently waited backstage with her 12 foot Boa Constrictor to come on stage. After three hours the snake had had enough and escaped from the basket. Total pandemo-nium broke out, with bodies flying everywhere. I think the act eventually got on just before midnight.

We did have tremendous fun and, of course, raised a lot of money for charity. The most satisfying thing for me was the many guide dogs we bought for the blind – very special.•

John Linsdell, long-time Concorde stalwart, reluctantly became a regular member of the panto cast after working behind the scenes for several years. He recalls: "I never had any desire to be on stage and I was very content to be a backroom boy helping to paint the scenery and make props. But as time went by I was coaxed to take part by being one half of what became a long running double act with James Karsenbarg as the Panto Cow.

"We went on to take part in many productions as Policemen, Gondoliers, and our favourite duo was the Farmers. The entire cast was a great fun-loving bunch, and although it was very time consuming we all thoroughly enjoyed ourselves. The best bit was that people actually paid huge sums of money to our various chosen charities to come."

Yes, the pantos have raised vast amounts for charities. Among those we have been delighted to help are the Royal Green Jackets Bandsmen (following the 1982 IRA bombing in Regents Park), the Guide Dogs for the Blind, Phonic Ears for Deaf Children, Listen for Life Infant Respiration Monitors, British Kidney Association, Hope Lodge School for Autistic Children, the Allergy and Inflamation Research Trust, Age Concern, Eastleigh Operatic Musical Society, CRY (Cardiac Risk in the Young), the Rose Road Assocation and the Wessex Cancer Trust, which is also our chosen charity for donations from the sale of this book.

Thanks to raising laughs with our pantos we have also raised enough money to pay for 12-seater minibuses for the Tankerville School in Eastleigh, the Riding Therapy Centre, the Hope Lodge School, the Red Lodge School and Salterns School in Totton, and in 1993 we were proud to hand over £11,500 for the purchase of a sailing boat for the Youth Challenge Trust.

Bob Kemp has been a vital and entertaining member of our panto casts, and it was particularly poignant for him in the year that we raised enough money for a Resuscitation Machine for use by the Special Care Baby Unit at Princess Anne Hospital. It had just been installed when Bob's baby son was one of the first to benefit from the machine. Bob dashed from our panto, still dressed in his lion costume, to be at his son's bedside.

The late and greatly missed Alan Froud was extremely prominent in the early pantomimes, both as a performer and scriptwriter and energetic member of the production team. He used to write amusing introductions for the programmes that revealed his waspish wit. This is how he set the scene for the 1986 production of *The Wizard of Oz:*

•This is naturally the time of year when one's thoughts stray to Easter eggs and hot cross buns, and ultimately, of course, to the Concorde Pantomime.

Why indeed, I hear you ask, when all other pantomimes in England are staged at Christmas do the Concorde players insist on performing their extravaganza at Easter? Good question. The answer is evidently simple: The Concorde members get so pissed at Christmas that it is not until early February that the fog lifts, the brain clears, sober thoughts come to mind and pens are ultimately put to paper.

This year we did consider for your continued edification (I hesitate to use the word entertainment to avoid charges of fraud) presenting such epics as *A Bridge Too Far* or possibly *Ben Hur*. Such suggestions had to be shelved when one considered the difficulty yours truly had when being lowered through the roof last year. We also had to take into account getting a

The Concorde Swing Quintet who were brave (and big) enough to give us the Full Monty: Mike Bagley, Rob Wiltshear, Andy Goodson, Phil Smith and Andy Sharpe.

supporting cast of 17,385 fully laden paratroopers on stage, and despite the many alterations Cole has made to the place it is still not big enough to stage a chariot race.

The choice therefore was simple, and lay between. *The Highlights of Cole Mathieson's Sex Life* or *The Wizard of Oz*. The committee gave serious consideration to the Cole Mathieson sex life story, but came to the conclusion that in return for their hard-earned ticket money the audience deserved something longer than four and three quarter minutes, and as leading man Cole would have had such a little part. Consequently, *The Wizard of Oz* was unanimously chosen. You will find the usual sick-bags under your seats. Enjoy it. Oh yes you will!.**

One of our funniest ever scenes was the classic Mona Lisa sketch. We showed Mona sitting for her portrait, and when she was revealed in full it was our much-adored Beryl Smith sitting on the loo! How we miss the wonderful Beryl, another of our late, loved members.

Cooking up a panto storm, our singing chef David Ophaus. Don't dare go near his kitchen! Gordon Ramsay, eat your heart out.

How best to represent the panto casts and the hard-working backstage staff? We decided to pick on three years from different decades to give a good cross-section representation of our talented performers. These were the wonderful volunteers who were game for a laugh ...

SNOW WHITE and THE SEVEN DWARFS (1981)

Snow White	**Alan Froud**
Queen/Gipsy	**Brian Kingsnorth**
Prince	**Simon Foderingham**
Seven Dwarfs	
	Doc: **Bob Kemp**
	Grumpy: **Bernie Thomason**
	Sneezy: **Kevin Clark**
	Bashful: **Howard Barker**
	Dopey: **Garth Burgess**
	Sleepy: **Cole Mathieson**
	Happy: **John Locke**
Chamberlain	**Andy Butcher**
Mirror	**Clive Hancocks**
Pages/Woodmen	**Simon Hartill, Nick Kington**
Girls	**Hilary Westmore, Sally Bence**
Fairy	**Jan White**
Horse Front:	**Andy Butcher**
Back:	**John Bonnet**
Director	**Simon Foderingham**
Script	**Simon Foderingham**
	Alan Froud
	Bernie Thomason
Script secretary	**Jan White**
Sound effects	**Dave Walker**
Music	**Peter Young**
Costumes	**Caroline Barnes, Jan White**
Make-up	**Maureen Freemantle**
Scenery	**Roy Roberts, Joy Roberts**
Lighting	
& Pyrotechnics	**Jim Budd**
Choreography	**Lisa Bradshaw, Alison Stables**
Paint supplier	**Geoff Bartlett**

DICK WHITTINGTON (1994)

Dick Whittington	**Sharron Karsenbarg**
Pussy	**Lesley Monaghan**
King Rat	**Brian Kingsnorth**
Fairy	**Kirstie Mathieson**
Town Crier	**Brian Wallace**
Fanny	**Gill Jeffery**
Alderman Fitzatreat	**Alan Froud**
Alderman's Clerk	**Dereck Robson**
Ratlings	**Peter Young, Bernie Thomason**
Idle Jack	**Simon Foderingham**
Sarah the Cook	**Paul Murray**
Dance	**Cole Mathieson, David Ophaus**
Captain Cockle	**James Karsenbarg**
First Mate	**John Linsdell**
Helmsman/Poopdecker	**Paul Stephenson**
Bosuns	**Garth Burgess, Cole Mathieson**
Peeping Tom	**Kevin Roberts**
Sultan	**David Ophaus**
Sultana	**Pauline Mathieson**
Harem Girls	**Rachel James, Roberta Pritchard**
Eunuchs	**Gary Evans, Rob Wiltshear**
Entertainer	**Kirstie Mathieson**
Written, produced and directed by	**Simon Foderingham**
	Brian Kingsnorth
	John Linsdell
Stage Manager	**Phil Smith**
Make up	**Rachel James, Carla Welsh**
Choreography	**Gill Jeffery**
Costumes	**Jo Pearce**
Sound	**Jim Budd, Matthew Budd, Brian Wells**
Scenery/co-ordinators	**John Linsdell, James Karsenbarg**
Painted by	**Barton Peverill College**
Musical director	**Peter Young**
Secretarial	**Gill Jeffery, Pauline Mathieson, Lynne Snow**
Treasurer/promotion	**Pauline Mathieson**

In harmony, it's the Singing Chef again, with my classically trained daughter Kirstie – giving their rendition of 1992 Olympics theme song 'Barcelona' by Freddie Mercury and Monserrat Caballe.

ALICE IN BLUNDERLAND (2004)

The Narrator	**Kirstie Mathieson**
Alice	**Sharron Karsenbarg**
White Rabbit	**Jane MacKinnon**
Duchess	**Beryl Smith**
March Hare	**Kevin Roberts**
Mad Hatter	**Karen Dolan**
Theatre Director	**Garth Burgess**
The Questioner	**Rob Wiltshear**
The Caterpillar	**Gill Jeffery**
Tweedledee	**John Lambourn**
Tweedledum	**Phil Smith**
Queen of Hearts	**Dereck Robson**
King of Hearts	**Bernie Thomason**
Knave of Hearts	**David Ophaus**
Mock Turtle	**Brian Wallace**
Ben the Dormouse	**Rachel James**
As Himself	**Jamie Mathieson**
The Voice of	**Paul Murray**
Dancers	**Karen Dolan, Rachel James, Gill Jeffery, Shelley Jory, Sharron Karsenbarg, Jane MacKinnon Kirstie Mathieson, Sue Smith**
Written, Produced & Directed by	**Richard Digance**
Choreography	**Gill Jeffery**
Costumes	**Jo Pearce**
Make up	**Rachel James, Debbie Riglesford**
Hairdresser/wigs	**Janice Martin**
Stage crew	**Ron Jeffery, Alan Martin**
Sound	**Barry Wells, Jim Budd**
Scenery painted by	**Kevin Roberts with Gary Evans**
Design & Printing	**Zip Imagesetters**
Secretarial	**Gill Jeffery, Kirstie Mathieson**
Treasurer/promotion	**Kirstie Mathieson**

THE CONCORDE CLUB: The First 50 Years
A Family Affair ... with a little help from their friends

WITHOUT input or interference from Cole, we invited members of the Mathieson family and a few close friends to make their contribution to this 50-year history of the Concorde Club. Naturally, the first word goes to Cole's long-suffering wife and business partner, Pauline ...

THE PERILS OF PAULINE

"Goodness, where do I begin? Let's go back to the days of the Bassett Hotel, circa 19-mind-your-own-business. It's impolite to ask a lady's age, but let's just say I was a 16-year-old student at Southampton Technical College doing a Secretarial Course – completely broke, as students usually are. I was spending all my spare cash in the Tudor Coffee Bar opposite the Civic Centre.

I used to go to the Balladeer at the Bassett Hotel with friends Brian Jones and Mick Gay, and then progressed to the Concorde to see Manfred Mann. We had so many enjoyable evenings there, and to this day I remember with a smile the great nights featuring Jimmy James and the Vagabonds and the marvellous Jimmy Powell.

Fortunately, I only lived up the road on Bassett Avenue so was able to walk home (those were the days when it was safe). It is needless to say that I was, of course, underage to go to the Concorde – one of many adding a year or two to our age to get ourselves in!

My luck changed when my friend, Liz Gay, decided to give up her job on the coats at the Concorde on a Tuesday night. "Would you like to take it on?" I jumped at the chance and, although it was hard work (nearly everybody then wore heavy Donkey Jackets or Duffel coats), I actually earned 10 shillings for doing this privileged job! This amount of cash made me break even on my pocket money!

I therefore met Cole – by this time I was 17 but still kept my age a secret until my 18th birthday, when I owned up! Our first date was to the Silhouette Club, then owned by that great character Brian Adamson. We had a wonderful time, and things grew from there.

The club was doing well when Cole received notice in early 1970 that we had six months to vacate, as the Bassett was being turned into a Steak House. The members started a 'Save the Concorde Campaign,' which made a tremendous impact.

What they didn't know was that a friend of ours, the designer Roland Tucker, had seen this old school in Stoneham Lane that was up for sale. How could we organise money to buy it? Cole and I visited so many banks and were told by all of them that a Club in Stoneham wouldn't work as it was too isolated. (The road of course in those days was a small lane – the M27 had not been built).

Eventually, with some help from the brewers Watneys, we managed to purchase the school.

Our family, Pauline in front where she belongs. Fiona on my right, and Jamie and Kirstie to my left. We look on all our Members as part of the Concorde family.

Then the work started. First job was to build a car park – not quite as important as it is today as most of our customers arrived by the No 41 bus which emptied out at approx 7.30pm and reversed the customer traffic at 10.30pm.

As Cole has stressed in the first part of the book, the members were great. They gave up all their spare time in helping to paint the place, and aid Jim Budd with the re-wiring. Everybody worked together as a team to clear the whole site of the rubbish that had accumulated, and all for free beer and pies from The Cricketers.

We eventually opened on the 18th August 1970 for the start of what has been a great adventure; not always easy but never ever dull.

I by then was working full time, first at the Norwich Union and then at the Staff Centre. I have a lot to thank to both of these jobs as they taught me how to do double entry bookkeeping, PAYE, and ledger work. So in 1970 I decided to concentrate on helping Cole full time, providing he paid me £5 per week to give my Mum for board and lodging!

I set up an accounting system but didn't have to worry about PAYE as we couldn't afford to employ staff.

It was frantic but fun. First thing in the morning we would stock the bar, do the cellar work, and after lunch sit and do the odd letters that needed to be written. Back home for a quick tea and back again for a 6 o'clock start. We only had a licence to 10.30pm in those days, so it was great to be able to go for a curry after work.

It was during this period that I bought my first car off Cole's brother, Ginger, for £30. Bessie, a two-door Ford Prefect. She gave me a new lease of life and, of course, became part of Concorde legend following the Charlie Mingus Spiral Staircase Story that Cole has already shared with you. That was as funny and bizarre as anything can possibly get.

As a Club Opening present I bought Cole Fergie, the Golden Retriever, because I was worried about him locking up at nights in the darkness – there were no street lights then. We didn't realise that Fergie would turn out to be the friendliest of dogs to the point that, if any burglar gave him a KitKat, he would show them where the safe was and possibly the combination.

In fact Fergie became quite a character, and it was not unknown for him to wander up to Eastleigh Ambulance Station in the evening to share their chocolate biscuits. Once they found out where he belonged he then used to be given a lift home in an Ambulance. Don't forget these were the days before Health and Safety took over our lives and the Nanny State introducing so many PC rules.

I know a lot has been written about Fergie, but the one night I remember was his first birthday. It fell on a Sunday, so we asked the Magistrates for an extension of licencing hours to celebrate an Honorary Member's birthday – one Fergie Mathieson. A bit tongue in cheek – but we got away with it.

We didn't charge any extra but just asked for birthday presents for Fergie. I think the supply of biscuits and chew bones lasted a good year. But true to form when the band played Happy Birthday, Fergie laid on his back in the middle of the dance floor and wee'd in the air with a tremendous fountain. He brought the house down.

After about six months we decided that we could afford a cleaner – what a luxury! And along came the wonderful Mrs Carter. She entered into the spirit of the Club, and used to come socially in the evening. Fergie would wander to her house (at the rear of the Club) and she would phone and say she had him and would bring him back in the morning.

As we had no kitchen we put up a table in the cellar and Cole's famous Billy Bunter Rolls were created. They were massive and certainly filled the customers up. Life in those early days was great and really enjoyable – although exhausting.

Then it all started – Cole wanted to expand. He knew that the only way forward was to get a late licence so we had to build a restaurant and kitchen. More visits to the Bank!

Once we opened the restaurant in 1972 it certainly signalled a change of my life. I was quite happy doing the books and wages, but suddenly I was asked to be a Chef one night a week. I did not have one lesson in cooking at school as I was put into the Latin section, so here I was asking people to pay good money for my cooking!

I suppose that because I had been brought up to go to good restaurants it came naturally to me, and in fact I quite enjoyed it. I couldn't have been that bad because within a few years I was cooking 100 meals on a Saturday night, with the help I must stress of the kitchen team behind me! One good thing happened when David Ophaus joined the staff – I was banished back to Reception.

When the restaurant had been opened Cole dabbled in a bit of cooking and made his famous fish pie for the Panto Cast Rehearsal lunch – shame he forgot to put n the sauce!

Cole and I married in March 1973 and lived in the School House, which is now the Moldy Fig. His wedding day gift to me of a mangle was, I suppose, meant to put me in my place, but I am delighted to report that I have never ever put it to use. Once our children arrived, we moved our home away from the business and my life was spent juggling work and a baby sitting rota so I could work in the evenings.

Cole's devotion to jazz is legendary, and can best be illustrated by stories surrounding the birth of our two children. I was overdue with Kirstie and after a regular check up with the doctors I was booked in for 22nd October to be induced. Shock Horror from Cole! "That is the day I have the World's Greatest Jazz Band booked," he wailed. "I won't be able to cope!" After a lot of chatting to doctors I managed to get it brought forward to 18th October, when Kirstie arrived a little earlier than she had planned. Cole enjoyed the World's Greatest Jazz band without any hassle.

I also had a problem with Jamie as they decided to induce him on 1st September. Aghhhhh … our membership renewal date, and one of the busy days of the year. But, with some reluctance, we decided to go along with that!

After the expansion of the restaurant Cole had itchy feet and Simons Wine Bar and Pepper Joe's Restaurant were born. Again – would I set up a bookkeeping system and do the wages?

It was fun working with Simon (a former DJ at the Club). As this is about the Concorde I will leave the history of those two places alone – they will need a book themselves.

Mums' the word, two special ladies: Gladys Le Bas and Edith Mathieson.

Then of course Cole started to realise his dream of having a Hotel on site. Another set of books! But at least I was spared from making the beds! Ellington Lodge has been a huge success thanks to a lot of effort going into the design and then the devotion of the staff over there.

In October 2003 I was taken ill with a brain aneurysm and was in hospital for four months following three delicate brain operations. My family were so supportive during these days – not that I knew what was going on half of the time as I became quite do-lally!   What's new???

On my release from hospital I couldn't wait to get back to work. Oh what changes had been made! It was if I had been away for years rather than months. We were now computerised! Help! Graham Martin, our Accountant, had designed a new way of doing the bookkeeping, so my famous Red Books were no longer allowed. Fiona and Kirstie had been helping Graham to do my work, so I came back with everything being up to date. I never thought I would say this but the new system is much easier – me praising computers; whatever next!! That's almost the equivalent of Cole praising Country and Western music.

My health now is fine, and although I am still working I don't do quite as many hours as I did and enjoy taking our two dogs, Teddy and Yoshi, for walks.

When I looked at our wedding photographs for this book I suddenly realised that I had not mentioned my dear old Mum, Gladys Le Bas. She was an incredible person who adored her family and grandchildren. My father died when I was 11 years old in tragic circumstances. My Mum found that she had to go out to work to get Mal and I through our final schooling. In fact my brother was due to go to University but took Articles instead with Paris, Smith and Randall where he eventually became Senior Partner.

I left school at 16 to do a secretarial course. Mum got a job at Chanelles Dress Shop in Above Bar and later the manageress, Mrs Phillips, opened up her own shop, Susan Gowns in Portswood and put my Mum in charge.

When she retired we had by then opened Simons Wine Bar and she became a part-time cook down there, producing some incredible dishes. When we left Simons I decided to open the Musicians Bar (now the Moldy Fig) and Mum agreed to do some cooking for me – all her wonderful pies, sausage and mushroom plait, and quiches. It gave her a bit of pocket money and put the Musicians Bar on the map for local businesses.

In the meantime Mum used to babysit for me whenever I asked – either the kids going to her or she would come and stay at our house. Every Wednesday she had her five grandchilden for tea and during the school holidays would have Kirstie and Jamie all day to enable me to go to work. I also had a regular babysitter in Katy Dean, who came every Wednesday to enable me to go to the Club to serve Interval Food – then served in the Green Room.

My Mum was the life and soul of any party going on and she adored the Club and would help me out whenever I asked. Sadly she died of kidney failure 15 years ago. Cole and I and the children still miss her terribly, and often have a laugh reminiscing about funny events that took place when she was around.

One Thursday morning when Jamie was about four he came down in the morning and said: "I didn't know Grandma stayed last night" She didn't I said. "Oh yes she did," Jamie responded firmly. "I have just got in bed with her and given her a cuddle." Shock horror! Who was in the bed? I charged upstairs and woke Cole, who drowsily explained: "Oh it's Georgie Fame – he stayed the night!"

My one claim to fame is that I once threw Rod Stewart out of the original club. He was a real rascal in those days, struggling along on a gravedigger's wages. There were French windows in the main room, and he tried to smuggle his way in without paying. I think it was a Manfred Mann night. I spotted him and showed him the way out. Now he could afford to buy the club!

Cole and I have had a most amazing journey, mostly happy and always eventful. I don't think either of us envisaged quite how the Club would grow when we bought it in 1970. We have had fantastic support from our Staff who have adapted to all the changes over the years with great enthusiasm.

Jamie, Kirstie and Fiona are now very much involved. They organised a superb 50th Anniversary dinner for us in October 2007, for which I can't thank them enough.

Now, whatever next? I am just waiting to hear Cole say: 'I've got an idea …'❜

The Mathieson sisters Kirstie (left) and Fiona, who is now Mrs Tony Giles.

A 1997 family affair ... Pauline, Kirstie, Jamie, me and our son-in-law Tony, married to Fiona.

FIONA, FERGIE AND THE MISSING Y-FRONTS

A memory from Fiona, Cole's eldest daughter from his first marriage to Mary Hagens. Now Mrs Giles, Fiona works at the Concorde with special responsibilities for Human Resources. She takes us back to her childhood:

'I remember as a child spending my school holidays at the Club when Dad and Pauline were living in what is now the Moldy Fig. Dad would collect me from my Mum's, and I was more or less left to my own devices during the day. Consequently much of the time was spent with our beautiful golden retriever Fergie!

I can clearly recall being given a blow-up dinghy for my birthday one year but without a footpump. I would spend almost an hour blowing the damn thing up by mouth and then launching the dinghy off the riverbank.

Fergie was most impressed with this and used to swim ahead of the dinghy. With me holding onto his lead, we would sail up and down the river.

I taught him, with a little help from Rufus the dog next door, who already had this skill under his belt (or paw), to retrieve bricks and large stones from the river that runs through the grounds of the Club. I would throw a brick and Fergie would leap in with enormous energy and enthusiasm, then manoeuvre the brick into position and proudly surface with the brick in his mouth!

As mentioned, Rufus belonged to the neighbour Ralph Hallett, who still lives next door to the Club. On one occasion just before we were due to go on holiday to South Devon, it was discovered that a pair of Ralph's blue Y-fronts had gone missing from the washing line. There was much discussion and laughter as to who may have wanted to steal a pair of old underpants!

The following day we left for our holiday and as usual stopped en route for everyone to stretch their legs, including Fergie.

We pulled into a car park, and let Fergie out of the car. He was promptly sick. Not unusual itself but to our amazement, he regurgitated the said pair of blue Y-fronts! The thief had been caught red pawed.

Fast forward now to a more recent memory. One Saturday in August 1992, Kirstie and I decided to spend an evening at the Club for a few drinks and a dance. We were approached by a chap who was clearly very confident in himself and we later found out that his nickname was Bungalow Bill!

He started off by telling us that he was a regular at the Club, to which we replied that we both were too. Then, to impress us, Bungalow Bill said that he knew Cole, to which we replied, "So do we".

He then went on to say that he knew Cole very well and had known him for years, to which we replied that we had too!

Bungalow Bill disappeared shortly after we dissolved into fits of laughter when we told him Cole was our dad.'

KIRSTIE AND THE CURSE OF MIKE HUNT

PAULINE and Cole's daughter Kirstie is a trained opera singer, who has become a motivational backroom force in the running of the Concorde. Here she reflects on what it was like growing up as the daughter of a night club owner:

•It was a 'different' childhood to most of my friends. I remember whilst at school I was always popular around about panto time of year with my risqué jokes going down a storm with my friends, although I'm not so sure I was so popular with my posh friends' parents! Friday morning was also interesting at school when my teachers looked a little bit the worse for wear after a Thursday night at the Concorde.

An early memory was when Pat Masom was Dad's secretary and I casually asked what the 'L' in C L Mathieson stood for. Pat replied 'Lazybones' – and for years that is what I thought Dad's middle name was. Dad was always one for telling porkie pies – one of my favourites is that he once told me he was the lion in my favourite film *The Wizard of Oz*. You take a look – it could be true; there is definitely more than a similarity.

The Pantos have always been interesting. I'm not so sure that my tutors at music college would be too proud of some of the things I've had to do or songs I've had to sing.

Singing, for example, the *Brindisi* from *La Traviata* whilst wearing a life jacket under a ball gown that, as the duet went on, had more air pumped into it so that by the end I was enormous; or singing *The Titanic* theme tune *My Heart Will Go On* whilst 'on board' the tastefully re-named *Tit-anic* complete with iceberg moving across the stage and life size penguins, or even a Nana Mouskouri duet with Demis Roussos.

But by far one of the most memorable 'roles' for me was in my first panto. Still in my innocent teens, I had one line to say. The panto was *Cinderella* and I was in the ballroom scene. I was a guest at the ball – the footman announces the arrival of the eminent Michael Hunt to which I responded: "Oh I haven't seen Mike Hunt for ages!" I couldn't look Mum or Dad in the eye for weeks!

Mind you, some of the things I've seen them do/say on the stage could have scarred me for life. Not only content with embarrassing Jamie and I in the small confines of the club, Dad and Richard Buswell went on to Tom O'Connor's TV show with their lederhosen routine and their sand dance was even performed (in full costume!) in Ibiza.

It is quite an experience to sing opera in what is essentially a jazz club. Several 'jazzers' in the audience were dipping their toes into the Opera waters for the first time and were quite sure how to react. My friend Sera Baines (who performs with me in the opera cabaret dinner shows I have put on at the club) giggles along with me at a rather strange occurrence that happens during the shows. You can picture the scene: a smokey (well, it used to be) jazz bar, the jazz pianist starts the tune, he plays the opening line with the audience nodding their heads, then recognising the tune applaud and acknowledge the band.

The Concorde went to the dogs long ago. The Club has been the domain of a procession of dogs, including the legendary Fergie (right) and now Boris (aka Stinky or Yoshi) and Teddy (above). The night that Fergie celebrated his birthday by peeing a fountain into the air is part of Concorde folklore. Teddy has taken over from Fergie as the character dog of the Concorde, and is famous for stealing chips from unsuspecting musicians as they eat in the dressing-room. It is perhaps fitting that Concorde members have raised thousands of pounds for Guide Dogs for the Blind.

Now switch the picture in your mind to the Concorde on Opera night. Our fabulous pianist Jeremy Limb (whose Dad was a jazz pianist who played with, among others, Chris Barber) starts the dramatic introduction, Sera the heroine soprano character is just about to kill herself in the name of love, she sings the first phrase and, yes, you've guessed it, a number of the audience start nodding their heads and acknowledging that they know the tune! You can take the jazz fan out of the jazz club but you can't take the jazz out of a jazz fan!

A couple of stories that stick in my mind from when I was working in the restaurant: One of the waiters (who shall remain nameless) had been dancing with a young lady and things were going well. Suddenly he was back in the restaurant.

When asked what had happened he replied: "We were dancing away when suddenly she stopped and started scrabbling around on her hands and knees on the dance floor. When I asked what she had lost she replied, 'Sorry but my teeth have just fallen out!'"

Another time I was working the bar when the great Bud Shank was headlining. One of the support band asked in a heavy American accent: 'A Scotch and a Bud.' At least that's what I thought he said, and I duly served him a Scotch and a bottle of Bud. He looked at me as if I was daft (me?), and said in a very slowly delivered way: "I asked for a Scotch for Bud."

The Concorde charity quiz and curry nights have been good fun – the first one my team won! (and no, it wasn't a fix). The next one I was hauled on stage to mark the answer sheets as question setter Geof Holt had forgotten the last round and had to dash home to get it. Geof (again!) also has been known to get the answers wrong even though he set the questions. One time his answers meant Lulu won the Rear of the Year award when only seven years old!

Dad has always enjoyed his glass of wine ("Never" I hear you cry!). The lovely, much-mourned Pat Sparling, who worked at the club for many years and passed on well before her time in 2006, had a long-standing bet with Dad that she would go before him. He vowed that if she did he would down a glass of *Lambrusco* in one go, and true to his word that is exactly what he did at her wake! A favourite memory about Pat was when one evening she received a phone call from Max Bygraves, who was very much into his jazz. Pat, not believing it was him, proceeded to give Max the third degree, finally saying: "Cole, stop mucking around. I know it's you, you plonker!" The penny dropped when Dad walked around the corner!

One of my most recent memories happened at Christmas 2007. Jamie's tribute band nights have always surprised me – I've never really been into copying an artiste, probably from my training at the Welsh College of Music & Drama and English National Opera Baylis programme, where you are taught to find your own voice and style. However they have grown on me and some of them are spookily similar. At Christmas Jamie put on 'A Night for the Ladies' which consisted of a George Michael tribute (Rob Lamberti) and a Robbie Williams tribute (Paul Warren). Neither had met before the evening. Paul did his Robbie set, then Rob as George came on. Rob got completely carried away and in the end it turned out to be an evening of karaoke with George Michael. He got Paul back onto the stage and they did a couple of unrehearsed duets. After his fourth or fifth encore Rob finally got off the stage and went back to the hotel to change.

I had gone to reception to get my coat when Paul suddenly came out and said could I call the hotel because he wanted to have a photo taken with Rob. What followed was one of those conversations that you never expect to be having: "Hello, is that George Michael? Hi, it's Kirstie here. I am at the club reception with Robbie Williams and he wondered whether you could come back to the club as he would like a photo taken with you!"

The Club has always had a good relationship with Hampshire County cricketers, annually supporting their benefits. I always remember Dad telling a story of how when Robin Smith signed up to Hampshire he was given a membership on the understanding that he was over 18 etc. It was all going well until Robin had a fantastic match and splashed all over the papers on the Monday morning – Robin Smith, Hampshire's hero and he is only 16!

One of the newer dogs on the scene is Stinky (otherwise known as Yoshi or Boris). He has appeared in the Panto as the Giant's lunch, and has become well known around the club. The other week one of the printers upstairs suddenly stopped working. After many hours wasted and

Jeff (Gill Jeffery's husband and our IT man!) coming in to sort it out, the problem laughingly became clear … Stinky had sat on the wires and pulled the plug out of the socket.

Before the club got refurbished we had a rather unusual wiring set up courtesy of Jim'll Fix-It Budd. As the club had got bigger and bigger more and more 'patches' had been added to the wiring. One Saturday night the fuse blew. Where was the fuse box… oh dear, directly above Table 6 in the restaurant. The puzzled diners had to be moved whilst the manager stood on a chair, removed a square of the ceiling and turned the electrics back on!

One of my cousins, who shall remain nameless, worked at the Club while not at Uni. Soon after he qualified he started working for a local accountancy firm. One evening he was asked by his colleagues whether he wanted to join them as they were going out to the Breakfast Club. My cousin had never heard of the Breakfast Club and asked where it was. The reply he got was, "Oh its real name is the Concorde Club but we call it the Breakfast Club, as if you get lucky you are guaranteed to get breakfast in bed the following morning!"

In recent years due to our close promixity to the crematorium we have been host to a number of wakes. On one occasion a lady called up to speak to Lynne about a wake. Lynne went through all the costs and various options. When Lynne asked whether she had a date the lady replied: "Oh no, he hasn't died yet but you can never be too prepared!"

Finally, a story of being made completely speechless. One evening the irreplaceable George Melly was doing 'An audience with….' type of dinner. I was sat next to George and was feeling rather shy and star struck. I offered him some water to which he replied 'Water – why would I drink water? Fish f**k in it!'

Only at the Concorde!

WHEN KENNY BAKER CAMPED AT THE CONCORDE

KENNY BAKER was adored by everybody at the Concorde, not only for his magical trumpet playing but also his magnetic personality. His widow, Sue, remains a welcome visitor: Kenny appeared at the Concorde Club many times, from the early days of the Club right through until his untimely death in December 1999. It would be too much to list every appearance so I will confine myself to mentioning one or two of the many great evenings. The first was in December 1996 when Kenny, with his famous "Baker's Dozen", which he had reformed in 1993, was invited by Cole to appear at the Concorde and then again in 1998.

As all true jazz fans will know, Kenny also ran "The Best of British". I well remember the evening of 26th June 1996, a full house, a truly fantastic atmosphere when the band – made up of Kenny on trumpet, Jack Parnell on drums and doing vocals, Don Lusher on trombone, Lennie Bush on bass, Roy Willox on alto sax and clarinet, and Brian Lemon on piano – gave a much acclaimed performance.

From the very beginnings of the Club, Kenny considered it one of his favourite venues. He loved the atmosphere and a drink or two in the Moldy Fig. Ellington Lodge had not yet been built, so Cole, kindly agreed that Kenny and I, plus our beloved dogs of course, could camp overnight in the Club car park, as we often did. For me, the Concorde will always have a special place in my heart. It's a quality venue for lovers of real music, especially jazz.

AFTER getting a degree in Sociology at the University of Exeter, Jamie eventually decided to come under the Concorde umbrella and has established himself as Club Manager in succession to Simon Foderingham. Among the innovations he introduced to the agenda – despite some opposition from Cole – are the enormously popular Tribute Nights. This is his tribute to the Club:

'I was born into the Concorde. Some of my very early recollections of my life were seeing my Dad dressed as a Pirate, a Chicken and even a woman. Fortunately this wasn't a cross dressing ritual but Pantomime rehearsal. I was dragged every Sunday to rehearsal and then repeatedly told not to mention anything I heard while at school. I now know why!!

I used to help with bottling up and glass collecting until I left for the University of Exeter. It was quite a magnet for the girls and a great chat-up line that my father owned a Private Members Club. Dreams of being the next Peter Stringfellow though were squashed once they visited the Club to find the party rocking for the over 40's!

After University I began a career in IT consultancy in London. When I was made redundant I moved back to Southampton to earn a few pennies behind the bar. I found myself enjoying it, and when Simon Foderingham left I took on the role of Duty Manager.

My eventual love for the Club was briefly tarnished on my first week by a group of Newcastle builders (each of them 18 stone and above) who wanted to batter me for not letting them into the Club on a Saturday night. I did succeed in stopping them!

I grew into my role at the Club and wanted to provide a different sort of entertainment on a regular basis. The jazz has always gone well but I felt that the 'Disco Members' wanted something different to just DJ's.

After much persuasion, Dad – who admits he is deaf to music outside jazz, opera and classics – agreed with my idea of Tribute Bands. He initially had reservations about it as he felt karoake would never work, but with the valued assistance of Terry Rolph, of Avenue Artists, we got the new project up and running.

Tribute Thursday was born on April 15th 2004, with Ultimate Abba the debut group. They sounded like them but were probably two to three times the size. Ultimate Flabba!

Tributes started as one every six weeks, then increased to every month and then – in May 2005 – to every week. They have been a resounding success with many dates having the 'Restaurant Full' sign months in advance.

There are too many favourites to mention because the quality overall is extraordinary. Some highlights and lowlights include:

A Beach Boys tribute band, who were appalling and not the sort of standard I require at the Concorde They finished a highly forgettable set of the magnificent singalong tunes of the original Beach Boys with some ear-challenging heavy metal by The Darkness – much to the

REMEMBERING OUR PAT

THERE will be hundreds of Concorde members who will fondly remember the face on the right. It is our former receptionist Pat Sparling, who is a legendary and much loved figure in the history of the club.

We have put her here in the family section because that's how we considered her, as part of the family.

Pat was the welcoming face of the club for many years, and knew just how to mix a friendly greeting with firm authority when required. We lost Pat all too early, and these irreverent yet lovingly compiled words at her funeral from local Knight of the Round Table Dereck Robson summed up how we all felt about her:

My memories of Pat are fond;
At Concorde she stamped her mark,
If you were pissed and wanted in
You passed the Matriarch.

The lady there, antennae tuned
Could tell if you were right,
And if you passed her searching glance
You could stay in there all night.

I remember first, when dying of thirst
From Round Table I had come,
I met her glare, and just stood there
Looking humble and somewhat glum.

"So where've you been you naughty boy,
And where is Shirl the Girl?"
"I've been Round Table, Auntie Pat,
Not with my little Pearl."

"Well you can come in, don't make a din,
Don't drive the people loco."
"Well thank you, Pat, I'll do just that,
And have a cup of cocoa."

bemusement rather than the amusement of the over 60's crowd.

An Evening with Frank Sinatra and Dean Martin turned into farce as – when having problems with sound – they fell out and refused to talk to each other. Dean declined to help Frank with his sound as feedback echoed around the club. The problem was overcome as our resident Tom Jones had popped in to the club to have a drink. He helped out the struggling Frank. At the end I had to be a mediator between the warring factions.

That is nothing to the Ultimate Tribute Fallout. We had an A-Ha tribute band who had performed very well. This was until they started to dance with the fans after their show. Jealousy struck when two of the men fancied the same woman. Nothing seemed to be a problem though until the end of the night when they were packing up.

Disagreements came to the surface and one punched the other and broke his nose. What then ensued was a chase around the Club until I managed to lock one of the warring band members in a toilet. I called the police and an ambulance to deal with the situation and I believe the culprit spent the night in jail. I managed to get away at five in the morning. Fortunately this all happened after all our members had left. This type of proplem is very rare at the club. For fifty years, the Concorde has famously been a non-violent place.

It is surreal that we tribute lovers (even Dad has to grudgingly concede how the standard has risen) refer to the artiste as the person they are trying to perform. It is quite normal on a Thursday for me to ring the hotel to tell them to let me know when George Michael or Elton John is on his way over.

Some of the lookalikes are amazingly so much like their original artistes. Navi, who performs as Michael Jackson, has not only performed for Michael Jackson at his birthday party but works for him as a double when Jackson is in London (and when he was on trial!) Most of the time on television you are looking at Navi and not Michael Jackson.

We have had every artist/band you can mention from Queen to Bill Haley from George Michael to George Benson and from the Village People to Status Quo.

Two exceptional artistes are Milli Munro who performs Tina Turner, Whitney Houston, Shirley Bassey and Diana Ross with equal aplomb, and Rob Lamberti, who transforms from builder to George Michael with some fantastic make up and a wig. My favourite has to be Alvin, a balding middle-aged man who switches to as good an Elvis as you can get. What a showman!

Cliff Richard lookalike Jimmy Jermain comes with his own tour bus, which he had great delight in showing me around. There were beds, TV, sofa and, of course, pictures of Cliff everywhere. I believe he really thinks he is Cliff.

The most memorable performance was by Cher, who featured after our *Beaujolais Nouveau* lunch and proceeded to ask Regular Reception Arm-Rester Geof Holt on stage to perform the worst Sonny impersonation of *I Got You Babe* you can imagine. All credit to Geof though. You should see the dread on men's faces when an artiste asks for a man to join him/her on stage. I don't think you have seen as many men run for the toilet, including me.

I love my Thursdays, and hopefully the call for tributes will long continue. I would like to thank Liz (don't mention Andrew Browning), Tony, Stuart, Sarah, Doug and Paul and Ian (the DJ's) and chef Andy Sharpe and the kitchen crew who over the last three or four years have made such a success of Thursdays in the club. It could be said to be a tribute to them.

The Concorde has always been part of my blood and is where I met my beautiful wife Teresa, and where I had a magnificent wedding reception in September 2005. For that I will be ever grateful. Dad and Mum have worked wonders and I am exceptionally proud to have played just a small part in their success.[9]

Jamie pays tribute to Jim'll Fix-it Budd after one of his retirement announcements

JIM BUDD (ALMOST FAMILY) SOUNDS OFF

COLE and I go back more than fifty years, all the way to the Yellow Dog Club days of the mid-50s. We were separated when we got our call-up papers. Cole got a cushy job in the local Netley hospital, but I needed a challenge. I wanted to get into the engineers or the signals. So I told the recruiting officer that I would like to be in catering. That did the trick, and they assigned me to the Signals section of the Royal Berkshire Regiment. I was posted to Cyprus, and learned loads about electrics and communications as a battalion instructor.

This gave me a good foundation for when I was reunited with Cole after my National

Service, and I became the man of all parts. I remember fixing up dimmer switches long before most people had even heard of them. That was at the original Concorde at the Bassett Hotel, where I also set up revolving lights for the DJ nights by using an old gramophone turntable.

Cole used to leave me in charge on Balladeer nights, and I would help out at the jazz and R&B sessions. I remember one night Cole and I putting out the tables and chairs for a session featuring Mike Vickers and his Quintet. Mike arrived early, and while we were still setting up he had written band arrangements for five songs. He was only a youngster, but a real genius.

Another time Cole and I went for an after-hours drink in a dive of a nightclub in Southampton. The place was raided by police because they didn't have a licence. It would have looked bad for Cole when he was seeking a licence himself for the new Concorde. But the police were only interested in the owners and did not bother with us.

When we got to the Old School I completely rewired the place. You wouldn't believe the mess made by the previous occupants, and it was a real team effort to get everything straightened out. Everybody pulled together, and that great spirit has lasted to this day.

My main job has been sound and lighting engineer, and I have been at the sound checks for some of the greatest jazz performers in history. I pride myself on usually getting everything right at the first time of asking. I have seen enormous changes to the technical side, and now so many things are computerised. But it was great fun in the old days when musicians worked with just tiny Marshall amps, and it was a real challenge for me to help to get the sound balance just right.

I have been involved with the pantomimes as the lighting and pyrotechnics specialist since the very first panto in 1975. The funniest incident was the night I singed Cole by accident. He was dressed as a chicken, and was in the wrong place at the wrong time when I let off a flash right between his legs. He must have set a world high jump record.

Cole and I have always had a great working relationship. I do the work, while he watches. That's a joke, but there is some truth in it.

He is very good at telling me what to do, and then watching me do it. I was once high up on a ladder with Cole holding it steady beneath me. I was lowering the lights, and asked Cole how it looked, meaning that he should look up and say. He decided to walk away to have a wider look, leaving me swaying on the ladder with nothing to hang on to. I won't tell you what I called him!

Another time it was decided to put a small bar in front of what is now the DJ unit. Watneys had laid in the beer pipes to the edge of the raised area. The engineers had signed off that Friday with the request: "Any chance of getting the pipes over to the bar?" They were beneath the pine-wood dance floor, which had a four foot cavity under it. I removed a couple of small planks and pushed my way down into the hole and out of sight. At this point the Concorde Club football team came in for a drink after training. Not wishing anybody to fall into the hole in the floor they thoughtfully replaced the boards – with me underneath! Fortunately, I had removed the nails so was able to get out.

It's all been great fun, and I can't keep away from the place. I've retired a couple of times, but keep on working because there's no place like the Concorde. It has been like a second home for me, and I am proud to have been associated with the club right from the start.

MALCOLM LE BAS, BROTHER IN LAW

THE memories I have of the early days in the Bassett are the hatch at the entrance, always forbidding – where your age was checked before they would allow you in. I recall seeing Manfred Mann and Mike Hugg on several occasions when the place was packed and full of excitement. Although I didn't know it at the time, my future wife, Sue, attended with her brother. I was to meet her later!

I was not into the Trad Jazz revival at that time, preferring travelling around – on my law student's meagre wage – to see the Orchestras of Duke Ellington, Count Basie, Stan Kenton and Woody Herman. We were very lucky in those late 50s/60s and early 70s once the Musicians' Union bar on the Americans coming over was removed.

Then, small world! My sister, Pauline, married Cole and it has been a delight to have him as my brother-in-law. I know just how hard he has worked - indeed with him working so hard at unsociable times and me heavily involved in my legal practice, when we saw each other - particularly over Christmas - we both struggled to keep our eyes open!

Quite the most impressive part of Cole's successs is that he has managed to remain himself – dry humour, self-effacing and very loyal. He has, of course, remained true to his love of jazz, which is why he is so respected in the business.

My favourite memories are, in no particular order:

■ Seeing Maynard Ferguson and his big band on a couple of occasions while crammed into the corner of the capacity-crowded Club – this was before the refurb and the new stage. Everybody wanted *Eli's Coming*!

■ Receiving a call from Cole on a Wednesday evening telling me that Charlie Mingus was doing a gig at the Club on the Friday of that week. Of course, we went and what a great experience. That was the night that Charlie famously got stuck in the spiral staircase, but my main memory is of his innate skill on the bass.

■ Seeing one of my favourite pianists, the Jamaican-born virtuoso Monty Alexander, play at the Club was a real treat. What a talent!

■ Watching George Melly down a couple of bottles of Port whilst doing one of his pre-Christmas gigs, again in the corner before the refurb.

■ Johnny M and the Midnite Follies Orchestra … Ralph Sutton … the list goes on. Now, as a sign of age, we have to rely on recreations of the greats such as the Benny Goodman 1938 concert at the Club. I would willingly go to listen and see that on a regular basis. I now look forward to the Gene Krupa recreation.

Of the British musicians, I find the work of pianists Dave Newton and Brian Lemon the most satisfying. Of the female singers, I love Clare Teal and keep hoping that Cole will get Claire Martin to perform at the Club.

It has been a delight listening with my wife, Sue, over a span of fifty years, and we congratulate and thank Pauline and Cole for all the pleasure they have given to so many people.❞

This is me with brother Derek, known to all as 'Ginge.' He and my sister Jan have always been there for me and have been supportive from way back in the Bassett days.

DEREK, COLE'S DRUMS AND THE OLD BILL

DEREK MATHIESON, Cole's younger brother, was known to everybody as Ginge, and was always ready to roll up his sleeves and help with the clearing up at the new Concorde Club in Stoneham Lane. He recalls when Cole still had ambitions to be a jazz drummer:

❝When Cole was doing his National Service at Netley Hospital he had really friendly hours, and was able to carry on playing the drums in the evening at the White's Home pub in Northam. This was before he helped launch the Yellow Dog Jazz Club at the Portswood Hotel. I was five years younger than Cole, and still at school.

When I got home I would pack his snare drum, cymbals and high hat in a case, balance it on the crossbar of my bike and push it to Northam and then take the drum-kit home after he had finished his session. He used to jam with whichever musicians showed up.

One evening I was pushing the case towards the pub when I was stopped and questioned by the police. They did not believe my story that I was taking the drum-kit to my brother, and they accompanied me home and asked my parents to verify my story.

It has been astonishing to watch what Cole has achieved from his start in the back room of a pub. He introduced me to jazz, and tried to teach me to play the drums. But I never took it seriously, and finished up playing a bit of banjo.

Our sister Jan used to help out on the pay-desk when Cole first started the Concorde at the Bassett, but then moved to Devonshire with her husband Derek Jones. Like me, she still gets to the Concorde whenever she can to see our brother's latest developments. We are very proud of him. ❞

R OLAND TUCKER, Cole's best man and designer supreme, has been a large influence on the first fifty years of the Concorde, the way it looks and feels. This is how he remembers the past 40 odd (sometimes very odd) years:

•It was sometime in the mid-60's that I became a member of the Concorde Club which was held in a small room adjoining the Bassett Hotel. There were several rock and blues bands which appeared there and apart from attending these I was drawn to the 'Modern Jazz' evenings on a Sunday.

The mid sixties was all about Watneys Red Barrel and Starlight Ale which featured across the bar, but in my quest for some refinement I made my first foray into wine. I recall the cloakroom attendant Stan Fry and I sharing a bottle of 'Justina' wine, whilst I did 'light shows' from behind the scenes.

During this time I worked in Southampton for an architect and fairly soon moved to work in London for a top design organisation. My visits to the Concorde Club were reduced but I would always get there on a Saturday night. One evening on leaving the Club I noticed a small poster, 'Designer Required'. That's me, I thought, and after a conversation and briefing with Cole, I put forward a design and colour scheme.

This was the age of psychedelic colours, oranges, purples, reds and yellows in vivid patterns, and with my knowledge of the London scene it was bang up to date! Cole and I struck up a friendship and we would often meet in London to look at bars and clubs, an enjoyable but necessary must to 'be cool'.

In London it was the Flower Power, Carnaby Street, Chelsea Drug Store and Watneys Birds Nest era. For the uninitiated, Birds Nests featured scantily clad girls dancing in metal cages! This inspired Cole and I to transport some of the 'in things' into the Concorde Club, including pyrotechnics (but sadly, some would say, not the bird cages).

Discotheques soon became the 'in' thing and I recall the Concorde Club started these on Wednesday evenings – we created a poster entitled 'Disco nights for Sophisticats'. The word 'Sophisticats' was contrived to mean sophisticated people who were 'cool cats', a well known saying from the jazz brigade in the States.

The name 'Sophisticats' certainly spread – it was mentioned in the *Daily Mail* and I recall a club member 'phoning to say he had read about it in a United Arab Emirates newspaper!

Some elements of the Club interior changed, including a timber louvred canopy over the stage. We were all on tenterhooks when 'The Strange World of Arthur Brown' appeared, his entrée for his act and hit number 'Fire' featured him wearing a hat which was on fire!

As time went by it was announced that the Bassett Hotel was to close and therefore The Concorde Club would need to be relocated.

During my travels I noticed an agent's board on a school in Stoneham Lane, Eastleigh, advertising that it was 'For Sale' – freehold. I approached the agents on Cole's behalf, to discover that it had been used as a social club by Prices Bakery (later Manor Bakeries) based

Days of Wine and Poseurs: This is me playing Champagne Charlie with design guru Roland Tucker, that fabulous performer Georgie Fame and – looking like James Bond – Jim Budd.

in Leigh Road. This was fortuitous in planning terms and Cole eventually purchased the premises. On a very tight budget but with lots of volunteer help from club members, the new Concorde Club evolved. I was fortunate enough to be commissioned by Cole and Pauline to carry out their architectural and interior design work over many years, including the Ellington Lodge Hotel.

Away from the professional involvement I have many happy memories of my evenings at the Club for jazz, blues and special events. In particular, on one of the first Summer Ball events, I recall sitting on the lawn edge next to Monks Brook. Among us were many young ladies in ball gowns, somehow they 'slipped' into the brook and several of us ended up doing the 'conga' throughout the brook.

Cole and I have remained very close 'buddies' over the past 40 years or so, a testament to his bonhomie nature which extends to all his club friends and members.

Thank you Cole.❜

MAUREEN CHAPMAN is the lady who built the foundation to this book. Without her facts and figures you would not be nearly so well informed. Here she gives the history of her history in the Concorde:

'A few years ago I went to the Club on a Friday night to listen to the Teddy Layton Trio. I'd done this many times but this evening was different, as during the evening Cole told me he had some papers relating to the Club and asked me if I would be interested in putting them in some sort of order. That night was the beginning of the Concorde Archive. The 'some papers' duly arrived in about six boxes which contained letters, programmes, photographs and other memorabilia of the Club from the Bassett and Stoneham Lane days.

When Cole started the Club way back in 1957 jazz clubs were not expected to last five years and certainly not 50! So although the programmes showed dates, in many cases the years were not shown. I had to work out which year an artist appeared by working out for instance which year 5th February fell on a Wednesday.

I compiled yearly lists and then tried to marry up the photographs and newspaper cuttings, the only way this could be done was to start an index. The index grew and now extends to over 140 pages. It reads like a Who's Who of the music scene in England over the last 50 years, and indeed of the entertainment scene in general as it contains the names of musicians, cabaret artists, groups, bands, disc jockeys, tribute bands and opera singers who have appeared at the club over the years, the year they appeared and who they appeared with. We try to give a small flavour of the lists at the back of this book.

For later years I had access to Cole's diaries, which enabled me to make lists of the performers and events for various years. John Mann let me borrow his *Echo* scrapbooks containing copies of his reports, which gave so much information about the events and details of all the musicians playing on a particular night. Ken Nutley and Gordon Sapsed gave me many photographs and other members have given me photographs and memorabilia.

Southampton City Library have a great archive of all editions of the *Southern Daily Echo* and I was able to glean much information from the advertisements – the first one I could find for the Concorde being Wednesday 23rd October, 1957. Coincidentally the night set aside for the 50th Birthday celebrations was 23rd October, 2007.

For those who remember the Bassett days the curtains were also a great help – as soon as I saw those curtains I knew the photo was taken at the Bassett. One photograph of a dog gave me a few problems, I knew it wasn't one of Cole's dogs, I discovered it was of Pedro, who was Tiny Smith's dog at the Bassett. The photograph is in the Archive together with those of Fergie (Maynard Ferguson), Tubby (Tubby Hayes), Woody (Woody Herman), Teddy (Teddy Wilson), Jamie's dog Buddy (Buddy Holly), and Yoshi also known as Boris (Boris Karloff)

From all these sources I was able to compile lists of performances and events for each year, and we know exactly which dates the likes of The Cream, Slade, Rod Stewart and Robert

Maureen compiling the club history. Without her, this book would be much slimmer

Plant as well as Coleman Hawkins, Teddy Wilson, Sacha Distel (as a jazz guitarist), Nat Gonella and Kenny Baker played at the Club.

In addition we are able to give details of charity evenings, pantomimes, benefits for Hampshire cricketers, cabaret artists, disc jockeys and tribute evenings. There are also programmes, menus, wine lists and Wine Society and Ladies' Business Club items.

We have the Concorde version of the Generation Game. Cole started as a jazz drummer, his daughter Kirstie has performed in her field of Opera, his son Jamie takes part in the annual panto, as does Pauline. Sir John Dankworth and Dame Cleo Laine's son Alec appears as a jazz bass player and their daughter Jacqui as a singer. Georgie Fame has his sons in his band.

We also have Willie Garnett and his son Alex, and Jimmy Skidmore and his son Alan. Ronnie and John Horler have both played at the Club, as have Stan and Clark Tracey, Bucky Pizzarelli and his son John, also Michael and Christian Garrick.

I really enjoy compiling the archive and doing the research, especially for the early years. I have a quantity of material which is destined for the National Jazz Archive. I went to see the Archive which is housed in Loughton Library in Essex, and they have an extensive record of jazz. Any duplicate books etc they receive are passed on to schools and universities.

Now when I go the Moldy Fig on a Friday, time has moved on. The Concorde building has

Local hero John Horler, piano genius, who followed his father Ronnie in the Concorde version of the Generation Game

changed but the spirit and ambience of the Club hasn't. Teddy Layton is no longer with us, I go to see the Dave Lewin Trio, possibly collect come more papers from Cole for the Archive, I look in the main club – there is a new cabaret artist tonight where once Bradley Walsh and Joe Pasquale performed and I know the Archive is again out of date.

On a more personal note the Concorde is special to me and many others. I am delighted that my research has been helpful in the compilation of this book especially as £1 of the cost will go to the Wessex Cancer Trust.

Twenty odd years ago I was diagnosed with breast cancer – it was discovered in its early stages and the treatment I had at the Royal South Hants was second to none. My daughter in Australia was recently diagnosed with the same illness – I contacted the hospital who found my records and the doctors in both countries were able to compare notes.

My research for the Concorde book will therefore help in a small way to repay them for my treatment and their help with my daughter.

There are many personal memories. Just a few ... the night when the drummer dropped a drum stick, we all watched fascinated as it slowly rolled through a crack in the floor of the stage. The drummer pointing out to the band that 'It's gone through the hole'. The jazz night when a member suddenly laid flat on the floor and local undertaker Stan Henstridge measured him. We were all worried, but he hadn't passed away – he was being measured for a coffin in the Panto. Many evenings spent with Pat Masom in the then Musician's Bar trying to find a tune that Ray Ember didn't know – we never found one. Teddy Layton playing a tune for me the night before I was due to fly to Australia. He chose *For All We Know We May Never Meet Again*. Only Teddy.❡

BEN WEBSTER AND THE BRANDY NECKLACE

ANDY CHAMPION is the widow of Bob Champion, one of Cole's closest friends back when he was first starting out in the business, and together they promoted Riverboat Shuffles to the Isle of Wight. Bob, Cole and a great character called Hugh 'Ugh' Collyns were often like the Three Musketeers, enjoying many liquid-loaded adventures together. These are among Andy's treasured memories:

'Anyone who knew Bob would remember his drink was Cognac. I recall the night Ben Webster appeared at the Concorde. Bob returned from the gent's cloakroom with a huge look of glee. He had just encountered Ben Webster and had noticed, on a string necklace around his neck (but concealed under Ben's shirt) hung a row of miniature Martell brandy bottles. Lifemanship!

At the time of these 'greats' touring Britain, rumours were rife of hard-drinking musicians, so it was somewhat amusing for Bob to enjoy buying Eddie 'Lockjaw' Davis a glass of milk, whilst discussing the merits of the latest tablets for stomach ulcers.

On the same bill that night was Harry 'Sweets' Edison, a member of the Duke Ellington Orchestra. It was surprising to hear he hadn't heard a recently released album here of 'Back To Back,' one of Bob's great favourites.

There was a wonderful evening with the World's Greatest Jazz band, and we had a long conversation with that superb singer Maxine Sullivan during which she recalled her eventful career. She was a delight.

John Edgar Mann in his *Echo* review that week summed her up beautifully. "... with winter in her hair and face, but springtime in her voice."

American drum master Butch Miles entertained us with tales of Hollywood musicians vying for the attention of leading ladies. We found that as entertaining as the brilliant music!

And wasn't it great to see two of the South's 'stars' Teddy Layton and Cuff Billet touring with Butch Thompson and the Oliver Centennial Band?

Going back earlier, Bob didn't drive so would talk friends into giving lifts. One occasion proved quite hazardous as we set out (from Botley) in a 3-wheeler car (Triumph Reliant) with snow gently laying. By the time we reached Bitterne, there was a blizzard and the car was skidding all over the roads. I don't recall seeing the one-man-band Jesse Fuller at the Bassett that night. I fancy we drowned our disappointment in the Bitterne brewery!!!!

Whoever talked a very swingy Polish Quartet into coming back to Botley (after the Club) en route to London? It was a freezing night and, perhaps because of the political climate, only the leader and a 'roadie' came in for a warm and some refreshment. I remember taking out hot drinks for the rest, but couldn't persuade them to come inside. They must have waited in that cold van for over an hour at least. I suppose they really were the days of the Cold War!

These are just a few of my memories of happy days. You needed to be there!'

'OFFICER' HALLETT BLOWS THE WHISTLE ON COLE

RALPH HALLETT is the next-door neighbour to the Concorde Club, a premises he had wanted to purchase to expand his tree surgeon business. But the Council selected Cole's club project. Instead of bearing any sort of grudge, Ralph welcomed Cole warmly, and they have been friends ever since. He remembers the day Cole turned him into a policeman:

•Way back in time when the Concorde was being launched and the sun was shining, I had a phone call from Cole.

"Hello Ralph," he said, without any pleasantries. "Could you pop round with your dog?"

"Yes," I replied, sensing a problem. "I'll be round in a minute.".

I arrived at reception to find Cole staring up at two large, threatening Irish gentlemen, one tall and the other wide.

"What's the problem?" I said, holding on to my very friendly Golden Labrador dog.

Cole said: "Sorry to drag you out when you are off duty, *Officer*! But I'm having a bit of bother with these gentlemen. Would you have a word."

I thought bastard! What's he getting me into? My dog was wagging his tail, waiting to be a great friend.

So in my most authoritative voice I said: "Look here, you two, you're being a nuisance. You are clearly not members of the club so clear off!"

I hoped at this point the dog would at least growl, but no. He preferred to be very affectionate.

Then, to to my amazement, the two gentlemen, instead of turning on Cole or myself, started to beat seven bells out of each other before disappearing across the car park. I don't know where they ended up but we had a hell of a laugh!•

RICHARD BUSWELL AND A COUPLE OF SLAPPERS

RICHARD BUSWELL, Cole's close pal and enthusiastic panto partner, recalls the day they got slap-happy on television:

•It was a chilly morning in October when Cole and I both turned into Guildhall Walk, Portsmouth, at the same time. This was surprising, as we had come from different directions. Cole from Southampton and me from Old Portsmouth. As we both stepped out of our S Class Mercedes saloon cars and took our suitcases out of the boots Cole said, perhaps with a hint of pride: "We look like a couple of old pros fresh from the music halls."

We had seen advertised that the Tom O'Connor Road Show was looking for locals to perform short acts on the daytime programme. I suggested to Cole that as we had always performed a double act in the Concorde Pantomime each year we should try an audition. Cole reluctantly agreed.

My great pal Richard Buswell and I show off the style that earned us a spot on Tom O'Connor's television show. What a pair of slappers!

As we entered the salubrious changing rooms called the Portsmouth Guildhall Gents we still hadn't made up our minds what we were going to do. We had the Maori Dance, the Sand Dance, Flag Dance and the Austrian Slap Dance under our belts. Even Fred and Ginger didn't have such a varied repertoire.

We opened our cases, retrieved the lederhosen and ten minutes later, fully adorned with makeup, silly hats and bells, we entered the audition room.

This room was filled with 10-year-old ballerinas, pet animals and strange-looking people. We of course looked perfectly normal! We waited our turn to perform before two young production staff ladies. As we commenced, one of the young ladies started to laugh while the second could not control herself and fell off her chair. We were in.

We went back to the changing room, and I said to Cole: "Why don't we black up and go back doing the Maori dance? They'll never know it's us." Spoilsport Cole did not agree, which was, in hindsight, a wise decision. PC and all that.

Came the day of the show, we arrived early and had time to chat to other hopefuls. Cole asked the man beside him what he normally did for a living. The man, Richard Digance, said that he just happened to be topping the bill. Well done, Cole. Another foot in the Mathieson mouth.

I myself stood next to a young lady who was very scantily dressed. We both thought she was fairly fit. This was former Page 3 pin-up Linda Lusardi. During the rehearsal she was picked up by some local body builder dressed as Tarzan, and with appropriate jungle-call noise thrown over his shoulder and whisked off revealing to the cameras her undercarriage. She was at that time noted for not wearing any knickers. Cole and I felt then that on the whole the day had not been in vain!

At the live show our turn arrived, Richard Digance had wowed the audience, Linda had put on some knickers and we brought a smile to Tom's face. In fact they liked us so much we were featured on the opening titles of the show every day for six weeks.

Not many can boast that. We were titled people.

Talking about other dances, when we performed the Flag Dance in the Concorde Pantomime we wore sailor's outfits with very baggy shorts, plimsolls and flags in our hands. With these we flag signalled during the dance.

Bobby Kemp and Alan Froud had been naughty boys during the show, according to Bobby's mother, and had uttered a few very choice words. When it was all over she accosted her boy, saying he had lowered the tone of the show and brought the Kemp family's name into disrepute.

She asked: "Why could you not be like Cole and Richard? They made people laugh without resorting to smut."

Bobby pointed out, rather unsportingly we thought, that she should have seen the words we were saying with our flag signals.

Suffice to say the second of the two words we semaphored was OFF. We deserved a good slap, without the lederhosen.❞

A SAINT TOASTS THE CONCORDE

MIKE JUDD, once a Saints footballer and now establishing himself as a fine professional toastmaster, looks back on three decades of Concorde experience: "Over the past 35 years, my involvment has been a mixture of business and pleasure. Being a part of the wines and spirits industry, I can vouch for the fact that the club has always been regarded as one of the most successful and professionally run establishments throughout the south of England.

I remember introducing Jas Hennessey (from the Cognac family), and with enthusiastic discussions with Cole, enabled support of the now infamous *Beaujolais Nouveau* days.

The club has always encouraged a 'relaxed but never casual' ambiance, and for the last 15 years it has featured a very successful Wine Society.

Being a professional sportsman, I know the importance of solid foundations along with a good team. In this respect the Concorde Wine Society – in fact, the entire Club – has been truly successful and I am sure they will continue to be so for many years to come."

THE DAYS OF WINE AND NOSES

MIKE BAGLEY was one of the chief motivators behind the launching of the enormously popular Concorde Wine Society in 1992. It has grown into one of the most successful Societies in the south, with a growing number of members proving they have a nose for the bouquet of the best wines. Mike recalls the sweet taste of success:

"At the club in the very early Nineties it was suggested that a wine-tasting circle be organized for the benefit of the members. A small commitee was formed consisting of staff and members, and in September 1992 the first ever Concorde Wine Society presentation and tasting was launched.

The tasting on that occasion was Spanish wines. Sixteen years later the Concorde Wine Socity is still very actively flourishing. During those years regular monthly presentations and tastings have taken place for members and guests, covering virtually every wine producing region in the world, with some regions being featured several times over.

Additionally, outside visits to English Vineyards in Dorset, Hampshire and Surrey have taken place and in Autumn of 2008 there will be the first ever overseas visit, when 40 members and guests fly to the Bergerac region of France.

The monthly presentations attract around 60-80 members and guests to the club and the atmosphere is relaxed and very convivial, particularly as the evening progresses!

I was honoured to be involved in the Wine Society right from the beginning, organizing presentations and tastings which turned out to be quite a pleasurable pastime! I stepped down from the committee after 10 years but still enjoy attending the monthly events. I feel sure that with the success achieved since 1992 the society is definitely here for years to come.

Let's all drink to that!"

The irrepressible, larger-than-life George Melly – they threw away the mould after he had been created. Here he is at the Concorde with Simon Foderingham.

THE 'LORD' AND THE STRIPPER

ANDY BUTCHER, long-time Concorde member, a former police inspector, pantomime regular and one of Cole's most trusted friends, remembers the evening the Concorde was stripped of its dignity: •Early 1970's and Screaming Lord Sutch (who later become the Parliamentary candidate for the Monster Raving Loony Party) was the live act. This was in the days when Cole had to re-new his liquor licence annually and then, as now, he never used any sort of entertainment that could possibly be detrimental to an application.

Lord Sutch appeared on stage, in a coffin, and did his full repertoire, during which, for a specific song, he had a "Go-Go" dancer dressed in a skimpy bikini, gyrating on stage. I was standing at the bar with Cole and he was becoming very agitated because of the girl's suggestive movements and kept saying: "This is going to affect the renewal of my licence." But worse (for Cole!) was to follow – as suddenly she whipped off her top and Cole came as close as anybody I have ever seen to having a heart attack.

Needless to say, it didn't affect his application, and the Club continued to prosper.•

RICHARD CARTRIDGE MEETS A LEGEND

RICHARD CARTRIDGE, master broadcaster and an excellent musician, recalls a day with a giant of jazz: "I was the presenter of the weekday afternoon show for BBC Radio Solent at the time that I met and interviewed one of the most unique and gifted artists to ever grace the stage of the Concorde Club.

George Melly, premier exponent of jazz and blues, journalist, author and modern art collector and lecturer. The most erudite and sophisticated man you could hope to meet.

He arrived at the studio wearing a trademark pink fedora hat, stitched into a suit apparently made of rather garish deck chair material! He greeted me with a warm sincere smile, the sort that ordinary mortals keep only for best friends. The conversation went well. We talked about his music, his art, his friends and his escapades!

He seemed to be genuinely delighted that I intended to watch his performance, with John Chilton's Feetwarmers, at the Concorde that evening.

I arrived early to find George sitting alone in the main room of the club catching up on his paperwork. "Good evening George, Richard Cartridge. We met earlier today, can I buy you a drink?"

Cole had told me previously that George had a penchant for wine from the Bordeaux region of France, which he liked to drink by the pint! "I understand you like a glass or two of Claret," I said.

"Well dear boy," George replied, "I have recently changed my allegiance to a delightful new blonde with a wonderful body. She's called Stella Artois!"

That evening George gave a dazzling performance. Jazz and blues, and the odd risqué vaudeville song. He was charismatic and had the audience in the palm of his hand.

Halfway through the show he mentioned the interview earlier that day. "Mr Cartridge is in the audience this evening," he announced. "Where are you my dear, I want to thank you for your meticulous research. At last, somebody who actually knew who I was!"

As a raconteur he was second to none and as our enthusiasm grew George got more outrageous!

I now pass on the story that he told, which brought the house down and serves as a memory of one of the most unforgettable characters of jazz and the entire entertainment world.

It was the tale of the London cabbie who picked up a naked young woman outside a nightclub in the early hours. No shoes, no handbag, nothing! On reaching their destination the cabbie asks her how she intends to pay him. She opens her legs and gives him a smile. "Ahh" says the cabbie checking her out in his rear-view mirror, "Have you got anything smaller?!"

Thank you George Melly for the laughs and the music. And thank you to Cole and the Concorde for giving him your stage so many times.

I had the pleasure of presenting the Concorde's 50th anniversary show, much to the surprise of Cole and Pauline. The warmth of all the tributes paid that night show the esteem in which Cole and his team are held. Here's to the next fifty years."

THE AIRPORT CHIEF AND THE MOLDY FIG

COLIN HOBBS, former Managing Director of Southampton International Airport, was a regular visitor to the Concorde and remains Cole's friend. He recalls the day he was 'set up' at the Moldy Fig: •Only seven minutes from my office, I used to take a never ending flow of guests to the Moldy Fig, where I knew that Cole and his team would painlessly see us through a splendid meal (three course or those wonderful baguettes) in less than an hour. Perfect for the busy businessman. And so the strategic direction of Southampton Airport and particularly its transition from a small local airfield to the Primary Business Airport for Central Southern England, not to mention its doubling in size, was often fuelled by a Moldy Fig lunch or snack and above all – THE GINGER BEER SPECIAL.

My life running the Airport was far too busy to allow alcohol at lunchtime, but what do you drink? Enter bar attendant Pammi, who had a magic touch with the ginger beer special: Two thirds ginger beer topped up with lemonade or soda and a few drops of Angostura bitters did the job.

It was the Concorde Club that became the scene of one of my most dramatic days. Despite everyone's best endeavours, incidents do happen and we spent many hours preparing for them, in training staff and in the swift liaison with the police, local medical and other services. This is to ensure that in a crisis everything works smoothly.

Everyone is aware of the resources that the media have at their disposal and their reaction to any incident is instantaneous. My staff and I could find ourselves at the wrong end of a TV camera at almost no notice with very few facts at our disposal. And so we had to rehearse that as well, and regularly hired professional TV and radio interviewers to put us through our paces with a variety of stories that often developed through a full day or more.

However incidents cannot be predicted, so the really useful training is that which is unexpected. Imagine my concern therefore, one day in 2000, when I received a 7.30am call to my car mobile phone from the airport. There had been an incident! I was told a runway had been closed, and it was serious. They did not know if there were any fatalities. I was told to go straight to the Concorde Club, where a Crisis Management team was being set up.

On arrival at the Club I was 'door stepped' (a wonderful expression for being ambushed by a camera team from the television station) for an instant interview as I got out of my car. I had no facts and was pretty cross at not having had any warning from my media team, although it was essential to show calm leadership and not get ruffled when on the air.

Well, we got through that and I went inside the club to find I had been on the receiving end of a very successful put-up job. It turned out to be another training stunt dreamt up by Jan Halliday, my Marketing and Public Relations Manager. The TV interviewers and the camera teams were real, even though the incident was not.

It was a valuable experience and helped when we did, regrettably, have a fatal incident involving a light aircraft. This – the real thing – aged me, but I was able to handle it because of the training. I wish I'd had one of the Moldy Fig ginger beers to ease me through it.•

KATH SMITH AND A ROLL ON THE DANCEFLOOR

KATH SMITH is married to former Hampshire and England cricketer Robin Smith. They were regulars at the Concorde, where they did much of their courting. Now living in Perth, they have maintained their close friendship with Cole. Kath recalls: •Having staged a number of events over the years, I can honestly say that the staff at the Concorde Club have been the most co-operative, helpful, and most importantly - fun to work with.

It is almost as if the staff are high on happy pills. Nothing was ever any trouble (whatever challenges I gave them), and they never stopped smiling!   Most strange if you ask me!

When I first met my husband Robin we would always spend at least one evening a week dancing the night away at the club – a regular haunt of the Hampshire cricketers.

You are guaranteed a good meal, and you always know somebody else there.

I remember laughing so much one night. God it was sooooo funny.....

It involved my lovely but extremely scatty friend (best not to name her as she holds a very powerful job now). She came walking out of the ladies' loo, looking unbelievably glamorous with her long dark and wavy glossy hair, beautiful brown eyes all a-sparkle, tiny little waist any ballerina would die for. My friend looked a million dollars ... from the waist up, at least. She walked straight onto the dance floor and sexily strutted her stuff.

Almost immediately she attracted the attention of a handsome young man. He tapped her on the shoulder ... not requesting a dance, but to tell her – much to her enormous embarrassment – that she had a long strip of toilet roll dangling from her.

Not only had she somehow caught the end into her knickers, she had tucked the bottom of her silky flowing skirt into them too!

One of the best, funniest memories that will stick with me forever! Robin and I have many happy memories of the Concorde. This tops the lot.•

SALUTING CITIZEN COLE OF EASTLEIGH

GODFREY G. OLSON OBE, three times Mayor during 53 years devoted service to Eastleigh Borough Council and an enthusiastic supporter of Cole and the Concorde Club. He (much to Cole's embarrassment) speaks for many people of Eastleigh:

•It was a very brave move for Cole to take over a redundant School and transform it, develop and enhance it to become a nationally recognized Jazz Centre. It was because of its importance that in 2003 I had the pleasure of proposing that Cole be made a Citizen of Honour of the Borough.

I describe the Concorde Club as the Mecca of Jazz, and have always found Cole a charming, non-demonstrative, modest man who has developed a facility second to none and in doing so has made an important contribution to the Social and culture fabric of Eastleigh. The Club has always made a considerable contribution to the welfare of the area with the support given so willingly to many Charities.•

THE CONCORDE CLUB: The First 50 Years
Behind the Boss's Back

WITHOUT Cole's knowledge, co-author Norman Giller went behind his back to ask members of his staff to submit contributions to the book. Not one of them had the courage to tell me that he is nothing like the nice, kindly, warm-hearted, charitable character being painted in these memoirs. He has attracted more treacle than Bakewell's Bakery. Leading the way is his current PA and the Concorde function co-ordinator …

LYNNE WICKS: •When people ask me what it's like to work with Cole I say that as a boss he is a pleasure to work with and a very good friend. Having worked with him as his PA for almost 22 years I have had lots of fun and laughter in a job that is simply quite unique.

There are so many stories to pass on, and we would need another book for me to tell them all. But when I look back, one which springs to mind is when I worked on Reception on Saturday nights. It was when the Chippendales were in town appearing at the Mayflower Theatre. Their manager rang to ask if they could visit the Club after their performance to "chill out."

Having taken the call myself, I said we would be delighted to welcome them and duly went through the Club's rules – no denim jeans, t-shirts, earrings, etc etc. The buzz quickly went round the Club that the arrival of the Chippendales was imminent and the girls started to gather in expectation at Reception.

And so the hunks arrived; one by one they came through the door, and to my horror – well, I suppose I should say relief actually as they were at least dressed! ... but in jeans, vests and an array of earrings. I think at that point my street cred as a Receptionist hit an all time low amongst the lady members as I said – as hunky as they were – they couldn't come in dressed like that, and I duly turned them away (I think I could hear some cheering in the distance from the male members!)

One of Cole's favourite expressions is when he rings me, having left the office five minutes earlier and says: "I've been thinking ….", which inevitably means that he's either come up with a new idea or he wants to change something we've already done.

There's never a dull moment with Cole, and his enthusiasm for the Club never fails to amaze me – which shouldn't really as that is why the Club is so successful and the reason I'm contributing to his 50-year book.

I've seen many changes at the Club, experienced the highs and the lows, watched it expand, lived through two major refurbishments, a flying visit by Margaret Thatcher in her Premiership campaign, several births, marriages and deaths, twenty pantomimes, the addition of a hotel, a fire, met many stars from the world of entertainment (including the

Chippendales!) and shared Cole's great pride when he was awarded Citizen of Honour of the Borough of Eastleigh.

All in all a great way to earn a living – and a very sociable one at that. And finally, when people ask me how do I cope with 'Cole's morning after the night before' knowing his penchant for the odd glass of wine – I say, it's easy; I just drink as much as he does.•

PAT MASOM (formerly Fry), Cole's secretary before Lynne: •In the 1970s I organised several coach trips to the 100 Club in Oxford Street, primarily for 'my' Sunday night people (I was the Sunday receptionist at the time). The trips were all successful and enjoyable apart from one notable exception. The coach broke down on the motorway and, as it was a Saturday evening, no replacement was available.

As we were not far from the Club we all scrambled down the bank on to Leigh Road and walked back to the Concorde. We were 'all dressed up with nowhere to go,' so some of us went to Simons Wine Bar where Cole bought wine that cost £6 a bottle – the most expensive wine on the list. We marvelled that we were drinking something that cost £1 a glass!

Because Cole was instrumental in arranging for bands to visit local prisons to entertain the inmates, he was invited with a guest (me) to a performance of Charley's Aunt at Kingston Prison in Portsmouth, performed by prisoners and members of the local Amateur Dramatics Company.

At the time the prison was used for male domestic 'lifers' – mainly unpremeditated crimes of passion. It was long before 'Porridge' so I had no idea what to expect. After signing in (and hearing the gate clang shut behind us) we were escorted to the theatre for a very enjoyable evening.

It was all very informal, and after the performance we met and chatted to the cast and backstage workers – a very friendly bunch of chaps! It was eerie to think that most of them were inside for bumping off their wives.

In the early Stoneham Lane days there were a couple of geese that frequently wandered round the car park, terrorising the punters (and the poor old postman!).

I can't remember their names – I think one was Gonzo. Cole said they were better for security than Fergie, who would have licked the hand of any burglar. One day they attacked world famous saxophonist Eddie 'Lockjaw' Davis when he arrived for a gig at the Club. The geese honked louder than Eddie ever did!

My first visit to the Concorde was all the way back in 1961 when, if I remember correctly, there was Morris Dancing on the lawns of the Bassett Hotel. Yes, it was a Balladeer Night. It was hardly Cole's jazz style of entertainment!

In those days there was all kinds of music and entertainment, jazz, folk, rhythm and blues, the start of Manfred Mann, The Cream, Mud, Rod Stewart, and a young keyboard player called Reg Dwight who later became Elton John.

We also enjoyed such delights as 'The Foot Game,' – too complicated to explain and very, very daft, but we were young and had lots of laughs.

I became Cole's secretary in 1972, and I used to take my son, Adrian, to the office with me from when he was about three. He grew up to play the music that Cole and I love, and I am so proud that he has often played at the Concorde, where Cole has always set the highest standards.

It has been quite astonishing to see the quality of musicians that Cole has persuaded to come to play; simply the best jazz artistes in the world. I feel privileged to have been able to hear them in informal surroundings where, like the punters, they stand at the bar and chat during the interval.

And to think it all started in the backroom of a Southampton pub!*

DAVID OPHAUS, Executive Chef at the Concorde since 1988:

*I guess you could say my job as Executive Chef at the Concorde is unique. My affiliation with the Club goes way back long before I joined as Chef.

My father had a butcher's shop in Fair Oak and as a child I would help out in the shop after school and at weekends. Cole and Pauline would use the shop and that was back in the late 60s. Later they would buy their meat from the shop via Mike, one of the former chefs here. And that goes back to the 70s.

I owned my own restaurant – The Angry Trout in Romsey – in the mid-70s for 10 years. Cole would often drop in, and so I guess by the time he and I first started talking about me joining the Club in 1988 you could say he already knew a bit about me.

I joined the Concorde on Halloween in 1988, and said I would give it a few years to see how it would go. Well, twenty years later I am still here. I have always approached my position at the Concorde as if it were my own business and Cole has always supported me in this role.

He is forever coming up to me and sharing his most recent gastronomic experience and exploring whether or not we provide the same dish at the Concorde. His passion for good food is as mine, always something we try to pass on to members at the Club.

In years gone by Cole and I would walk the streets of London trying out various restaurants, even popping in to Ronnie Scott's for a glass. I have been privileged to work with Cole and Pauline at the Club in what has become for us – and especially Cole – a unique phenomenon on the south coast.

Cole has always made me feel part of the family. I even met my wife, Caroline, at the Concorde, on a Thursday evening back in the 80s.

My love for music and amateur dramatics came in to play, having performed in 20 pantomimes and Echoes of Pantos dinner shows and many 'singing chef' occasions - from Opera dinners to Burns night, Beaujolais Nouveau and Christmas Carols. And I was once Tweedledee to Cole's Tweedledum, and have shared many duets with Kirstie.

What about the jazz I hear you ask. I have heard about the best there is over the years but I still can't tell you whether its modern, old, be-pop etc – but I know what I like and what I

The team making the Concorde tick in 2008: Gill Jeffery, me (the weakest link), Pauline, Lynne Wicks, Jackie Baker, David Ophaus, Mark Pinn and Philippa Davies, and at the back Kirstie, Jamie and Fiona. And we have a great back-up support team, but we could not squeeze everybody into the picture.

don't like. That's as far as my expertise goes.

My kitchen staff and I are always getting compliments from visiting musicians on the food that we serve them, so we must be doing something right.

I have estimated that I have worked around 1000 Wednesday jazz nights and Cole asks me every time: 'Have you made the band's sandwiches yet?' You'd think he'd know by now, wouldn't you!

I have always had the utmost respect for Cole; trust and integrity in a business like this are very important and I am sure they are among the reasons why I have been here so long and certainly why he has been here so long. Cheers Cole, here's to the next 50.❜

SIMON FODERINGHAM, once chief of staff at the Concorde in his days as manager and former partner of Cole in the Simons Wine Bar and Pepper Joe's restaurant businesses: ❛I first became involved with the Concorde Club back some 40 years ago when it was situated in the annexe of the Bassett Pub in Burgess Road, Southampton.

Already quite a successful DJ along the south coast, I approached Cole Mathieson with a view to introducing discotheque to the Club. This was not easy, especially as the Concorde had made its reputation as one of the top live music venues in Southampton. However, eventually Cole agreed to give us a chance and with my partner at the time, Jon Ferris, we started to work on Wednesday nights, initially introducing some of the bands and playing in the interval. It was not long before we had a regular discotheque on Wednesdays, which became a really popular night.

Following this success, we were then given Saturday evenings which again took off almost immediately and there used to be a regular queue of people to get in (oh happy days). The 'Disco Nights' integrated well with the live music and provided an excellent choice for the members. In 1970 the club moved to Stoneham Lane and the disco nights increased. Mondays were 'Revive 45' nights, which were always full and great fun.

Thursdays took over from Wednesdays and became the biggest night of the week. It was probably responsible for more matches, hatches and dispatches than any other factor in the whole of the area. Saturdays were still as popular as ever and, with the added dining facilities at the club, became the perfect venue for a social night out.

By this time Jon and I had been joined by a young apprentice, Joe Craen, who had an incredible record collection. Between us we were responsible for taking the club nights to a new level. Subsequently new DJ's were introduced, such as Dave Walker, Geoff Bartlett. John Clarke, Stuart Bennett and Gary Evans. I'm sure all of us would agree that the Concorde was the best 'Gig' on the south coast and we will always have fond memories of our time there.•

MARK PINN, Manager of the Ellington Lodge Hotel, gets closest to pricking the image Cole has for efficiency and perfectionism: •The funniest memory that sticks in my mind was that we had an old Japanese-style bridge that went over our pond, and it was looking a bit tired and needed some attention. So Jim and Cole decided to repair it. This was in 2007.

Out comes Jim with a bit of wood and a drill and Cole, as usual, the Supervisor. They both get on the bridge, Cole holds the plank of wood while Jim gets ready with his drill and guess what happens? The bridge collapses and Cole and Jim fall into the pond and get soaking wet from head to toe. Bloody funny! To this day the drill hasn't been found and bits of the bridge are still on the bonfire.

Just a week before the Mayor of Eastleigh was having photos taken in the garden whilst standing on that very bridge!•

JACKIE BAKER, long-serving membership secretary and the welcoming Receptionist on Wednesday jazz nights, reveals that it's a dog's life working with the Boss: •My little story goes back about ten years. I asked Cole if he was interested in giving a homeless golden retriever a home. I had little response to the question but he did take the phone number of the shelter. A few weeks later I had a phone call at the club late one afternoon from Cole asking me if I had a spare dog's lead and bowl!

I was absolutely thrilled, and realised immediately what he had done. Soon after he walked in with a very sad, shy-looking beautiful retriever – the beginning of a wonderful relationship between Cole and Teddy (Wilson), who has become a favourite with all regular Club members.⁹

LESLEY MONAGHAN, Concorde Receptionist circa 1979-89, submitted this imaginative contribution to the club's history:

RANDOM DIARY OF A CONCORDE CLUB RECEPTIONIST

Wednesday night – jazz night. This is fab - I'm with Elaine Tanner. It's Georgie Fame and the atmosphere is buzzing – fantastic sound coming out from the club, and we sit gossiping at reception when Alan Price walks in unannounced. How lovely and he joins in quietly. Still got to cash up and sort stuff out with the band. 03.00 am finish. As usual Elaine is in charge! Georgie Fame and Alan Price stand at reception and we bring them cups of coffee – smashing guys.

Thursday night – disco night. Hooray – it's me and Jo Pearce. We always have a hoot ... sorry guys but we take the mickey out of everyone coming in through Reception. Thankfully we've got Brian Kingsnorth as our manager sorting out the riff raff. Jo and I used to laugh at everyone quietly and then loudly! We got nicknamed Pepsi and Shirley!

Friday night – Grab a granny night. Oh Lord, here we go. Me and the one and only Pat Sparling – very funny. Grown men begging to be let in the club, and Pat just giving them the look, then Pat and I giving them marks out of 10!

Saturday night – It's me and Joan Tucker and the footballers are in full force. Sorry Joan, got to tell the Kevin Keegan story: Me being a Scouser I, of course, know KK – my fellow receptionist quite rightly asks KK for proof of identity and bless him – he produces his card and as a Scouser I'm curled up under the desk. Well done that girl for being the true receptionist.

Sunday morning – Panto rehearsals – 11.00 am – great. All the gang are there. It's *Dick Whittington* and I'm Pussy, to Sharron's Dick. Loved being every part of the panto – chorus, dormouse, princess, pussy ... Oh Lord, Robbo is getting worked up about his tights! Butch is in a panic about his lines and Bobby is as cool as ever, hey another panto – and I know it will all be all right on the night.

Sunday evening – It's a busy night, so it's Tall Lesley and Little Lesley working. Although Sunday evenings are usually quiet there's a big party on but we have a ball and the Sunday jazz crowd are always so nice. Simon's working so we have a bit of a laugh with him.

I'd like to dedicate this to the memories of two desperately missed Receptionists who have gone missing in action – to Pat and Jo.

GILL JEFFERY, a legend of the Concorde pantos as dancer and choreographer who. amongst other things, runs the Ladies' Luncheons, reveals that Cole is a bit of a polisher: ⁶It could have been about 1992, anyway back in the days when I was fit and able to get my legs up. There was a group of my dancing friends who performed the Can-Can on *Beaujolais*

'Les Tartes de Panto' 1988 – left to right, Rob Wiltshear, Paul Stephenson, Lesley King, Jo Pearce and Pauline Mathieson. Rob and Paul found it a bit of a drag.

Nouveau (now called the French Day) which takes place every November. In fact, one of them is still doing it to this day!

On this particular Beaujolais occasion Cole had the dance floor polished to shine like a new pin, which of course also turned it into a skating rink. Health and safety was nowhere to be seen and you took your chance just like all those idiots on 'Dancing on Ice'.

The Can-Can is always one of the highlights of the afternoon, enjoyed by everyone after a few tastings of the new wine, and the atmosphere was electric with anticipation. We dancers limbered up and preened to stop ourselves thinking of the pain and exhaustion we would be feeling after the three minutes of frenzied kicking, spinning, cartwheeling and splitting.

We were given the get-ready signal from Jim Budd in the DJ booth and listened for the first few notes of the well known 'Orpheus in the Underworld' Can-Can music. Hearing this tightens all muscles with fear. Then off we galloped, the four of us, smiling and squealing as we went, swishing our beautiful red and white skirts. What an entrance!

One after another my dancing buddies reached the dance floor … and one after another they fell in a heap on top of each other.

I was the last to reach the dance floor and stopped in my tracks as this picture of chaos developed in front of me. Not thinking to help them to their feet, I turned and ran back in the direction I came. They spent what seemed like quite a while untangling themselves from each other before following me off to hide away from the audience's raucous laughter.

Luckily there were no serious injuries, only fits of giggles and we regained our composure and went for it again, this time stepping gingerly onto the dance floor and performing with a little more restraint. We finished all in one piece to rapturous applause and requests that we do the first version again the following year!

I don't think the dance floor has ever been polished since, thank goodness, but there was always a little reminder when we talked about performing the Can-Can again: Don't Can-Can when the floor shines ... because you can't can't! My fellow dancers: Jane MacKinnon (still performing the Can-Can on the French Day), Karen Dolan and Julia Watts.•

BRIAN KINGSNORTH, who was a giant force at the club (particularly when playing the panto giant) before emigrating with his wife, Beth, to the United States: •Having been an Honorary Member and staff member for many years at The Concorde Club, I have a myriad of memories, but a few stand out.

From the early years at The Bassett where all the lads drank Manns Boilers, a mixture of Manns brown from a bottle and draft mild. The main reason was, if you were well in with the barmaid she would pour almost a pint of mild and give you the bottle. Thus, you got almost a pint and a half for the price of a pint. Needless to say, Cole never knew or he would have had a stroke!

When the Club moved from The Bassett to Stoneham Lane, many evenings were spent cleaning up the Old School House, painting walls and much more, getting ready for the Grand Opening. We were kept going by Cole or Pauline bringing in Party 7's and meat pies from The Cricketers Arms, which was just up the road.

And who thought about putting in a spiral staircase to the upstairs? It was a hazard to everyone who went up it, or worst of all, came down it! Some, like bassist Charlie Mingus, got stuck, to their embarrassment and much amusement to everybody else.

Years ago, we formed the Concorde Football Club and played in one of the local leagues on Sunday mornings. All we wanted was something to do on a Sunday until the pubs opened. We eventually got quite good at it and won several trophies over the years, and became something of a force to be reckoned with in local football.

It is fascinating to me how so many lives have been affected by The Concorde. So many people have met at the club, relationships have developed, those people have eventually married and their children have used the club. I'm sure by now, there are some of the early members' grandchildren using the club as well. My wife Beth and I met at the club and have been happily married for over 20 years. There are so many like us, whose lives changed because of The Concorde.

As I have said before, I have so many memories of The Concorde Club, it would take forever to tell them all. These are just a few, and I have added other recollections for the chapter on the pantos, which brought me so much laughter and satisfaction over many years.

I thank Cole and Pauline so much for their support over the decades, and for what The Concorde Club has done for the local community. The best of luck to all our old friends from Beth and me in Louisiana.•

GRAHAM MARTIN, Cole's accountant and erstwhile golf partner: •There are times that Cole may ask, "Did anyone go to the Concorde at the Bassett?" There is often surprise when I raise my hand because I am much too young to have been there officially. My brother Richard is seven years older than me, and with our parents away he was left 'baby sitting' his 14 year old brother.

Richard's idea of 'baby' minding was to take me to the Concorde at the Bassett, buy me a coke and sit me at a table in the corner. He only returned when it was time to go home and by now he had a girl in tow to whom we gave a lift home. It was a two seater van, but we all squeezed in. Ever felt you might be in the way?

Several years later as a trainee chartered accountant, I would spend my social time at the Stoneham Lane Concorde, dashing to get there before 10pm so I did not have to pay Jan on the desk the five shillings entrance fee.

Move on a few years and I can even claim to have been a musician at the Concorde, when my band played there. The year I am not sure of, but it was April 5th and it was a private function for NALGO. It was my Mum and Dad's anniversary and they gate crashed the do. My memories are not just of the only time I ever played the anniversary waltz for my Mum and Dad to dance to but of Cole, Pauline and Mum and Dad polishing off two bottles of Champagne.

The biggest surprise, however, was about 20 years ago when I received a phone call asking me to come and see Cole and Pauline. The invitation was a mystery, but all became clear when I was told that their existing accountant was retiring. They needed another and asked me. To complete the circle, my brother Richard and I were back at the Concorde on October 23rd 2007 to celebrate not only the Club's 50th Anniversary but also Richard's own 65th Birthday. With our 89-year-old Mother, and Richard's wife Christine we enjoyed yet another fantastic night.

I know that Norman Giller is doing his best to get somebody to dish the dirt on Cole. No chance! He is a thoroughly nice man, and a gentleman of the old school.•

CHRIS SHEPHERD, manager of the Moldy Fig: •I started work at the Concorde 16 years ago when my son Mark was four and he will be 21 this year!! I applied for a weekend Christmas job behind the bar of the main club thinking I would earn some extra pennies for the holiday and leave in the New Year but, sixteen years on, I'm still in situ looking after the Moldy Fig wine bar, so as the Club has grown and developed over those years I like to think that I have grown along with it!

We have a great all-round staff at the Concorde who are not only colleagues but also friends to me and most of us seem to have been there a very long time, which speaks a great deal. I suppose any one of the long-standing team will have many memories. There is the bonus, of course, of working with the wonderful sounds of the musicians and singers in the Fig, like Shirley Morgan and, for years, there was the brilliant Teddy Layton Quartet who were hugely popular.

They were Moldy Fig favourites – Teddy Layton with the saxophone that he played as well as almost anybody, drummer Arthur Ward, bassist Alan Duddington and pianist Dennis Taylor. This picture was taken on the 20th anniversary of the band's debut as Concorde residents.

My personal main memory has to be the fact that I met my husband Tony, a long time member, while still working on the Planter Bar in 1993. After a slow courtship we eventually went out for a "just good friends dinner" and the rest, as they say, is history. We had our tenth wedding anniversary last year and I still remember his favourite tipple at that time – "vodka, bottle of coke, lots of ice, no lemon, thank you."

The Concorde started as a place of work for me, but over the years has become a great deal more and will always hold many fond memories.◗

JOE CRAEN, club DJ from 1967 to 1979: ◖It's 1973. It's the three day week. There are miners' strikes. There are lots of power cuts. Jim Budd, Cole's right hand man for many years, managed to come up with an idea to keep the Disco nights running. He got members to park their cars in a line so that he could connect their car batteries up, and as the power grid shut down he could use the power from the cars to keep the music going. Tests showed that it worked. But when it came to putting the idea into action for the first time the owner of the car nearest the club decided that he wanted to go home, which of course meant everyone else had to move their car. Don't know who it was but word is that his membership was cancelled.◗

JOHN CLARE, former Concorde Club DJ, was with Henry's Records in Southampton from 1969 to 1988. He now lives in Perth, Australia: •My love affair with the Concorde club is twofold. First of all as a fan who attended many classic gigs from 1968 when it was still at the Bassett Hotel, right through to 1988 when I emigrated to Australia.

And secondly, after starting work at Henry's Records in St Mary Street and getting to know all of the local disc jockeys as a result, I was offered the job of second disc jockey there, by my great friend Joe Craen, replacing Simon Peterson/Foderingham when he retired from DJ-ing to concentrate on his wine bar.

I only did it for two years from 1975 to 1977 and was replaced by Dave Walker when I gave it up. I enjoyed it immensely, especially "Revive 45" night.

Amongst the many great gigs that I was lucky enough to witness, some of the best were by some of the finest jazz musicians ever with the mighty Charlie Mingus topping the list, followed closely by an amazing set by Mose Allison and the legendary Stephane Grappelli with the Diz Disley Trio and the awesome Maynard Ferguson Big Band.

On the rock front, there was The Nice, Manfred Mann, David Essex, and Ashton, Gardner and Dyke to name some memorable ones.

We also got to see a few really good local bands and it was at the Concorde that I first saw The Bob Pearce Blues band, the Mick and Bob Williams and Judge Lee line up, and a very youthful Sid Carter got up and jammed with them at the end of their set and was mightily impressive!

Then there was the incredible Smiling Hard who I saw on several occasions. The best line up being the one with Larry Tolfree on drums (now with the Peter Green Splinter Group) and Nick Hugg on bass (youngest brother of Manfred Mann's Mike Hugg) plus Kevin Gilson, Spike and Andy of course, completing the classic line up.

I also got a lot of listening pleasure from many Fo'c'sle club gigs – Alistair Anderson, Nic Jones, John Renbourn and Jacqui McShee, a youthful Pete Harris, later to be another keystone in the local folk and blues scene. The list is endless! Happy days.•

From an Englishman living in Australia to an Aussie working at the Concorde. **TONY FILGATE**, manager of the restaurant: •My plan when I came here from Tasmania was to be back home by now, but I'm enjoying life too much at the Concorde. It is an incredible place to work, with a team that is very professional but loose enough to have a good laugh when the time is right. I had only been at the club a short time when Cole grabbed me and said, "We want an Aussie song." Before I knew what was going on, I was on stage struggling through a version of *Tie Me Kanagroo Down Sport*. That would only happen at the Concorde.

You only have to see how many of the staff have been here for years to realise what a great atmosphere there is behind the scenes. We pride ourselves on our service, and David and his kitchen team are the tops. I had to live through England winning the Ashes, but then had the last laugh with our whitewash victory Down Under. I have made good friends with many of the members, and the banter adds to the fun. Like so many people, I feel very lucky to have found the Concorde.•

CHRIS GOLDEN, club disc jockey whose stint straddled the seventies into the eighties before he emigrated to Canada: :•My memories cover quite a small time in the history of this amazing club. In the fall (sorry autumn) of 1979 I took part in the only audition I've ever had, to become the new resident DJ, taking over from Joe Craen who had been there forever.

Having been resident DJ at The Pier for nine years I was hoping my reputation would go before me….however like all the other hopefuls I had to show my stuff.

Fortunately I was chosen and spent the next three years happily entertaining the wonderful Concorde members. Apart from the fabulous pantos, the highlights for me were the New Year's Eve discos.

I remember playing *Nellie the Elephant* with dancers cruising around the floor with their hands between their legs like trunks, and shortly after having everyone on their knees while I played *Hi-Ho-Hi-Ho It's Off to Work We Go* from the Snow White soundtrack.

This was followed by *Singing in the Rain* with Cole jumping around the dance floor with an umbrella until someone soaked him with a soda siphon, and to cap it all, just after midnight a wonderful rendition of *Land of Hope and Glory* sung magnificently by the members.

I was also fortunate to meet my wife Kate at the club. When I joined she was the receptionist and a romance quickly flourished. It was always a pleasure working at the club and Cole is a great boss.

If I had not emigrated to Canada in 1982 I would like to think I could have stayed there for many years. Thanks to Cole for providing me with an opportunity to join the Concorde staff, albeit for such a short time.•

PHILIPPA DAVIES, one of the latest in the long line of Concorde receptionists: •One Tuesday evening as normal – nothing on in the main Club, Shirley Morgan, Tony Day and John Hibberd playing in the Moldy Fig, and me working on Reception.

Cole sits on the settee opposite me looking up the corridor to the Moldy Fig and he gets fairly excited by his standards as he sees someone in the doorway.

"You didn't tell me Jamie Cullum was in the Club tonight," he says.

Surprised, I leave the Reception desk and come to have a look, and I see a young man wearing spectacles. I recognise him as one of the hotel guests.

"That's not Jamie Cullum," I say. "He doesn't wear glasses."

"He does," says Cole.

"I don't think so," I say, returning to the desk.

The young man walks down the corridor and comes into Reception.

Cole says to him: "Has anybody ever told you that you look like ..."

The guest finishes the question: "Harry Potter? Yes, all the time."

"Uh, I was going to say Jamie Cullum," says Cole.

"Nobody's told me that before but thanks very much," the guest says. "I'm really chuffed about that."

Oh well, at least Cole had made a guest happy.•

Young Jamie Cullum. pictured here at the Club, was a popular performer at the Concorde before his career went into orbit. I was one of the first to recognise his talent, and I thought I had recognised him on an unannounced visit to the Club. I was wrong, but I made a hotel guest happy. We are here to please!

PAMMI FERNANDES, who has worked behind the bars, served at the tables and is a greeter-and-seater on jazz nights, is one of the more unconventional members of the Concorde staff, as these memories will help illustrate: •One bright summer morning Emma and I were chatting behind the bar in the Moldy Fig, having done all the preparations for lunch. We were, as usual, generally putting the world to rights when a little boy ran in. Looking towards us, he threw his arms in the air, then ran back to the door and disappeared. The little boy was dressed in Edwardian clothes, boots, breeches, shirt, tank top and wore a cap. Emma shouted: "I've just seen a ghost of a little boy." As the Concorde was an old school and the Moldy Fig was the headmaster's house, it was reasonable to assume that the ghost was that of a former pupil. Other people have since seen him, and Cole's son, Jamie, admits he finds it spooky when he has to lock up the Moldy Fig late at night.

One day a local businessman – let's call him Mr. P – came to the Moldy Fig with his secretary for their usual long, drawn-out lunch that always included the slow polishing off of a bottle of wine. He could be very long-winded and would almost lecture to us waitresses and barstaff on any topic that came to mind. This particular afternoon he went on and on about how important it is to give people time, always to be polite and listen, even if they're door-to-door salesmen, or flogging double glazing or telesales. We were now running late, and to try to shut him up I said in sheer desperation: "If you say so, Mr. P., but what about if one of the old Jehovah's Witnesses knocks at your door?"

He replied: "I am one ...!"

While I waited for the floor to swallow me up, the other girls disappeared to giggle out of sight of Mr. P. I was left alone behind the bar, trapped.

"And what do you do when one of us knocks at your door" asked Mr. P.

"I tell them I'm a little witch," I said, "and I'm in the middle of making a spell. Then I watch them run away up the drive." Well, that shut him up.

Another regular customer, let's call her Miss L, used to like just the 'nob' ends of the baguettes becasuse, she said, they were nice and crunchy. When I handed her a basket of just nob ends, she said: "Oh honey, I like you. You always know I just love the nobs."

More giggling in the background.

We were honoured to have the Heath Brothers from New Orleans lunching in the Moldy Fig, when Teddy, Cole's Labrador, came waddling in. The Heath brothers stared wide-eyed at him as if he was a visitor from outer space.

"Gee," said one brother, "have you ever seen a big yella dog like that? Where you get a big yella dog like that?"

The other brother said: "And how d'you feed a big yella dog like that?"

"Well I guess" said his brother, "that's why Cole has a restaurant. You need one to feed a big yella dog like that."

Teddy got bored with the attention, and wandered out into the garden. Lunch was served and the Heath brothers were soon tucking in. One of the brothers looked out into the garden, where Teddy was, um, doing his business. "Hey, will ya look at that," said the brother. "That big yella dog is shitting bricks!" For some reason, they suddenly lost their appetite.

One more story. One Friday evening we were working behind the bar listening to the wonderful tales from Teddy Layton and his band colleagues when one of the girls entered carrying a mystery object in a large velvet bag. I guessed what it might be because she hosted Anne Summers' parties.

"Oh good," said one of our crowd behind the bar. "You've brought it. Let's see."

She unveiled the mystery object from the velvet pouch. It was a large battery-operated dildo, with controls. Ooh! She slapped it on the fridge in the kitchen and proceeded to put it through its manoeuvres. We innocent ones all stood looking on in amazement.

"I've sold three already," she said.

Suddenly somebody hissed urgently, "Quick, it's Cole. He's coming to the kitchen."

Somehow the dildo had got stuck to the fridge. Panic! Someone threw a tea towel over it, and Cole came and went, not knowing why he had found us gaggle of girls with fits of the giggles. I have kept the secret – until now.

There are many more wonderful stories of life at the Concorde. It is a great place to work, and offers lots of opportunities for laughs. Cole takes it all in his stride.⁹

THE CONCORDE CLUB: The First 50 Years
Memories of the Musicians... those fit enough to print!

MUSICIANS queued to get their memories into the book because of the high regard they have for Cole and all he has achieved with the Concorde. Joker Alan Barnes said it could also be something to do with the fact that they want to get more bookings at the club. We wondered in which order to place the memories, not wishing to upset the egos of the nororiously sensitive jazz musicians (another joke, by the way). We finally decided to run them exactly as they arrived. For anybody who missed out – musician or member – we are very happy to add your comments to our website at www.concordebook.co.uk. All those who failed to come up with a memory are now on the blacklist of Cole, who is determined to show he is nothing like as nice and accommodating as everybody keeps saying (another joke!).

DAVE GREEN, London bassist who has made more Concorde appearances than any other non-resident jazz musician (over 100 at the last count): •I feel very honoured to have the distinction of being the musician having made the most appearances at the club over the years – unfortunately that means that I must also hold the record for having eaten the most of the excellent chips and sandwiches that Cole provides for the band at the end of each night's music. Oh well, it was worth it!

I think I'm right in saying that my first gig at the old Bassett hotel in Southampton was with the Humphrey Lyttelton Band in 1965. I had just recently joined Humph for a month long tour. Big Joe Turner and Buck Clayton were the guests. I'm happy to say I stayed with Humph for the next eighteen years. My next appearance at the Bassett was with the Don Rendell Quintet. That was the night Don tried to talk Cole into becoming a Jehovah's Witness.

The word 'GREAT' springs to mind when I recall all the wonderful times I've had at the Concorde, great club, great food, great hospitality and above all great music. I've had some of the most memorable nights of my career playing there over the last 45 years or so.

There have been so many memorable sessions that it's hard to pick out one above another, but I particularly remember wonderful nights with Benny Carter and Herb Ellis, Kenny Davern and Ralph Sutton and – the one I would really have liked to have on tape –– Billy Butterfield, Dick Wellstood and Allan Ganley on drums.

May Cole and the good ship Concorde sail on for ever.•

LEN SKEAT, another London bass player who – with his late brother, Bill – has won the hearts of Concorde fans over many years: •Whenever I play the Concorde I always see the same faces, from sound engineer Jim to the receptionists, the bar and restaurant staff and, of course, the people in the audience. That speaks volumes for the way Cole runs the club. He is a fair and honest man who wins everybody's loyalty. There is not a better-organised jazz club in the country, and I always consider it a privilege and a pleasure to play there. They really appreciate their jazz, and Cole treats all musicians with respect and makes us feel welcome. Congratulations on the 50 years. It is a remarkable achievement, and thanks on behalf of all my fellow musicians for all that you have done to promote jazz in the best possible taste.•

ALLAN GANLEY, the magnificent drummer's drummer who gave us this comment just two weeks before he died in March 2008: •One night with the Pizza Express All Stars, we wore evening dress, and trombonist Roy Williams forgot his black shoes. With me being in the background we decided that he could wear my black shoes and I'd have his brown ones. Well, it was okay for the first number, and then my feet started to hurt because the shoes were pinching, so I ended up playing in my socks. And not very well either! I think it was Cole who made the request for the band to play, "Your feet's too big!"

I had my one rotten experience at the Concorde with American star Bud Shank, who complained about my playing. I can accept critcism, but NOT ON THE STAND! So we had a big argument backstage and he apologised, but I pulled out of the rest of the tour.

That gig apart, I've always loved playing the Concorde. And I go right the way back to the start in the 1950s! Cole looks after the musicians, and makes sure everyone is comfortable. It really is the best jazz club in Britain, no doubt.

Cole and I have become good friends over the years, and there was one time when he sat in for me after I had strained my back. I was playing with Benny Waters at the Pizza Express in London, and could not go out after the interval, so Cole took over and did a fine job. He could have been an outstanding drummer if he'd stuck at it, but preferred the much easier job of running a club! All of us in jazz should be grateful that he chose that path, because he gives us the best possible stage on which to play.•

JOHN MADDOCKS, almost like part of the furniture at the Concorde: •I first played at the Bassett Hotel with my band – the Black Bottom Stompers – in 1967, when it was a tidy trip from London in those days prior to the M3 and swift cars! I was based with my band in South London at the time and we had the reputation of being 'hot and frantic,' playing in the King Oliver and Jelly Roll Morton style. At that stage I was 21 years old as were two others. The oldest as I remember was 32. He seemed to us youngsters like a real veteran!

We did several gigs for Cole at that time. I have always remembered the dog [no change there then], and the welcoming atmosphere that greeted us at the Bassett plus the packed room and the dancing – smoke and all! Remember those days of smoke-filled halls and pubs?!

I moved to Poole in 1973 and started up my own band – the John Maddocks Jazzmen. Cole was very kind to allow me the opportunity to play and to establish myself in a new area. This eventually led to a residency every Sunday for many years, by now in the School house as originally designed. In fact there is a photo of a record cover taken outside the building when you could actually see the brick walls. The band were considerably younger than they are now as well.

OUR SHIRL – Shirley Morgan – who sings for her supper in the Moldy Fig with Tony Day and John Hibberd. She first sang for Cole at the Red Lion, Totton, in 1955.

The weekly residency has long since ceased but the Jazzmen have continued to flourish from those far off days. I cannot emphasise enough the encouragement and support Cole has given me and my band over the years. Indeed I would like to go on record by saying that whatever Cole has done at the Concorde, whether in its humble beginnings to the very impressive establishment it is now, he has never forgotten the local musicians. I really respect him for that. Cole has allowed us to use the club for CD recordings and photo shoots over the years.

The band has established itself as a national favourite and plays on the jazz club circuit. We do however especially look forward to playing at the Concorde, usually about six times a year now, and particularly so at the Christmas Party which we have played at for many, many years.

We always try to think of something different to do at the Christmas Party and on one famous occasion Dave 'Shady' Thorne, who sadly died some years ago, decided he would sing *When I'm Cleaning Windows* – the George Formby song. That night he appeared in overalls, had his ladder and bucket of water, and delivered the song from the dance floor accompanied by six collapsing jazz musos trying to keep up with him and laughing at the same time. It was a hoot. I, like many others, regard the Concorde as home.•

SHIRLEY MORGAN, resident singer at the Moldy Fig with pianist Tony Day and bassist John Hibberd, and co-leader with Tony Day of the Concorde Big Band: •I think I can safely say that I have known Cole Mathieson longer than almost anybody else connected with the Concorde. We go all the way back to the mid-1950s when he was running gigs at the Red Lion in Totton for the Ronnie Horler Band. In those days he also did a day-time job delivering bread to people living in the New Forest area.

I wish I could excite your readers by dishing the dirt on Cole, but I'm afraid I have to be boring and tell you that he is one of the greatest human beings I've ever met.

I owe him so much, including being responsible for me meeting my husband of 46 years Terry Morgan. He gave me a gig singing with Ronnie Horler, and one evening the trombonist Ken Grinyer walked in with his mate Terry. It was love at first sight, just like in some of the songs I sing. I was knocked over the moment I saw him and chased him hard from that day on, despite Ronnie Horler telling me it would never last.

When my dear Terry died in 2006 Cole was one of the first people at my side, helping me through my grief by insisting that I kept on singing at the Moldy Fig. It was a wonderful gesture, and it helped pull me through those dark days. Cole did it for me, and would do the same thing for any of his friends.

I call him Mr Jazz. I can think of nobody who has done more for our music, and he is always there for anybody in trouble. Why he's not been given a major honour is beyond me. He has raised thousands of pounds for all sorts of charities, and never ever boasts about it.

He is one of Southampton's greatest sons, and we are all very proud of him and what he has achieved.•

RONNIE KOLE, New Orleans-based pianist and entertainer extraordinaire: •My first memory was back in 86 when our bus pulled up to the Concorde, and my thoughts were, "This is a jazz club?" After walking inside, my second thoughts were, "This is a jazz club!" The outside looked anything but a night club of any kind, and after going inside, it was so beautiful and nothing like the jazz joints that we've all come to expect ... and what a wonderful piano and sound system and to be treated with respect.

We were so impressed with the bulletin board, pictures and schedules of acts that were coming to the Concorde – so very diversified and compelling. Since that first experience we've returned to the Concorde every time we were in the UK, both to perform and also to be with two wonderful people, Pauline and Cole Mathieson. The addition of the hotel and naming the rooms for jazz greats was another mind boggling experience.

We so enjoyed showing Cole and his friendly solicitor Adrian Lightfoot around New Orleans, and also answering a request to see how our Judicial System worked. We took them into an Appellate Court where a friend of ours was a Judge, and was holding court. Yes Cole and Adrian were introduced to the court, and that just started off many fun experiences.

Cole's concept is so unique: diversification in the acts, room, food, so many charity functions et al. I don't know of another club that is so diversified with world class musicians and/or acts. Bravo to a trend setter. •

CLARE TEAL, who has developed into a mega star since her early appearances at the Concorde: •I just love singing at the Concorde. It has an intimate atmosphere and an audience that appreciates every note. When I first played there a BBC film crew accompanied me, and Cole wondered why they were following me around. He did not bat an eyelid when I told him that I was taking part in a documentary programme about a notorious con man. His reaction was to order tea and sandwiches for everybody. Typical!

On my second visit I was signing CDs in the foyer when a woman informed me in slightly hysterical terms that she'd just found out her husband was having an affair. She punished him by ordering six of my CDs on his credit card, which left me feeling just a tiny bit guilty for profiting from his infidelity.

My thanks to Cole and his excellent team for all the great support. It is much appreciated, as are those amazing chips he always sends into the dressing-room at the end of the show! They are real diet destroyers.•

DAVE NEWTON, whose piano playing has won him the support of many who argue that he is the best in the land: •I have played piano so often at the Concorde Club over the last (at a rough guess) twenty years, and I have fragmented memories from so many nights with so many different bands. If I pieced them altogether, it might make for a tremendous night, in my head anyway. There are many constants.

The first ones that spring to mind are the warm welcome from Cole and the patient smile from Jackie as she accepts yet another box of CDs to sell at the interval. Into the main room and there will be Jim going about his sound-checking business with quiet efficiency. Not one howl of feedback in twenty years to my knowledge, which is pretty incredible.

The fragments: I see Mark Nightingale at the far end of the stage in full flight, Alan Barnes hunched over a half swallowed microphone pacing his gags as only northern comedians can. The look on the face of American drummer Jeff Hamilton as he sees the drum kit that's been hired for him to play that evening (a huge orange affair with Salvation Army sized bass drum I seem to remember), Bud Shank and Allan Ganley exchanging pleasantries in the dressing room, people keeling over at the bar (after the gig) ... the shadowy mountain range of figures standing at the bar when the lights go down.

There was a time when I did a few Friday nights in the Moldy Fig with Teddy Layton and Arthur Ward and the welcome was always just as warm. Many nights with Stacey Kent, with folk hanging from the rafters to see the show. An abundance of wonderful nights shared with so many delightful people and the main reason it all works is because of Cole's appreciation of what makes a club a great club. And what a discerning crowd too!

Whenever we have played at the Concorde the Trio has had a ball and if there was a club like it in every town up and down the land, we would be the happiest bunch of wandering minstrels to be found anywhere in the world. We could quite possibly be the fattest too if they all dished up the vast quantities of sandwiches and chips that are prepared for us after the show's over. Sorry there is not a specific recollection, but everything comes together pleasantly in one long extremely satisfying memory.•

ALAN BARNES, one of the most popular visitors to the Concorde, both for his sensational sax playing and his razor wit: •I can remember my first appearance at the club with the Pasadena Roof Orchestra in the 1980s. The first thing that strikes you is what a great venue it is. I thought there must be jazz clubs like this all over the country. I'm still looking – there aren't any! Then there was the gallery of photos in the Moldy Fig, real American giants who had been at the club and pictures of British greats looking slim, with full heads of hair – something for the audience to compare their present state with!

The leader of the P.R.O. was a master of the malapropism – 'My room is so small, you'd have to be a ventriloquist to get in there' being his finest contorted moment.

I came to the club early on with Stan Greig's Boogie Band, a small group playing Big Band classics with no music. Fortunately, one of the great riff setters of all time was on the gig in the shape of Willie Garnett. After we picked up each riff, he would turn a huge imaginary page to the next one.

I'd arrived for the pick-up with my alto sax, forgetting I'd been booked on baritone and quietly confided as much to John Richardson in the back of Stan's car. 'Don't worry, the old c*** won't even notice' he whispered back. Stan's grating Scottish brogue broke the peace: 'The Old C*** has already noticed!'

Another time, with Bob Wilber's big band, Spike Robinson was one of the guest soloists. I saw him light a cigarette and inhale deeply as three-quarters of the fag disappeared. When he breathed out, no smoke appeared! Somehow he'd retained the lot – a virtuoso smoker as well as saxophonist!

When I joined the Humph band, one of the first gigs was at the Concorde. I had become very ill two days before with what turned out to be severe salmonella poisoning (diagnosed by the NHS six weeks after the consultation), and I was not at my best. The illness really was quite violent and I startled a few users of the gents that night who had previously chatted with me. They viewed me with new respect!

After a couple of weeks I'd lost a stone and we were in Germany. Humph, never one to tolerate illness in himself or others announced: 'I'm going to buy you the biggest plate of greasy noodles you've ever seen. That will sort it out'. He dragged me off to a Chinese, ordered me to eat the noodles and next morning I was fine!

I was in the band on the one night when Cole was fleeced by one of the greatest jazz musicians in the world. So that I do not line the pockets of the lawyers Sue, Grabbit and Run I will not name him, just suffice to say he had an unconventional way of doing business. He thought that being in the town he was playing in was a fulfilment of his contract.

Having been paid in advance, he failed to show for the gig, offering the excuse that he was having trouble with his chops. We played without him and Cole honourably offered money back to anyone who wished to leave. I don't think more than two people took the option. Cole says that he learned from that day never to pay musicians in advance!

Cole, of course, has a whole raft of responsibilities in running the club – the most important being his role as chip tester general. A huge plate of Sarnies (or in musicians rhyming slang Georgios – Georgio Armani's or Harry's – Harry Carney's) appears after the gig accompanied by a pile of chips. Cole takes responsibility for quality control on the latter, a duty he takes more seriously than lesser men would!

His constant companion is 'Teddy Wilson', a gentle Golden Retriever who has little or no piano playing ability but a huge sexual drive. I've known a few musicians like that! Advice to musicians new to the club, don't leave bags or piles of clothes at ground level. Teddy is apt to "make friends" with them.

Whenever a punter says to me: 'I suppose you are most at home in a sleazy, smoky dive' I always think: no, I like to play in a clean, well run place with a comfortable dressing room, good food and drink (always an excellent local real-ale), friendly staff, where the owner greets you as an old friend. That is the Concorde Club.

I've only played there 31 times. Come on Cole we can do better than that!⁹

TONY DAY, Shirley Morgan's piano accompanist and arranger/conductor for the Concorde Big Band: ⁶I remember a wannabee Sinatra complete with phony American accent (all the way from Portsmouth) and a *Sinatra at Blackpool with Billy Ternent* LP under his arm who wanted to sing with the trio one night in the Moldy Fig. I asked him what would he like to sing and he replied *I like New York in June*, so I said, "How About You," giving the number its correct title. His response: "Yeah...well we can do that later"! Priceless.⁹

Recognise anybody you know? A jam-packed Concorde Club for a Wednesday Jazz Night visit from the king of the cornet, Ruby Braff, in 2002.

JOHN CHILTON, famous for his trumpet, his Feet Warmers (and the warblings of George Melly) and a respected jazz writer and historian: ❛I'm pleased and proud to say that during my thirty years with George Melly I saw the Concorde Club develop from its early days into what became just about the perfect jazz club. Many of its merits are due to Cole Mathieson, who combines a keen love of jazz with an admirable eye for décor and a knack of offering his customers a fine selection of excellent food and drink.

But Cole doesn't only provide fodder and facilities for the punters, he makes sure that the same comforts are readily available for the musicians. Unlike many other club owners he also installed an excellent sound system and bought a splendid grand piano.

Whenever we played at the Concorde I enjoyed chatting with Cole, who kept me up to date with tales of visiting American guest stars. His description of the time the hugely talented, but much overweight, Charles Mingus got wedged on the spiral staircase is still vivid in my memory.

We got to know quite a few of the Club's regulars, one of whom donated a striped suit to George, which became one of his favourites. Apparently the man (a larger-than-life tailor called Des Goodenough) bought the outfit in the hope he'd resemble George, but his wife felt the suit was much too bold for her husband and said, with admiration: "There's only one George Melly – give it to him." Happy memories.❜

BRIAN PEERLESS is one of the hidden aces of the Concorde Club. He is a manager, promoter and agent who makes Cole's life so much easier by helping to bring in the world's greatest jazz musicians to light up our little corner of Hampshire. These are his memories:

•My first trip to the Concorde Club was on 3rd October 1975 with the World's Greatest Jazz Band of Yank Lawson and Bob Haggart. The previous night had been a good one in Eastbourne, but the Concorde night was made more memorable, not just because of the great music, but because of a misunderstanding within the band. Towards the end of the second set Yank called a tune, but the band started by playing quite a different number to that indicated. As the nine-piece band was spread out in a line across what was at that time the far end of the club, with pianist Ralph Sutton playing an upright facing the wall, it was something that was perhaps inevitable – particularly towards the end of the day after a fair amount of alcoholic refreshment had been taken by many. The result was that at the end of the number Yank retreated up the spiral staircase, packed his trumpet and stated his intention to return home.

I was left with the job of trying to convince him to change his mind while the band played what turned out to be a very long version of *Caravan* featuring the trombones of George Masso and Sonny Russo and the bongo playing of Bobby Rosengarden. I pleaded my heart out with Yank to return, as a favour to me even if only to say good night to the audience. I'm not sure how many trips I made up and down that staircase trying to sort things out and reporting back to my on-stage band contact, Peanuts Hucko, on any progress. In the meantime the number had finished, and Sonny declared that if the leader was going home, so was he, and went off to sit in the band bus.

After some more pleading, Yank agreed, as he put it because we were pals, and returned to the stage to lead a third set into the early hours with the full band, which also included Billy Butterfield, Al Klink and Maxine Sullivan on vocals.

Later, at the hotel I called in on Yank and Billy, who were rooming together. Both were in their beds and sharing a drink, with Yank asking Billy, "We're friends aren't we, Billy? You wouldn't take my band, would you?" To which Billy replied, "What would I do with it?" and gave me a Butterfield raised eyebrow look. I rejected their offer of a drink, left them reminiscing and took to my bed. Next morning Yank was almost first to breakfast, with not a hint of what had gone before. I also remember that the night before Yank had introduced George and Sonny to the audience as part-time musicians, and that they were actually Masso & Russo, funeral directors. Years later when I was with Yank down at the club, a guy came up and asked how Sonny and George were getting along with their undertakers business!

Later in the same month I brought ex-WGJB member Bob Wilber down for a more peaceful evening. My trips to the Concorde have been numerous in the intervening years, particularly after I started organising tours in the early 1980s, at the instigation of Kenny Davern and Yank Lawson, for many of the American jazz players, including great musical nights with both of them, and also with Maxine Sullivan, Dick Wellstood, Billy Butterfield, Ralph Sutton, Dave McKenna, Warren Vache and Scott Hamilton, who must rival Kenny for the most appearances of an American artiste at the club.

Every trip has been an adventure, and those with Kenny, full of anticipation as to how he would deal with microphones and the acoustics. One I remember clearly was a date we set up in May 1988. This was with Art Hodes, whose tour was being arranged by Dave Bennett and for which Cole had thought would be a good idea to have a full group. Pat Halcox, Campbell Burnap, Andy Brown on bass and Stan Greig on drums were duly booked, and in talking with BBC producer Keith Stewart he agreed it would be a good date to record for broadcasting.

The evening went admirably of course, with a number of Kenny's very humorous, if somewhat long, introductions being captured by the BBC, although through some technical fault not all the music was recorded!

Over the years the excitement of travelling to the club has never diminished, whether it has been with all star American bands featuring great musicians including Jake Hanna, Howard Alden, Michael Moore, Dan Barrett, John Bunch, Butch Miles, Houston Person, Harry Allen, Marty Grosz, Jim Galloway, Jackie Williams, Jon-Erik Kellso, Randys Reinhart and Sandke, or solo tours supported by the best of our own players. Ken Peplowski, a regular Concorde performer, was so taken with the evening's events in January 1999 with John Pearce, Dave Green and Martin Drew that he arranged to have the the taped session issued on two CDs.

I often think of trips with magnificent pianists Brian Lemon and Colin Purbrook, both great raconteurs, and usually on the road with Concorde favourites Dave Green and Allan Ganley. What a sad loss when Allan passed on this year. He was truly a master drummer.

In recent times it has been a pleasure to introduce new talent to the club, including Italian pianist Rossano Sportiello, who has endeared himself to all who have heard him. He also did the same for Cole, and for a different reason on his first Concorde booking. Rossano, a dog lover, was introduced to Teddy and after much stroking and searching for the right words he haltingly said in his charming accent, "In Italy we call these Golden Retrievers." Cole replied in a flash and almost Michael Caine, *Italian Job*-like, "That's what we call them here."

Whenever Rossano phones one of his first questions is, "Have you seen Teddy Wilson lately?" I hope to see him, Cole and the Concorde team for many years to come.•

CRAIG MILVERTON, exceptional young pianist from Devon who is heavily influenced by Oscar Peterson but with a distinctive style of his own: •My generation is so lucky to have a wise and experienced man like Cole Mathieson to encourage young jazz musicians and to give them the chance of playing at one of the greatest venues in Europe. I think that it should be compulsory for student jazz musicians to visit the Concorde, and to get a taste of what a *real* jazz club atmosphere is like. I have been lucky enough to play at some of the jazz haunts in New York, and the Concorde matches them for ambience and beats them for facilities.

I had been privileged to play the Concorde several times as a support member of the band, but when I got the call from Cole to pay my personal tribute to my idol Oscar Peterson with my Quartet (Andy Cleyndert bass, Dominic Ashworth guitar and the awesome Bobby Worth on drums) I felt like a footballer must feel when he gets his first call up for intenational duty. Yes, in football parlance, 'I was over the moon!'•

Photographer Gordon Sapsed captures the moment when Scott Hamilton (right) meets one of his heroes, Tommy Whittle. Scott said he was realising an ambition when he played with Tommy at the Concorde for the first time. Bassist Spike Heatley completes a trio of masters.

The following contributions come from tenor sax legend **TOMMY WHITTLE** and his singing wife **BARBARA JAY**, who tours keeping the sounds of Ella Fitzgerald alive.

TOMMY: ‘I first played for Cole way back in 1958. It was in the pub in Southampton, the first Concorde. He had a nice little resident trio there, Monty Worlock on piano, Ron Andrews on bass and Kenny Harrison on drums. Then a couple of years later I played there with the Arthur Ward trio. Who could have dreamt that 50 years later I would still be playing at the Concorde and that it would have grown into the club as we know it today. It is absolutely amazing what Cole has achieved, and in that time he has always put jazz at the top of his promoting list. For that, we all owe him a big thank you.’

BARBARA: ‘The first time we took our Ladies of Jazz show to the new Concorde it really was still just like an old school, full of charm but very basic. I remember that Maxine Daniels, Tina May and I were in hysterics changing in a dressing-room that was like a cubby hole. Now it is one of the great jazz venues and Tommy and I always look forward to our visits there because the audience is so knowledgeable and Cole is the best of hosts.’

RAY LEWITT, a regular with Gerry Brown's Band at the Bassett from 1960: ● I have wonderful memories of playing the bass with Gerry's band in the early days of the Concorde. People of a certain age may recall my little interval comedy act when I would play the tuba and do solo renditions of the Temperance Seven hits *Pasadena* and *You're Driving Me Crazy*. Later I did a similar so-called comedy spot in the new Concorde, adding some ukelele playing. It used to amuse Gerry, who is always good for a laugh. I am very proud to be an honorary member of the club, but cannot get down from my Northamptonshire home as much as I would like. In the old days, my mother used to live in Bassett so it was always very convenient to drop in and see her whenever we were playing at the Concorde. They were lovely, lovely days. ●

BUD SHANK, world-renowned American saxophonist and flautist, makes a confession: ● In May of 1984 I appeared at the Concorde Club with the rhythm section of John Critchinson piano, Ron Matthewson bass, Kenny Clare drums. We had been working at Ronnie Scott's and I had a terrible case of the 'flu at the time. I slept in the car all the way down from London to Southampton, and slept some more in Vic Lewis's car after we got there.

The band set up everything and had dinner without me. When I did my warm-up before the show I discovered an extra unused bar room at the Club near the main room. Lo and behold there was a fully stocked bar in there with many varieties of lovely single malt scotch.

I went back into the concert room and found Ron Matthewson, a guy always ready for a good time, and we decided we would play bartender and customer. We each took a turn at these roles, and proceeded to get totally blithered. Ron just for the fun of it and me because I was so bloody sick.

We started the first set during which we played *Here's That Rainy Day* – all of eleven minutes long! This ended up on the recording (Mole Jazz). This record also included Manny Albam's concerto.

After the first intermission, we returned to the wonders of the secret bar. Miraculously nothing from this point on was recorded. I have often felt that I should have told the people at the Concorde Club how much of their scotch we consumed ... but I am telling them now!

If Cole wishes to send me a bill I will be delighted to pay up. Cheers!

Seriously, the Concorde Club was always a great place to play, with a knowledgeable, attentive audience. I made many friends there. Congratulations on reaching the 50 years milestone. ●

BUTCH MILES, former Count Basie drummer and arguably the greatest of current American jazz percussionists: ● I've been lucky enough to play the Concorde a few times since the early 80's. I'd heard about the club many times from great British musicians (who also happened to be friends of mine, like Roy Williams, Len Skeat, Dave Newton and Digby Fairweather to name a few).

They had told me that the Concorde was, as far as many musicians were concerned, THE place to perform. Naturally, the first time I played there I was expecting a lot and I wasn't disappointed. The club WAS a great place to perform and Cole treated musicians the way artistes should be treated – with respect. I always looked forward to coming back whenever I was lucky enough to be booked there with all the various bands I've worked with. Then a number of years passed by and I didn't get back that way for one reason or another until 2006. I was travelling with the Statesmen of Jazz and we were booked back at the club.

I was astounded and delighted at the changes Cole had made to his place. The sound and the ambiance had always been wonderful but now it surpassed itself. The food was even better than I remembered and the Ellington hotel was a true revelation, with the rooms named after jazz greats a neat and unique touch. It was a lovely sort of home-coming for me since I had been away for a long time and yet the entire experience seemed completely new to me.

It's a marvellous thing to realize that a well-run establishment like the Concorde can do everything right and still be a success. I congratulate Cole and all of the talent that has passed through those doors over the decades. Now, when do you want me back?'

BOBBY WORTH, one of the world's most accomplished drummers: 'To give you an indication of what it means to play the Concorde, I remember being as excited as if I had reached a Cup final when Spike Robinson invited me to play drums for him in 1991. It was my first gig at the Concorde and I felt that I had arrived. Next to Ronnie Scott's, I cannot think of a venue that means so much to jazz musicians. The audience appreciate everything you do, and it brings the best out of everybody playing.

The way Cole looks after the musicians is second to none, and we always feel respected. A jazz club surviving more than fifty years! That's just incredible. Promoting jazz is famously like a minefield. I was told this by a jazz promoter who is a millionaire. Before becoming a promoter he had two million! Congratulations to Cole on his long survival, and may he and the Concorde continue for many years to come.'

SIMON SPILLETT, voted the UK's Rising Star in the 2007 British Jazz Awards and also a rising author of note: 'The Concorde is everything that a jazz club should be; comfortable, amenable, civilised and with a menu that has caused many a musician to wobble on stage after a visit to the excellent restaurant. Thankfully it's also run by a patron who has built upon a genuine love for the music and its practitioners not just on business-for-business sake. Above all – and all jazz clubs ultimately thrive or fall on this point – it's full of enthusiastic fans, whatever the style of music being presented. I have some profound memories of the night I shared the Concorde stage for a Three Tenors evening co-fronted by Bobby Wellins and Alan Barnes, with John Critchinson, Andrew Cleyndert and Bobby Worth. It was typical of Cole to put on this sort of band, with its focus on good hard swinging jazz, and a very enjoyable time was had by all; not least by the band backstage afterwards! Fifty years is a long, long time in the jazz business, and with other much more celebrated venues coming and going, sometimes in a flash, sometimes in a long slow decline, the Concorde has every reason to be proud of its unique place in UK jazz. It's a one off and long may its singular existence be guaranteed.'

Three of the Dankworths at the Concorde: Sir John, Dame Cleo and bassist Alec

SIR JOHN DANKWORTH, the Great Knight of Jazz: •When the Concorde Club was refurbished not so long ago we musos were delighted, and for one special reason. Most of the face-lifts for concert halls and clubs (multi-million pound budgets accompanied some of them) spent 99.5% on the public access areas and the other half per cent on the stage and back stage areas for the performers, although the above only applied to the more generous managements. Many allowed a budget of 0% for our comforts.

As it happened, Cleo's 2007 debut at the Concorde took place a short time after a knee replacement, which for a few appearances restricted her movements during her set, requiring her to sit in a chair whilst on stage. The problem, however, was getting her on and off, which on the three gigs before the Concorde date required stairs to get on.

It was the first thing Cleo checked on arrival, and to her amazement she found that the level of the club's main floor was identical to that of the stage – so no stairs! Cleo was jubilant and mentioned her pleasure to Cole. Cole replied deadpan: "Yes, we heard about your temporary incapacity, and felt an artiste of your calibre was well worth the one-hundred-and-fifty grand it cost to alter the floor level of the entire club to make your life easier."

Cleo thanked Cole sweetly, while Cole and I exchanged glances. Of course, he was joking and what's more I knew he was joking. And he of course knew that I knew he was joking, but I'm just not sure whether he could tell that I really knew that he knew I knew that he knew I was well aware that the floor-level of the club and stage had never been changed. I hope we were sharing a tongue-in-cheek 'little white lie' joke, but I'll really have to ask Cole one day – just to be sure that we both knew what the other one knew.

Congratulations on making the Concorde one of the world's very finest jazz clubs, Cole. All we Dankworths appreciate your loving support of jazz over so many years. You have our total, collective admiration. I know that you know that!•

VIC ASH, clarinet and tenor sax virtuoso who has always blown it HIS way (often with Frank Sinatra): •I had a great time playing at the original Concorde at the Bassett Hotel in the late 50s, which was either as a solo guest playing with local musicians or with the various quartets which I had in those days. Cole had a top-class resident group that provided excellent backing. Since then I have played at the current Concorde club with several bands and singers, including the lovely Rosemary Squires, the BBC Big Band and other pick up groups. The last time was 4 July 2007 with my newly formed quintet. I think that the club is the best in the UK in every way - premises, sound and treatment of musicians. Cole is a great fan of middle of the road jazz, which is my own preferred style, and he is one of the best guys to work for. I always look forward to playing at the Concorde, and congratulate Cole on the club's golden anniversary. It was a privilege to be there at the start of it all.•

ROSEMARY SQUIRES, one of Cole's all-time favourite female singers and a legend in the business: •I have been singing at the Concorde since Benny Green invited me to be part of his show when the club was voted one of the top three jazz venues in the country. In particular I remember performing the Ella Fitzgerald Song Book with Maxine Daniels and Barbara Jay, and on another occasion it was wonderful singing with Ted Heath's former vocalist Dennis Lotis and the Vic Ash Quartet. I have only lovely memories of a superbly run club, and my husband Frank and I always look forward to meeting up with Cole. Where else could I get a kiss on one cheek from Cole and a good wash on the other from golden retriever Teddy? Every time we go to the club we find Cole has added a new dimension. It is quite incredible what he has achieved.•

KEN PEPLOWSKI, American clarinet and sax maestro: •I've played the Concorde Club many times, and it is without question one of my favourite venues in the world. The nicest staff, great food, great sound, Cole's marvellous rakish personality and wonderful hospitality, and even a big, friendly "house dog"! (Not to mention the sandwiches and great chips afterwards, and, yes, Cole, I feed half of each to your dog!).

I even recorded a CD there with my favourite rhythm section, John Pearce, Dave Green, and Martin Drew, with the help of the great house engineer, Jim Budd. I had started that particular tour of England with the last remnants of pneumonia (never a good idea), but the Concorde Club audience soon "revived" me (some, literally – I had to keep asking Martin Drew to refrain from his shameless attempts at mouth-to-mouth resuscitation). My recovery was such that we produced a memorable performance that we felt should be released.

It's always nice to walk into a room knowing the audience is "up" for anything, and, as I have more ham in me than one of Cole's sandwiches, I and the band always respond in kind. I tend to do some of my more loose, relaxed shows there, and I remember some great nights with not only my aforementioned "band", but players like Ralph Sutton, various all-star groups, and my comic foil, Marty Grosz. The Concorde staff prove that if you have great food, a warm atmosphere, and consistent booking, you can make a club not only last, but thrive!•

Ken Peplowski in harmony with guitar genius Marty Grosz. Bassist John Rees-Jones awaits, enjoying the moment along with a capacity crowd at the Concorde Club. What the photograph cannot convey is the sheer entertainment that Ken and Marty provided, not only with their stunning musicianship but also with their humour. It was a night not only of great jazz but loud laughter.

BOB KERR, wonderfully eccentric leader of his Whoopee Band: •We arrived early in Hampshire for a gig at Southsea, so we decided to have some fun with Cole. We drove into the Concorde car park, and unpacked our band bus and started to set up on the stage, where we were due to play the following week. Cole came in as we were putting up the drums, and you could almost see his brain spinning. "Good to see you, Cole," I said, as casually as possible. "How have the tickets gone for tonight's gig?" He mumbled something unintelligible and then disappeared in a cloud of dust to check his diary. He thought he'd double booked. When he came back in we were on the floor laughing. Typical Cole, he laughed with us, gave us coffee and waved us on our way. I'm still waiting for him to try to get his own back.•

GERRY BROWN, who has been playing jazz since he was seven years old in 1938, when he was already an accomplished harmonica player before switching to trumpet: • I go back on Cole more than fifty years. My band was resident at the Portswood Hotel and when we left in 1956 it was the Climax Jazz Band that took over, featuring Cole on drums. He regularly booked us when he opened the original Concorde at the Bassett Hotel, and it has been astonishing to watch what he has achieved since starting in the back room of a pub. We loved to party in those days, and there was never a dull moment.

It was my privilege to support Louis Armstrong on his 1962 tour of the UK, and Cole was imaginative enough to put on our 45th anniversary of the tour in a special tribute to the Louis Armstrong All Stars at the Concorde. That's typical of Cole to have his finger on the pulse, and I have always found him fair and supportive.

A few years ago somebody from a Southampton pub wanted to book my band in what was really Concorde territory. I felt duty bound to tell Cole, who was genuinely moved and thanked me for my loyalty. That's Cole. He is always loyal to those who are loyal to him.•

DIGBY FAIRWEATHER, trumpeter, bandleader, broadcaster: •Thinking about the Concorde is a pleasure. It is all so efficiently run that it's one of the few major venues in Britain which – for me – doesn't recall some Technicolor happening; the collapse of a stage (or a musician!), some appalling disaster or trumpeted triumph. There were certainly some musical highspots; one of them on what, for me, was an early visit with Keith Nichols' 'Midnite Follies Orchestra'. The MFO was making some small headlines of its own at the time, and I remember thinking that playing at the Concorde was a very big deal indeed.

The Concorde Club had already been going for twenty years and people thought of it as the South Coast equivalent to Ronnie Scott's. It was a marvellous night. And since then I've come back to the Concorde countless times with everyone from George Melly to Paul Jones, and with Don Lusher's 'Best of British Jazz' show after the death of dear Kenny Baker.

I was there too for Nat Gonella's last recording session of all at the club … with Kenny Baker! That was a big, big event.

Other memories though are more random. I recall the late-ish start to any concert and the early sound check with Jim Budd (one of the best soundmen anywhere in British jazz). I remember the strong coffee, and the delicious platter of chips that feeds the hungry visitors.

The acoustics of the club; so much improved since the ceiling over the stage was raised, giving the performer an impression of blowing into something close to a cathedral - or a church at least. And then of course there's the dog, Teddy, who patiently follows his owner about until energy is exhausted.

We shouldn't forget the owner either! Everyone loves Cole; not only for his faithful support to fifty years of British jazz but, well simply because he's such a nice bloke!

The calm he exudes dispatches performance nerves before they arrive; his solid slow-talking friendship and regularly-expressed affection for the great men of the profession is both reassuring and heartwarming.

And – considering he never thinks to mention that he's accomplished anything – the growth of the Concorde to include its state of the art hotel and jazz-titled rooms is even more of a visible triumph. I love staying there whenever there's a room free! So what can I say? Except – what would we do without him? Thank you Cole for a bookful of memories, random and otherwise.•

STACEY KENT, adored at the Concorde long before she took off into the stratosphere of international stardom (along with her husband, arranger and saxmaster Jim Tomlinson): •I could share a musical anecdote, but there are so many wonderful musical moments for us from the Concorde Club in these last 10 years. The audience always love to have fun there and give so much to the artistes. There is a real sense of giving from both the stage and house and the atmosphere has never been anything other than full of pure joy. And Cole's love of the music is so infectious, it has become part of the building itself.

BUT here's something a little more personal and a memory Jim and I just shared that made us both smile.

Sometimes, the concerts we remember are because of the concert hall itself, a perfect acoustic or all of us in the band being in exceptional form on one night or another or sometimes it's a great meal we've shared in some local spot in Taipei or France, say, but we often remember spots on account of soundchecks and the things that go on before we even play.

Since the start of our career, Jim and I have always travelled with a little rubber ball so that if we arrive somewhere early and if there is a nice outdoor space, we can run around beforehand and get a little exercise by playing catch -- this is one of our little joys on the road. On one sunny afternoon in spring, Jim and I arrived at the Concorde Club pretty early and decided to play some catch in the parking lot before the soundcheck.

The parking lot was empty so we had plenty of space. We had had the same emerald green rubber ball for years, that had travelled on tour with us to many countries across five continents. We had always expected to lose that ball someday but the same ball had managed to last for years.

This very ball had also been caught and thrown by musicians around the world; Humphrey Lyttelton tossed it around in our own back yard in London and James Garfunkel (Art's son) played with us in a town outside Madrid. But on that fateful day in front of the Concorde Club, just as it began to grow dark, we lost the ball in the bushes next to the front door. We hunted for a long time and even enlisted the help of Cole's dog, Teddy, to join in the search but we never found it.

If, some winter, when the bushes are bare and someone wants to go have a look, you may just find our ball. If you do, keep it for yourself, ours has been replaced!•

KENNY BALL, band-leading legend, whose first appearance at the original Concorde was back in 1967 when he featured Terry Lightfoot on clarinet: •When I played the Concorde in February 2008, an elderly gentleman came up to me from the audience and asked if I would mind playing *That's A Plenty* to mark his eighty-second birthday. He told me: "Last time you played that for me here was for my sixtieth!" It dawned on me how long I had been playing the Concorde, and the fact that he and I were both back at the club speaks volumes for how popular the place remains.

We, the audience and the musicians, always come back. I've been playing the Concorde since the Bassett Hotel days, and have seen it grow into an incredible entertainment complex.

Some years back I was at the Savoy Hotel in London at a reception of some sort. I found myself standing next to Georgie Fame, and we found we had in common an affection for Cole Mathieson and the Concorde Club.

We spent much of our time together talking about our gigs there, which we both always found special. Many of us look on Cole as our spiritual leader. While he and the Concorde are going strong jazz is alive and well.♥

GEORGIE FAME contacted us from Hong Kong where he was about to give a sell-out concert: ♥I played the first Concorde Club in 1964 after Cole had seen me playing at the Flamingo, and I have been coming ever since. Along with Ronnie Scott's, the Concorde is the club I like playing best in the UK. I always really feel at home there, and respond to the great reaction we get from a discerning audience. Whether I am singing *Getaway* or jazz standards the reception is always the sort that makes musicians go that extra mile. I consider Cole a good friend, and I congratulate him and everybody at the Concorde on making it to fifty years. Now for the next fifty ... ♥

JOHN HORLER, local hero who followed his late great trumpeter father Ronnie as a Concorde regular and for the past 20 years has been first-choice pianist for Sir John Dankworth and Dame Cleo Laine: "The most lasting memory I have is when Dad and I performed together at the Concorde Club, but in different bands, for the Monty Worlock tribute. That turned out to be the last time we played on the same gig.

I was with bassist Paul Morgan and he said at the time how beautifully he thought Dad played. Sadly, he died shortly after that which gave extra significance to that Concorde visit. Dad, of course, played at the original Concorde back in the early days, and so it has special meaning for me.♥

SAMMY RIMINGTON, respected world wide for his classic New Orleans clarinet and sax playing: ♥I first played the Concorde back in 1979, and have always found Cole supportive both of myself and of jazz in general. He has helped so much with his promotion of American jazz artists over many years. The Concorde always has a good P.A. system and a great, real acoustic grand piano and the restaurant is excellent. I can't praise Cole enough for all his good qualities and wish him all the success in the future. Cole has asked for stories showing him in a bad light, but I can't think of any and I will be amazed if anybody comes up with one.♥.

NEVILLE DICKIE, a master of the keyboard who has travelled the world with his entertaining boogie-woogie and stride piano playing: ♥A very good friend of mine – Roy Cooke – was a big fan of Fats Waller, so much so, he became involved with the British Fats Waller Appreciation Society and eventually became the Honorary Secretary.

When French RCA issued 35 LPs of Fats Waller, Roy was commissioned to write the sleeve notes for each LP, quite a task. He would often invite my wife Pat and me to his home in Caterham, Surrey. Hundreds of LPs were neatly stacked in the living room – every one featuring Fats Waller. He had dozens of copies of the same LPs and many of them had only one Waller track, but anything with Fats on it would be snapped up by Roy – no one else was allowed on that record player. Just Fats, Fats, Fats!

Roy worked in the City of London and by the time he got home, he was too tired to go out in the evening. I mentioned that I had a couple of gigs coming up with my Fats Waller Revival Band, one at the Concorde Club in Eastleigh and the other at London's 100 Club in Oxford Street. He said he hadn't heard any live jazz for years, but he would make an exception and come to both concerts – "as it was the music of Fats Waller".

Roy kept to his word, and showed up at the Concorde – finding a seat directly behind the piano. The band started and launched into the Waller programme. After about 30 minutes I turned around to see Roy, a smile on his face, eyes closed, obviously enjoying the music. We finished the first set and I walked off the stage, headed towards Roy, whose eyes were still closed, but there was no smile. I nearly spilled my beer as a loud snore erupted.

He woke up and apologized, but during the second set, I looked over my shoulder to see Roy's seat was empty. I presumed he had gone to the bar, but he was never sighted again that evening. I telephoned him the following day and asked him if he had enjoyed himself. "Great night" he said, "sorry I didn't say good night, but I had to catch my train home". In the background I could hear the music of Fats Waller – Roy was listening to the real thing in the comfort of his own home. I said I would pick him up and drop him back home for the 100 Club gig. Same thing happened – he had had enough after an hour and had scarpered and caught the train home.

One tries – but one can't win 'em all!

A quick word of thanks to Cole and also to Teddy, who always waddles on stage to pay me during my gigs at the Concorde, a club where it is always a pleasure to play.•

MARLENE AND BILLY VerPLANCK, regular and welcome American visitors to the Concorde, with Marlene bringing her great repertoire of songs beautifully arranged by husband Billy: •Working at The Concorde is like a dream come true. Let's start with Cole Mathieson. He is a very handsome, cool guy who knows how to run a club, knows how to treat his customers and his employees. Over the years we have worked there more than a half dozen times and the same people greet us. Cole, of course, with his beautiful dog always at his side, Jim, the sound man, Jackie at the desk and the patrons who are as loyal as his staff. It's like a beautiful home with dear friends and family. The club is elegant and beautiful, complete with excellent food, great piano, great sound and folks that come to listen. We said it was like a dream and we hope we never wake up.•

PAT HALCOX, who has blown lead trumpet with Chris Barber even longer than the Concorde has been in existence: •I first played the original Concorde back in the 1960s with Chris when the club was in the back room of the Bassett Hotel. It's extraordinary what Cole has achieved since then. When I ran my summertime band – a sort of busman's holiday while Chris took a break – Cole was good enough to give me a booking every year of its existence. I was extremely grateful for this, and I have only happy memories of these sessions. It was particularly pleasing to play so often in Hampshire because I have a lot of musician pals who come from the area, so it was a home from home. We also played there several times with Sweet Substitute, that excellent singing group from Bristol. There's always a discerning audience at the Concorde, and this has to be down to Cole's good taste and enthusiasm. It's got to be one of the best clubs in Europe with a most impressive history. •

CHRIS WALKER, local Forest FM broadcaster and jazz historian who leads his own Swingtet: •My memories of Cole Mathieson and The Concorde Club go back to the 1960s when I came down from London on a couple of occasions as a member of The Mike Daniels Band to play at the club when it was at the Bassett Hotel.

After the move to the old school house I worked at the club regularly, during the 70's and 80's with The Real Ale & Thunder Band (we filmed a TV show for "Southern" from there). From 1980 to 2006 I was producing and presenting the regular jazz programme on BBC local radio, and I was often at the club interviewing both national and international jazz stars before or during breaks in their sets.

I have fond memories of talking to Stephane Grappelli, Peanuts Hucko, Buddy De Franco and many, many more renowned jazz celebrities during their visits to the Concorde. More recently, clarinet maestro Dave Shepherd and I have completed a three-year Monday night residency in the Moldy Fig, which has an intimacy that lends itself to a perfect setting for our improvised jazz.

It's amazing how the club has grown since those days when it was in a garden room at the back of the Bassett Hotel, and it is a credit to Cole and his staff that visiting musicians always feel it is a special place to play and they invariably come back•

MIKE BLAKESLEY, who first played the old Concorde as trombonist with the Gerry Brown Jazzmen in 1962 and has since been a regular with various combinations including his own band:

•There are so many memories that come easily to mind. I recall Cole asking me to lead a band to accompany the highly regarded clarinettist Peanuts Hucko. He was very charming when we met and I made a faux pas almost immediately when he introduced me to his wife Louise Tobin [who had been vocalist with Benny Goodman and married sometime to Harry James] and I think my reaction at the time showed I hadn't heard of her!

To make matters worse - after the band played a couple of numbers on its own I made a big build up for Peanuts to join us. As I finished the announcement [I could see him walking through the audience towards us] the bass player said in a loud whisper, 'Mike I need a pee.'

I had to let him off stage and together with our star we all waited for him to come back. I think the rest of the evening was OK!

Again I was in the band when local musicians accompanied Billy Butterfield, the great trumpet player who had played with Artie Shaw, Bob Crosby and The World's Greatest Jazz Band. He'd arrived straight from a recording session in Birmingham with Dick Wellstood and was in a 'tired and emotional' state. He was also very friendly and charming with everyone.

Part way through the performance we were playing *Pennies From Heaven* and I gradually realised that during his solo the piece had changed to *I Can't Give You Anything but Love*, so naturally the rest of us went along with it. At a later date I had the pleasure of playing with him again when he was on top of his form.

Around this period I led a local band to back Bud Freeman, the famous tenor saxophonist, who had played with Tommy Dorsey, Benny Goodman and various Eddie Condon bands. He was known as a dedicated anglophile and wore suitable tweed jackets.

The band, like many others, would drink pints of beer, so it came as a shock when I asked him what he'd like to drink and he said: "Ah, I think I'll take a glass of sherry, old chap"!

Some time later I was playing in the band backing Wild Bill Davison, the exceptional Dixieland cornettist, and in the middle of a solo by the late Ray Ember [who'd travelled all the way from Woolston] Bill turned to me and said: "That guy's a hell of a piano player", which indeed he was.

It was Eddie 'Lockjaw' Davis who dubbed Ray 'The Bank Manager' because of his sophisticated look, and he played the piano as well as anybody ever could. Ray deserves a special mention in your book, because he was a greatly appreciated regular at the Concorde Club.❞

CAMPBELL BURNAP, trombonist and respected broadcaster and jazz historian: ❝I first played the Concorde with the Alan Elsdon band in the 1970s, and I have nothing but the fondest memories of playing there. I always liked being on the road (that feeling of "setting out" on the highway with a band gave me a kick). Eastleigh didn't take that long to get to from London though, and we knew that there would be a warm smiling welcome from Cole – plus an enthusiastic crowd and even magical sandwiches and chips at some time during the evening.

There was always a good atmosphere, and I remember that our pianist – the late Brian Leake – had an especially warm rapport with Cole whom he'd known since back in the 1950s. Our early appearances were, of course, in the original schoolhouse section of the club before the glamorous extensions!

I've appeared there over the years with various combos, including Marty Grosz, Pat Halcox's old 'Summer Band', and my own group. I've also visited the club as an interviewer for BBC radio jazz programmes when international stars like Clark Terry and Phil Woods were in action.

Another memory is as a paying customer – driving down from London with a young girl friend to dine in the restaurant and listen to Scott Hamilton. I'd promised her 'the most attractive jazz club in Britain, with great food.' Things got off to a less than perfect start, though, when she was informed that she couldn't enter wearing jeans (despite the fact that they were a top fashion label, and that she'd paid a fortune for them).

A quick visit upstairs to the panto props room yielded an unflattering corduroy skirt, but it qualified her for entry. She was frosty about this but thawed out under the combination of Cole's charm, Scott's music, and some great food.

However, when you say 'Concorde' to me I would always think of a night in 1988 when I was part of a pick-up band gathered together to spotlight the clarinet work of the late American, Kenny Davern. I remember that Stan Greig was playing drums that night, not piano, and that Mr Davern threw one of his purist tantrums when he noticed that we would be using microphones.

Kenny was a devotee of natural acoustics. This is all very well unless the show is being recorded for radio. At first Kenny demanded that the mics be removed. Then he was reminded that no mics meant no broadcast which in turn meant no cheque from the BBC. He meekly relented.•

ADRIAN FRY has the distinction of being the youngest of our musicians ever to appear at the Concorde … three years old, to be precise. His mother Pat Masom (previously Fry) was Cole's first secretary, and used to take Adrian along to the office while she took dictation from 'Uncle' Cole. Adrian has since developed into a brilliant jazz trombonist. These are his recollections:

•My memories of the Concorde Club begin in the mid-1970s when my Mum, Pat, began working there as Cole's secretary. During the school holidays I used to spend days there, often with other children whose parents were also working; notably Maureen Pickering's daughters, Karen and Louise. We'd play by the stream, Monks Brook, and sneak through the fence into the neighbour, Ralph Hallett's garden to the rope swing which hung from a branch over the riverbank.

One afternoon I was driving my red pedal-car on the patio and fell down some steps, incurring a head injury worthy of a trip to casualty; thereby joining the select group of children involved in vehicular accidents on licensed premises who arrive at hospital bandaged with a bar-towel.

It wasn't all play though – I would sometimes make myself useful and particularly recall helping Derek Griffiths stock the bar shelves. I approached this task with considerable enthusiasm as the reward was a bottle of low-alcohol beer with my lunch. Whilst I'd like to say that I developed my taste for ale at this young age, the beverage in question, Barbican, actually tasted like carbonated dish-water. Nonetheless, it said it was beer on the label, and that alone made me feel like a grown-up.

As both of my parents love jazz, it's not surprising that I too developed an affinity for the music for which the Club is so famous. Having started learning guitar and then piano, I only began to show notable musical promise (and less reluctance towards practising) when I took up the trombone. Whilst my initial inclination was towards Dixieland I was drawn towards mainstream jazz, and it was this blend of styles that were represented by the trombone band 'Five-A-Slide', led by Pete Strange.

Because Mum worked at the Club she was on first-name terms with all of the musicians, and she took me to meet Pete and the band's lead trombonist and featured soloist Roy Williams before their first gig there in April 1981. I'd been listening to Roy's new album with the Eddie Thompson Trio – *When Lights Are Low*, and from this recording had learned the tune *It Never Entered My Mind* pretty much note-for-note. I played this to them after their rehearsal, so maybe this loosely counts as my first performance at the Club! They both seemed to think that I did pretty well, especially considering the key of D flat, and as a result of this meeting Pete kept in touch; sending me tapes and his own hand-written Jack Teagarden transcriptions which he later published in book form. Both Pete and Roy continued to offer support and encouragement, and also gave me the opportunity to sit in with them on several occasions.

My first performance on stage at the Concorde was during the Christmas Eve lunchtime later that year, with 'Santa's Jazz Band' led by Dave Davis, and featuring two local musicians who have had a profound effect on my musical development – Teddy Layton (clarinet and saxophones) and Mike Blakesley (trombone).

Ted led the trio that was resident in the Musicians' Bar (latterly Moldy Fig) for many years, with whom I regularly sat in from the late 1980s. He was a truly beautiful musician, and I am both proud and grateful to have worked with him on many occasions with the Andy Dickens Band, and in the uniquely laid-back environment of the Friday night sessions at the Club.

Since Mike and I play the same instrument we don't meet so often on gigs, but we did form a two trombone band, and he has influenced my style considerably. This is borne out by the fact that when I do Dixieland/mainstream gigs with Paul Lacey (with whom Mike worked regularly on cruise ships), Paul comments that my style is very much like Mike's.

Many Friday night regulars will remember that Cole sometimes joined the trio, playing just a snare drum with brushes. I've always been interested in trying different instruments and he once lent me his snare for a month or two, which I augmented with a bin lid, a suitcase and a few tins to form a rudimentary drum kit.

Sadly my percussion skills were somewhat limited and I was certainly lacking in the innate ability that I was able to demonstrate on trombone, but it was good to have had the experience – although my parents might disagree.

The Club rules strictly prohibit anyone under 21, but Cole slightly relaxed the rules for me and from around the age of 14 onwards I was allowed to watch the first set of certain gigs whilst hidden in the DJ's booth by the side of the stage. This really was one of the best seats in the house and I particularly remember Gus Johnson beaming at me from his drum stool, just a few feet away.

Given that I'm now a professional jazz musician and appear occasionally on Wednesday nights at the Club, I can truly say that the Concorde has had an influence on my life. And perhaps the blow to the head in my pedal-car accident knocked some sense into me? No – upon reflection I'm sure that many would disagree with that, especially my parents!❡

DAVE BENNETT, renowned jazz agent and recording specialist: •From the long list of memories of the club I would single out Cole's usual generosity of making the room available for what was to become Nat Gonella's last recording session. That happy occasion had Nat in the company of Kenny Baker, Digby Fairweather, Teddy Layton, Martin Litton, Diz Disley and Jack Fallon. The "at home" atmosphere ensured a fitting end to Nat's gloriously long recording career.

Memorable among the musicians I have brought to the Club was Ruby Braff. He could be pretty intolerant at times: one of his pet hates was a drive of much more than half an hour. In consequence the two hour drive to the Concorde from London could be a burden to him and the last time I brought him he was very ill.

Any slight deviation in temperature from his personal requirements and you knew about it. He was not backward in letting Cole know, also throwing in a few other gripes. The average person confronted by such a verbal battering as this would usually feel under enormous strain. Cole's cherubic grin remained transfixed and he was unperturbed, did the best he could and Ruby was soon in great spirits. I was very grateful.

I was once told that Ruby used to share an apartment with Kenny Davern, and I asked Ruby if this was the case. He told me that Kenny had an apartment beneath him, "WHERE HE BELONGS!" A short time after Ruby had died was the last time I saw Kenny at the club and I thought, mistakenly, that he might be amused now by Ruby's remark. His response: "DID HE SAY THAT?" made me wish I hadn't mentioned it, and my laughter at his reaction didn't go down too well. Poor old Kenny, I miss him and Ruby very much. Both wonderful characters and Cole ranks alongside them.•

MEMORIES OF THE MANFRED MANN DAYS

WE move away from jazz for memories of the early rhythm and blues days at the original Concorde Club, kicking off with the recollections of three founder members of the Manfred Mann group that had a residency in the days of the Bassett Hotel:

MIKE VICKERS, a legend in Concorde history who went on to fame with Manfred Mann and beyond:• I think I actually played at the Concorde on the very first night. The takings were fairly small, I imagine, because there weren't that many people there, but Cole seemed happy about it. I don't think he knew then that the club would last 50 years and counting, but I can truthfully say in perspective that I feel honoured to be among the first to play there. This was Concorde No 1, of course, at the Bassett Hotel, and it was very small, but so were some of the other jazz clubs of the time. At least there was room for the band, unlike the possibly even tinier Half Note in New York, for example, where John Coltrane had to stand on the actual bar to play, floor space being so limited.

The times I most enjoyed at the Concorde were when I played with my jazz quintet, on Sunday evenings. It was a great chance to try out new pieces I'd written - some of which I later reworked for various career projects. I even did the announcements, and tried out some jokes, which the attentive audience graciously tolerated.

Cole was always the most pleasant and gentlemanly person to work for, and his enthusiasm and optimism about his chosen path shone through, although it must have been tough for him at times. He started booking guest stars from London, and I got to play a tune or two with them sometimes, including a memorable evening when Jimmy Skidmore, a heavyweight tenor player of the time, and his son Alan Skidmore, now a brilliant international heavyweight in his own right, were playing there together, a sort of cross-generational battle of the saxes. I had to try and play a lot louder than usual that night! Alan subsequently played for me on quite a number of commercial recording sessions, and I always tried to give him a solo or two, if at all possible.

I've visited Concorde No 2 only a couple of times, and obviously everything's much more up-market now, and bigger – which helps. Good luck to you Cole. May you and the club thrive and prosper for a long time to come.•

MIKE HUGG, another early legend of the original Concorde, who went on to huge things with Manfred Mann and whose composing has embraced such things as the signature tune for *The Likely Lads:* •They were happy days for me, getting to play with some of the top jazz musicians of the day at the Concorde. As I remember they were all gentlemen, easy to get on with and just loved playing. I never wanted those sessions to end, they were my dreams coming true. I used to practice a lot but my playing made a massive jump when I started performing in their company. They made you reach for new standards.

When we first started playing there as Manfred Mann we were still making the final transition from Jazz to R&B, which made for some odd musical moments. We would be on stage silent with a ticking alarm clock, as the alarm started ringing we would erupt into free jazz improvising for several minutes. A short while later we would be playing something like *What'd I Say.* It must have been very amusing/confusing for the punters.

We soon got ourselves sorted though, and we learnt how to use our jazz expertise in a more commercially acceptably way, and the place was soon full.

At the height of our residency we had the most fantastic time. The place was packed to the rafters, they were yelling, screaming and singing along, it really made us play to our limits, and sometimes beyond. I remember I was always soaked with sweat and literally steaming when we came off stage. AND we started attracting a lot of attention from all the pretty girls. Happy days indeed.•

PAUL JONES, lead singer with Manfred Mann when the group was first starting out at the original Concorde: •I played the new Concorde for the first time in 2008 with the Digby Fairweather Half Dozen, a little matter of 45 years since my last gig at the old club at the Bassett Hotel. Many in the audience told me they had been there at the Bassett when I was singing with Manfred, Mike Hugg and Mike Vickers. They were such exciting days, and we were so proud and pleased to have a residency. We were all secretly jazzers, but went with the popular flow. Even when we took off in a big way we still kept close to our roots, and used to drop out-and-out jazz numbers into our gigs. It is mind blowing what Cole has achieved from what was just a back room to a pub. The new Concorde is a magnificent venue, and no wonder so many jazzmen set their sights on playing there. When I returned there with Digby it was like being welcomed home.'

TONY HOLE (aka **Tony Benson**), whom Concorde members from back in the Bassett Hotel days will remember on vocals, harmonica and guitar with his R'n'B group, the Meddy Evils: 'I think it must have been late '62 that I started going to see The Mann-Hugg Blues Brothers every Monday or Tuesday night; initially not many turned up, and those who did sat at the tables arranged around the front. To me this band were quite different as they played a 'stylish' type of jazz with a blues feel, or maybe it was the other way around! They played mainly instrumentals featuring Manfred Mann on keyboards and Mike Vickers (who went to my school, although we hadn't met) on alto sax. Paul Jones, the vocalist, sang a few great jazz/ blues numbers and played really good harmonica.

During the instrumentals I got to know Paul quite well and every week we would chat over a pint at the bar. But then things started to change as the word spread that there was something very special happening at The Concorde every week. The crowds started to grow as the 'group' changed their style somewhat to embrace the more earthy Rhythm and Blues that was becoming very popular in the clubs.

In March 1963 they changed their name to Manfred Mann, having just been signed to HMV, and although their first two single releases were not hits, their loyal legion of fans lapped up their exciting, catchy style of R'n'B.

The emphasis on keyboards, sax and vibes, together with harmonica, made the Manfreds really stand out, and it wasn't long before Mike Vickers started playing guitar in the group.

Throughout 1963, the crowds really grew and Cole had to remove the tables as everyone wanted to dance. The jazz instrumentals were gradually replaced by vocals as Paul Jones took over as an outstanding 'front-man', although the crowds still loved tunes like Cannonball Adderley's *Sack O' Woe*. Paul would really whip up the audience with their version of *Got My Mojo Working*, with everyone screaming the answer back.

At this time it was so crowded that if you leapt up in the air you could only land on top of someone else as there was literally nowhere to land! The atmosphere was fantastic. With the release of *5-4-3-2-1* at the beginning of '64, it was pretty clear that Manfred Mann would 'chart' and, of course, they did and the rest is history.

The group played on for a few more weeks at the Concorde, and there were crowds queuing down Burgess Road to see the now nationally famous band.

Cole Mathieson clearly knew what was going on in the R'n'B scene as he managed to attract many bands who were on the verge of making it. The best known, of course was 'The Cream' and those of us who were lucky enough to be there when the first 'Supergroup' played the Bassett Hotel will never forget it. But we should not forget the wonderful 'Graham Bond Organisation,' with Jack Bruce and Ginger Baker and sort of forerunners to The Cream.

They would put on a very exciting soulful show whenever they played and Graham Bond would always allow me to lean on his Hammond throughout the show. What great nights they were ... as were the nights that Jimmy James and the Vagabonds played the 'Bassett'. It would be so packed, no room to dance and sweat dripping from the ceilings. I've not seen bands that exciting in recent years. That's why the '60's were so good because it was all new and fresh!

It was a great privilege to eventually play the Concorde many times with my group: 'The Meddy Evils.' We too had some smashing evenings there as did so many other local bands that Cole had faith in to draw a crowd. I think it just proved that the Southampton crowds were something very special, and they proved it again over 40 years later at the 2008 'Sixties Reunion' at the Concorde in Stoneham Lane.•

DAVID ST JOHN organized the reunion and gives a full report on his fascinating website at www.davidstjohn.co.uk He recalls: •I was one of the lucky ex-musicians (vocal/harmonica) who used to play the odd gig at the old Concorde during the early 60s R&B boom as well as going to watch other bands play there. A couple of my favourite nights featured John Lee Hooker and early Free, although I missed out on many of the early fledgling superstars of the future! My early groups were blues-orientated, thanks to the influences of the Stones, Yardbirds and other British bands who combined hard driving electric sounds mixed with the American classics of previous years.

I spent some ten happy years on the local Southampton group scene and my last band played at the new club shortly after the big move to Stoneham during the early Seventies, before I left the area in 1972 to concentrate on my solo career, which morphed into the comedy side and much more. The 'Sixties Reunion' night at the Concorde 40 years down the line was a complete sell-out and it showed that the magic lingered on with many people who rocked through through that memorable era.•

BOB PEARCE, whose Blues Band kicked off the reunion night: •I first remember playing the Concorde Club when it was at The Bassett Hotel, feeling very excited to be standing on the same stage that one of my blues heroes – Sonny Boy Williamson – once stood. I missed him the night he was there because I had a gig at The Blue Indigo (Bay Tree Inn). But I was there for many other acts, including Graham Bond Organisation, Brian Auger, Free, John Lee Hooker (Mississippi Fred McDowell was playing at Southampton University the same evening!), Joe Cocker, Champion Jack Dupree and, of course, The Cream.

The night they played there, I remember being told that they'd made Ginger Baker come down on the train as they refused to travel with him. How true this was, I really couldn't say, but he did arrive late, and he stayed overnight in Shirley because I had a chat with him the next morning as (a) I was waiting for my lift to work and (b) Ginger was on his way to the local newsagent for his supply of Rothmans!! This was at Foy's Corner.

I played at the 'new' club quite a few times during its early years – as support for Detroit Bluesmen, Baby Boy Warren and Boogie Woogie Red (they stayed at our place that night and oh, the stories that could be told ... but that's for another time!!), Dr. Ross the one man band, sat in with Sunnyland Slim and watched as Lightnin' Slim spent vast amounts of change on the then present "one-armed-bandit".

My last memories of playing at The Concorde Club were Friday nights, the midnight 'til one slot after the featured jazz band, Monty Sunshine, Max Collie etc. The list is pretty long. It was a solo gig, me, my guitar and amp, plus a harmonica in a 'neck-rack'. I was making £10 plus a meal each Friday night!! All good training though.•

TERRY DASH, of the Hertfordshire-based Terry Dash Music Agency: •I have been lucky to know Cole for many years as he has booked several of my Artistes for appearances at the Concorde. Among them were Lillian Boutte and her Music Friends from New Orleans, The London Ragtime Orchestra, Butch Thompson and The King Oliver Centennial Band, Juanita Brooks, and The Charleston Chasers.

It is always a pleasure to visit the club as everyone receives a warm welcome and enjoys the excellent hospitality. I remember well my first experience of the Hotel as there had been a mix up with the rooms, and instead of the single room that I had asked for, I had to share a room with the American Cornettist Charlie Devore, who featured some heavy snoring!

The Concorde Club is a prime example for future club owners of how to run a business and to earn the respect from the local community. Take a bow Cole.•

JOHN BUNE, owner of the excellent jazz-specialist company Zephyr Records: •In the late 40s I had fallen for the big bands of Ellington, Goodman, Herman, Kenton and Basie, with all their featured musicians. From the 60s to the 90s family business affairs took over and I no longer had the necessary time to keep up with the trends in jazz. While taking a break in Bassett from my Upper Shirley home in the 1960s, I vividly recall somebody saying there was a jazz club there but I did not follow it up.

Watching a French television programme in 1993, I saw Scott Hamilton playing and suddenly all my love of jazz came flooding back. My daughter stumbled on the fact that by sheer coincidence Scott was playing at the Concorde Club in Eastleigh that following Wednesday. Not a member, I rang up to find myself talking to Cole. He put me on to Jackie, who organised tickets for me. That night I was blown away by Scott, playing to his peak with the support of Brian Lemon on piano, Dave Green on bass and Allan Ganley on drums. Brian was just sensational and completely stole the show, thanks largely to the generosity of Scott in allowing him so much solo work. As they came off at the end, Allan Ganley quietly murmured: "You were great this evening, Brian." I got talking to Brian, and this led to him being my guiding light when I started Zephyr Records the following year. With Brian showing the way, we won the British Jazz Awards Best CD for both 1997 and 2000.

Since that first visit to the Concorde our family have spent many wonderful Wednesday evenings at the club, which is the perfect setting for jazz. Thanks to Cole and his team at the Concorde, Zephyr Records had been given a dream start.•

Finally, from the musicians, comes something completely different, We wondered how best to feature it in these memoirs without readers thinking we should be in straitjackets. It is the story of the legendary concert given at the original Concorde by the Gutta Percha Elastic Band. We decided that the most sensible way to convey the history and hysteria of the times was to go to the founder of the band, **MIKE SADLER**, for his recollections of what were mad yet wonderfully happy days. This former schoolmaster is now living in retirement in the heart of Surrey, and has lost none of his zany, Goonish sense of humour:

•In the opinion of relatively few people, one of Cole's promotional coups was engaging the services of Gutta Percha's Elastic Band. This organisation, or disorganisation, had its roots in a pub called White's Home, Northam, just down the road from the Prince of Wales, and the opposite side of the road from the Plaza Cinema before its transformation into a TV studio.

It was there that the first performance of the Caractacus Flywheel Piffle Group took place, marking the début of the esteemed *Daily Echo* journalist John Edgar Mann on Pasteurised Milk Bottle. His services had to be retained when the group morphed into Gutta Percha's Elastic Band for two reasons: firstly, John thought of the name, and secondly the unique sound of the aforesaid bottle. This was a quintessential component of the band's sound, a sound which no other band in the history of music has come close to equalling. There are some who may say this is a good thing.

After performances at the Yellow Dog Jazz Club at the Portswood Hotel, the band was as ready as it would ever be for the big time. To his everlasting credit, Cole not only agreed to give the band its big break, but provided the personnel (to call them musicians would be stretching it a bit) with a barrel of beer – a good move this, because many of the players would have spent more time at the bar than on the stage.

Excerpts of songs written with the intention of advertising the band's 1963 appearance at the Concorde have recently been discovered. One song, based on the unashamedly plagiarised tune of King Oliver's *Sweet Lovin' Man* goes like this (all together now):

Bring all your inhibitions, come along and hear
Gutta Percha's Elastic Band
Remember your subscription goes to buy more beer
For Gutta Percha's Elastic Band.

We've never had a practice, we never have rehearsed:
We know if we'd tried it, it'd sound a damn sight worse
Besides, the police would come and stop us
And tell us to disperse from Gutta Percha's Elastic Band.

What did Gladstone say in eighty-five
'Bout Gutta Percha's Elastic Band?
It's the only one to which Her Majesty can jive –
Gutta Percha's Elastic Band.

Gutta Percha won't be with us – he's doing time
For diggin' his potatoes on the Rock Island Line.
It's time to stop this rubbish 'cos I cannot find a rhyme
For Gutta Percha's Elastic Band.

The role of the pasteurised milk bottle has already been shown to be of crucial importance (today's semi-skimmed would have changed the entire sound of the band and we would not have made nearly as much impact). We featured an electric plank, which was just that – a piece of wood with bass guitar strings. John Moxham, one-string phono-fiddler par excellence, doubled on frying pandemonium.

The leader took the occasional solo on izalbumphone, comb and paper, plus the inside of a toilet roll.

Sadly, no recordings of the band exist. What I am proud to put on record is the fact that during our fairly surreal concert we had a collection for a Persian earthquake fund and raised the amazing amount for those days of fifty quid. And we got top ratings from our Puke Box Jury panel.

A section of the band went on tour to Winchester Prison, organised by Cole who said he had found us a captive audience. They counted us in and they counted us out. Our washboard player John Lindsell managed to fall off the stage. A request from the inmates for one of our delectable singers to 'get your knickers off' was not acknowledged – much to the disappointment of the band.

As for the lead singer, sometimes known when not preparing schoolchildren for their exams as Gutta Percha, he attended the very last night of the Concorde at the Bassett Hotel. He vaguely remembers that Cole, who used to call him 'Uncle Gut', spiked his beer with whisky, leaving him with a massive hangover. And the morning after Uncle Gut moved house.

And that's the end of my moving story, and the tale of how Gutta Percha's Elastic Band lit up the old Concorde with a fairly bizarre concert that was perfectly summed up by one of the patrons who said: "I've never heard anything quite like it before in my life."

He may also have added that he never wanted to hear the like again, but on that I could not possibly comment. Critics will always have trouble defining the band's place in contemporary music.

Was it, as was claimed by its leader, ahead of its time? Was it a fusion or a defusion band? Were there elements of world or even out-of-this-world music?

For all the concerts Cole has promoted over the past fifty years, there has been nothing quite like that produced by Gutta Percha's Elastic Band. Here's to the next fifty years.

WE now come to the memories of the most important people of all in the history of the Concorde Club – the Members. For many years, the slogan of the Concorde has been: "The Members Made It." Cole stressed throughout his personal story in Part One that he could not have made such a success of the Club without their loyal and continuing support.

Now they get their say, and we start with **GORDON SAPSED**, a 20-year member from Bassett who gets close up and personal with the musicians. He is a skilled photographer and jazz historian, whose striking pictures feature on many of the pages of this book. Gordon, a retired nuclear scientist, gave us his memories in the form of quotes he had heard while working with his camera close to the Concorde stage:

•Much-loved Jazz and Blues pianist **Gene Harris**, taking his seat at the Concorde for the first time in the 1990s: "This is wonderful. Why has it taken me so long to get to this place?" (Gene's first major public appearance was as a child playing piano with the Harlem Globetrotters in the 1930s).

Digby Fairweather in a BBC Broadcast: "Our live gig today comes from the Concorde in Eastleigh, where Cole Mathieson has demonstrated that you can maintain one of the finest jazz clubs in the world, without spending a fortune on Central London real estate."

Famed New York pianist **Dick Hyman**, musical director for most of Woody Allen's films, after the Concorde audience had given a standing ovation in mid-set for a stride piano rendering during a live broadcast: "I can tell what you like."

Veteran tenor sax player **Spike Robinson** was struggling as he ruffled through his music, looking for the next chart. Co-bandleader/arranger **Derek Nash**, standing next to him hissed: "They're in alphabetical order." Spike replied: "That's okay if you can remember the damned alphabet."

Concorde favourite **Conte Candoli** – a trumpet player in bands led by Woody Herman, Stan Kenton and hundreds of film and TV orchestras, on one occasion brought to the Club his brother Pete Candoli, who similarly had a top-class career in Hollywood, but rarely toured in later years. Just before the duo went on stage one Concorde fan said: "Can I say thank you very much Pete for the last twenty years of great music." Conte responded: "Is that how long you've stayed away from this place Pete?"

Drummer **Martin Drew**, who played with Oscar Peterson's Trio and other top groups all over the world was approached by a fan at the bar in the Moldy Fig, and asked: "Can I have a word please?" "Only if you're quick," said Martin. "They always have good food here in the musicians' room."

Singer **Clare Teal:** "This place has the greatest chips on Earth."

(A great, possibly even treasonable compliment from somebody who comes from Harry Ramsden Yorkshire territory).

New young singer **Gwyneth Herbert** on her Wednesday night Concorde debut: "This is fun – we don't often do Saga gigs."

Finally, the one and only **Alan Barnes:** "We're running a bit late, so if you don't mind we'll do our encore now."

I have travelled the world with my wife, Pauline, photographing jazz concerts, and the Concorde stands comparison with any jazz club anywhere. All the musicians I talk to always say how much they look forward to playing there. They know they will be properly appreciated.•

JUNE and DON GREENING, Bishops Waltham, Hampshire (and Western Australia!): •We have been members of the Concorde for many years, but we left it behind in 1999 when we decided to retire to Western Australia to be near our daughter. We bought a house and went for a trial run. It didn't work!

One of the main factors for changing our minds was the loss of our social life and friends at the Concorde. We missed it so much – the friendly welcome we always get, the great jazz evenings, Shirley Morgan and her guests on Tuesdays, and so on. So we came back home, and now go off to Oz to see our daughter for holiday stays, knowing we can come back! Thanks for all the wonderful years.•

GILL HOLLOWAY, Christchurch, Dorset: •I am making this contribution to the memories on behalf of my husband Tony Holloway, former bass player with John Maddocks and Gerry Brown's Mission Hall Jazz Band. He was friends with Cole even before the original Concorde started, so they go back a long, long way. Unfortunately, Tony is now paralysed down his left side following a stroke in 2005. But we still enjoy a full life, and we just want everybody to know that we often think warmly of our visits to the Concorde. I was a member of the old Concorde in my days as Gillian Foley, and Tony describes me as his groupie!•

JOHN PADDY BROWNE, Colden Common: •It was *Daily Echo* columnist John Edgar Mann who introduced me to the Concorde – or rather to the Balladeer Club, which was a sort of subsidiary of the Concorde – in 1961. While I knew something about folk songs back then, I knew nothing at all about folk clubs (or jazz clubs for that matter). Through JEM I met the Balladeers – Dave Williams, Vic Wilton and Pete Mills, as well as Cole Mathieson who seemed never to come out from behind the cloakroom counter in the annexe of the Bassett Hotel. All were immensely friendly and welcoming.

I never called myself a singer, yet somehow I was soon MC-ing those evenings when the Balladeers were otherwise engaged, and even being got paid for it. Cole, or sometimes Jim Budd, would slip a ten-bob note (that's 50p, folks!) into my hand and I would walk all the way home to Bitterne Park knowing that I had at least part of that week's rent covered.

I played in only one performance of the Gutta Percha Elastic Band, with its "Puke Box Jury" and record "reviewer", the witty and urbane John Francis of Francis Records, who played a selection of old 78 rpm discs on an ancient phonograph, complete with a massive horn, before smashing them into smithereens.

Of all the memorable evenings I spent at theclub, appreciatively sipping the occasional gratis Guinness that Mr Mathieson bought me (Cole's Porter), one evening stands out. It was in the middle of the worst snowfall for years. Southampton traffic was at a standstill; people were not getting to work. But somehow there was a full house at the Bassett, and we made the most of it, and the atmosphere was pure gold. Cole Mathieson, who must have anticipated a dead night, smiled so much you could have roasted chestnuts on his face!•

JOHN KING, Stockbridge: •I remember Cole turning up at the White's Home Pub at Northam (Ace of Clubs) in his Army uniform ready to play the drums. I was a friend of Terry Conroy at the time and remember he and Cole getting together to start a club at the Bassett Hotel. Terry went on to be the entertainments manager for Cunard. When Cole moved into the old school house in Eastleigh it was the first time there had been a permanent home for jazz. It's a real tribute to Cole that the Concorde Club has been in existence for 50 years and is recognised as one of the best around.•

DIANA and KEITH PASKINS, Winchester: •We both joined the Concorde at the Bassett in the mid-sixties but did not meet until 1977 at Stoneham. We were married in 1978 and moved to Surrey but kept up our membership. For twenty years we frequently made the 100 mile return journey to dance at the Sunday night sessions. The John Maddocks Jazz Maniacs were the resident band in 1977 and it was like his exuberant Christmas party every week.

Keith remembers seeing Maynard Ferguson at the Bassett. The tone of the evening was set when the drummer arrived and nailed his kit to the floor. Diana saw legends Sonny Terry and Brownie McGee, also Norma Teagarden. Later we both particularly enjoyed the Great Guitars (Charlie Byrd, Barney Kessel and Herb Ellis) and the incomparable Stephane Grappelli.

We moved back to Winchester in 1998 and can now enjoy great gigs on week days as well as being part of the furniture on Sundays. We will always be grateful to the Concorde for bringing us together.•

ROBIN CULVERHOUSE, North Boarhunt: •The Concorde evening that really blew me away was when the Maynard Ferguson orchestra was 'in the house' back in the early 1970s. I arrived quite early and joined a gaggle of blokes around the bar. The club was quite quiet apart from these chaps. Suddenly, following a signal of some sort, most of this crowd left the bar and headed for the bandstand. They were the orchestra!

It was clear from the first tune they played that this was going to be a special evening. Part way into the second number Maynard made his entrance, striding down from the back of the club extrovertly clad and clutching his horn, a real star. The high notes of his trumpet playing *MacArthur Park* stay with me clearly today.

The impact and orchestration of Maynard's English band was phenomenal. It was a wall of sound of the most beautiful sort, and despite many other big band appearances at the club that was the one to beat them all.

That was the night that Cole's dog Fergie helped himself to a slurp of beer from each of the glasses of each of the sax and brass section. The rascal also took a mouthful from my pint. We all learned not to leave our pints on the floor while Fergie was around!•

TONY MARTIN, now in Kenmore, Perthshire, takes us right back to day one of the original Concorde: •As I remember it, the original Concorde Club opened at the Bassett Hotel on Good Friday 1957. I attended that first evening with Terry Paine and John Sydenham, good friends of mine who were both just starting out on their exceptional football careers with Southampton. We all really enjoyed the new jazz scene that Cole Mathieson was introducing to the town.

Our dear mutual friend, the late Ron Andrews, was playing bass and it was the first of many great evenings that we enjoyed.

In later years I served you as Video Director of Hamilton Electronics in London Road with all your audio visual needs and appreciated the trade you bought us during that period.

I trust Shirley Morgan is still singing at the club and all the members are continuing to enjoy the wonderful jazz evenings you brought there.•

PAUL MURRAY, a Concorde member since 1969 and successful local business man, who is a driving force behind many of the Club's money-raising charity events:

•A small number of clubs become institutions: Ronnie Scott's, Annabels, Tramp, The Cavern Club to name a few. The Concorde Club also falls into this category. Why? Not only for its music, which is its *raison d'etre* and which is well documented in this book, but also for the myriad of other functions that it hosts as well as the other functions it serves. With regard to the latter, it is also an hotel, a restaurant, a wine bar, a meeting and conference venue and a theatre. I am sure that this list is not exhaustive. And as far as the functions for which it provides a venue are concerned, the list is endless!

There are functions that the Club organizes itself, such as the legendary pantomime and the Wine Society, and many others organized by others, such as the BNI business club and other business networking groups, fund raising dinners, wakes, charity events, fashion evenings as well as providing the meeting place for two Rotary Clubs.

It is this other side of the Club that has made me into a regular at the Concorde. In the 80's and early 90's for a period of twelve years I attended most Monday lunchtimes as a member of the Rotary Club of Eastleigh and from 1983 for about twenty years, I used to eat in the Moldy Fig on most Thursdays when I would buy my parents lunch. And early each year, I would be at the Club on a Sunday rehearsing my part for the Pantomime, the best parts of which would be turned into another show in October of each year.

As singing and dancing were well beyond my capabilities, I would attempt to deliver monologues interspersed with a modicum of acting. To this day, I am reminded by others of such topical soliloquies as "Bollocks to the butterflies" delivered at the time that the M3 was being cut into Twyford Down, a scar that can still be seen today.

My other involvement at the Concorde was organizing or helping to organize functions, charity events and fundraising evenings. The first "do" I organized was a birthday party for a friend on Tuesday, 17th May 1977.

Luckily, the birthday fell on a Tuesday, the only day that Cole would hire out the Club for such functions, as he was booked with regular slots on all the other nights of the week.

Another involved turning the Concorde Club into the Cotton Club for an evening in May 1989, when even the signs outside the club were changed to read "The Cotton Club". The entertainment put together for the first time that night was Harry Strutter's Hot Rhythm Orchestra, the Jiving Lindy Hoppers and Jo Chisholm, the American tap dancer, singer and comedian. This group were to perform together a number of times subsequently.

The compere was Johnny M and a highlight of the show was the appearance of the legendary trumpet player, Kenny Baker. I joined Paul Philp, the Solent Stars, England and Great Britain basketball player, on stage for a two minute tap dancing routine that had taken us months of training to perfect!

A few years later we did a similar thing and turned the Club into "The Cattlemens Club" for the Oilbarons' Ball, to reflect the popularity of the TV programmes "Dallas" and "Dynasty" at that time. This included getting Colin Croll of Millbrook Industries to build a nodding donkey oil well in the car park, along with a real American car outside the club's entrance. Stetsons were in evidence everywhere! The money raised was to plant trees in a wood in an area behind the Club. An early green project!

There were also annual functions to help the fortunes of Hampshire cricketers, who were enjoying their Benefit Years, with a number of "Dodgy Dinners" that led on to a number of "Slightly" nights. In fact the Cotton Club event was also billed as "The Slightly Dubious Night". For the life of me, I cannot remember why! Perhaps that is just as well.

As the local fundraising chairman for the Rose Road Children's Appeal at the time, other functions followed for this charity that benefitted and continues to benefit from Concorde Club generosity, as evidenced by "The Concorde Room" that still provides music therapy at the Rose Road Centre in Lordswood, Southampton today.

Going even further back to the late sixties, my father looked at the present site as a possible place into which he could move his business from its building in Market Street, Eastleigh. Just imagine, it would now be a warehouse and offices rather than a thriving Club and Hotel.

Things turned out differently and we went up to Chandlers Ford, where I still work. Ironically, one of the events I organized at the Concorde was my father's funeral in 1994, so it certainly has played a big part in my life – and still does. Its close proximity to Eastleigh Football Club, where I am much involved, has allowed the Club to be used for prematch meals, a fund raising venue and more often as an extra car park on the biggest of our match days.

This is yet another function for a Club that has become an institution. It has put so much into local community life as well as being renowned for its contribution to the musical heritage of Eastleigh and far beyond. Long live the Concorde!⁹

Band leader Georgina Bromilow, making a big impression in her Concorde debut in March 2008

RAY PAULL, Southampton, a regular member of the Wednesday night jazz audience with his wife, Pam: ❛I clearly remember the Manfred Mann days at the Bassett Hotel back in the 1960s. That was when the Concorde really started to take off, and I've watched it develop into a superb jazz club. We are so lucky to have it all on our doorstep, some of the greatest jazz musicians in the world coming here to our corner of Hampshire.

It's not only the established stars who get a platform, but also the young up-and-coming players. For instance, we were recently treated to a concert by a fabulous trumpeter called Georgina Bromilow, who started out with the Wigan Youth Jazz Orchestra. I don't know where she gets her breath from, because she sings as well as blows an awesome trumpet, with her cheeks filling out in the style of Dizzy Gillespie.

She has learned her trade playing in theatre orchestras for shows like *Chicago* and *The Rat Pack,* and led her own big band at the Concorde. It's great for young musicians that Cole is willing to put them on and give them the experience of playing to an audience that really knows its jazz.❜

GEOF HOLT, who describes himelf as an honorary and hopefully an honourable member: "It was a sunny Saturday afternoon in May of 1968 and a couple of my older friends, John Byrne who was a year older than me, and John Davies who had just had his 18th birthday a few days before, and was five months older than me, told me they were going to try the Concorde Club.

What's the "Concorde Club" I asked. "It's a Jazz club" came the reply. Before I could tell them that "we don't do jazz", they added that they have a Disco on a Saturday nights. One of the Johns – I won't embarrass him by telling you which one (told you I wouldn't mention your name Mr B) – said it was a members' club. We would HAVE to join, even though it was over 18s only. Now the more intelligent of you will have worked out I was only 17.

"Don't worry," one of the Johns said. "I work with one of the girls on the door. I'll distract her and we'll doctor some ID for you." So I spent the afternoon changing 1951 into 1950 on my Judo Club membership card and that evening off we went.

The problem was I made a terrible job of "doctoring" my ID, a partially sighted eighty year old would have realised it was faked. But luckily Jan wasn't working then. To this day I have no idea how I got my membership. Maybe John's friend took pity on me, I don't know, but I did get my membership and that's when my life took one of those paths that change your life for ever, and thank God it did.

Since that fateful day in 1968 the Concorde Club has been the backbone of my social life. It has provided me with a host of friends, one or two girlfriends and a social life that would be the envy of many.

I even go to the odd jazz night. Does that qualify me as a music lover at last Cole?

To me the Concorde is not just a jazz club, a night club, a disco, a restaurant, a hotel or a place to have a late drink. It is of course all those and so much more. Many of my friends believe the Concorde club is my second home.

Two of the greatest days in my calendar are the Summer Ball and *Beaujolais Nouveau,* and if you haven't been to them you don't know what you're missing. A thespian I am not but I have participated, in a very small way, in two of the many Concorde Charity pantos, but I have watched all the rest. For many of those my friend, David Markinson, and I were appointed as authorised hecklers, and any of you that have heard the jokes will know why they needed hecklers to get a laugh.

More recently I have helped Jamie with the quiz nights. These started in 2002 and have grown from just two in the first year to at least one a month, and Jamie tells me there a big demand for more from people who enjoy the unbeatable atmosphere of the Concorde. I am so glad I help with the questions and the marking because I would have no idea of the answers if I hadn't helped set the questions.

I was very lucky to have been born in Southampton because there is only one Concorde Club. They say that in life you only get out what you put in, I don't think that's true because I have got far more out of the Concorde than I could ever put in.

What will become of me now Cole knows I joined illegally?"

Note from Cole: "Geof, you're barred ... joke! For all of you who 'fiddled' your way in back in the Bassett days, I am offering an amnesty. Just make sure you buy the book!"

MICHAEL LOUGH goes on a memory trip from his home in Toronto: •I was a "Conc" regular from circa 1966-1969, a fairly interesting period for me being 18 in 1966. My memories are those of just a lad really enjoying the period. I liked jazz and Friday night was a favourite night – stomping all over the place with great friends that became a sort of musical and drinking "family". The Bassett was no doubt the greatest pub in the world to us, and to have a steady stream of music right next door was wonderful. I can't remember every event but I am sure my hearing was affected! I live in Toronto now, I've been here for nearly forty years, but one of these days I'll get back. Oh, by the way, thank you Pauline for letting me in for half price sometimes when funds were low…•

ROGER M. SMITH: Mayor of Eastleigh Borough: •It has been my pleasure to have known Cole Mathieson for 45 years, which is half a lifetime (if we're lucky!).

I remember the old Concorde Club in the Bassett Hotel, Southampton, and I used to be able to gain free entry to see all the golden oldies perform because the hotel's landlord – 'Tiny' Smith – was the father of my friend, David. We had the job of collecting up and washing all the glasses in the little club situated on the side of the hotel. This was a small price to pay for being able to enjoy the great entertainment.

In the later years at Stoneham Lane we have enjoyed many happy occasions and seen some great acts, and as Mayor of Eastleigh this year we have had such great support from Cole and his staff. Our twinning visitors were made so welcome in the Ellington Lodge Hotel and are looking forward to returning next year. Congratulations on 50 fantastic years.•

CHRISTINE E. WILLIAMS, Ringwood: •As a jazz and folk enthusiast, I have many happy memories of the very early days of the Concorde Club when it was just starting out at the Bassett Hotel in the late 1950s and early 1960s.

My late husband, Dave Williams, was a member of the Balladeers, a popular local folk group who performed at the 'old' Concorde Club every week.

An evening which stands out in my memory was a visit to the club by a group of cadets from two Russian training ships docked at Southampton. Their singing and dancing was memorable, as was the entire evening with lots of alcohol involved!

My brother Mike Sadler, otherwise known as Gutta Percha, organised the famous Gutta Percha and his Elastic Band evening at the Concorde. I also went and played with them (on the wobble board) when Cole organised a visit to Winchester Prison. We entertained the inmates with one of the most bizarre concerts ever. Happy days!•

TRISH CHRISTIE (used to be 'Little Pat' O'Farrell): •My first memory of the Concorde was autumn 1965, when Pauline refused to let me in because I didn't look old enough! This was at the Bassett Hotel. I became a member in 1967/68 and was a fairly regular visitor, coming to discos and to see some fantastic bands. I used to help out in the cloakroom, and I recall going on a couple of 'Riverboat Shuffles to the Isle of Wight. When the club moved to Stoneham Lane, I used to help out and I painted a bit of wall! I remember the excitement of the opening night.

I think my name was second in the new members' book. On disco evenings I used to get the dancing going to numbers like *All Right Now by Free* and *Metal Guru* by T.Rex. I worked as a barmaid and remember Cole checking that we girls understood the new decimal currency. I met my husband of 33 years at the Concorde in 1973. We are now back as fairly regular visitors, mostly on a Wednesday Jazz Night and also enjoy staying at Ellington Lodge.•

JOHN and BUBBLES TREE, Waterlooville: •One of our most enduring memories stems from 1986. We had always admired and enjoyed the singing of Maxine Sullivan, and she sang at the club accompanied by pianist Keith Ingham. It was the perfect gig.

Maxine sang like an angel, with Keith providing the most sympathetic accompaniment. But there is more ... Maxine and her daughter, who was travelling with her, joined us at our table for the interval and we talked about her life in Jazz.

She was so easy to talk to and as charming and gracious as we imagined she would be. Before leaving us, she autographed one of her LP's for us. Unforgettable.

We were extremely proud to be appointed Honorary Members of the best Jazz club in the world (just ask the musicians!). Thanks Cole, Pauline and everyone involved for fifty remarkable years at the Concorde Club.•

PHIL LATHAM, a devoted Wednesday night jazz regular at the Concorde: •My wife Anne was resident singer with Teddy Layton in the Musicians' Bar and then the Moldy Fig in the 80s and moving into the 90s. She loves animals as much as she loves singing jazz, and one freezing winter's day she found two white Aylesbury ducks struggling to survive on a small lake near our Southampton home.

Anne started feeding them every day, and she was just getting them back to something approaching full strength when she was devastated to find one of the ducks had been shot dead and the other one shot in the foot. The duck had its wings clipped, and had somehow managed to get itself to a small island in the middle of the lake, where it was stranded.

The temperature dropped to way below freezing, and Anne decided the water was frozen over sufficiently for her to walk to the island to rescue the duck. But twice she went through the ice into the water, and finally persuaded a group of children on half-term holiday to help her form a linked-arms chain across the lake. A little lightweight boy was last in the chain and got to the island, and then the duck was handed back until on safe ground.

Anne brought the duck home and nursed it until it was well enough to be returned to its natural habitat. She had told Cole of the adventure, and he volunteered to give the duck a home at the Brook that ran behind the Concorde.

The story made the local papers, and the members started calling Cole St. Francis of Assisi, but he said all the credit belonged to Anne. She has been a wonderful singer, and is a remarkable lady who is battling ill health without complaint. We are both warmed by our memories of Anne's happy days singing with Teddy and the boys and we will always have a special place in our hearts for Cole and the Concorde. Oh yes, and the duck!•

TED BOTTING, Murcia, Spain: ❛My earliest memories of the Concorde were of seeing the great Buck Clayton and Ben Webster at the 'old' club. Eventually the 'new' club opened and by then I had a wife, Kristina, who enjoyed jazz. It was there that we met the lovely Spike Robinson and his wife, Susan. Spike, of course, played many times at the club, and we eventually became good friends.

He and Susan stayed with us on numerous occasions at our home in Locks Heath. Sitting and talking with him into the early hours about jazz and jazz musicians while drinking a brandy or three is something I will never forget. On one such night it was starting to get daylight, and Spike said, on glancing through the curtains, 'We had better get to bed, Buddy, I'm beginning to see the light!'

Thank you Cole for inadvertently being responsible for that, and also thank you to all at the club for so many wonderfully memorable evenings.❜

JACKIE JONES, Andover: ❛The Concorde Club has meant so much to me personally since I first found it a few years ago. I had moved to Andover to take up a new job a while before, and thought it about time I got out and about and made a few friends. I signed up for a meeting of a Supper Club, which was to take place in a venue called the Concorde Club in Eastleigh, about which I knew nothing. When I arrived it was immediately obvious to me that this was a jazz club. I could not believe my luck, having been a jazz fan since I was about eleven (I am much, much older now!).

During dinner I was chatting to the person next to me, and I was told that if I was interested in hearing the jazz at the Club I should speak to "that lady over there" – who turned out to be Doreen Iredale, who has now become a good friend of mine. We regularly attended the international jazz nights on a Wednesday, and I have to say that the Concorde became like my second home! I no longer needed the supper club, having found what made me happier than I had been in years – a wonderful, friendly, welcoming jazz club with fabulous music.

I remember being blown away by the drumming of Bobby Worth at a gig in early 2005 (Digby Fairweather's Half Dozen with George Melly). What I really recall from that evening is Bobby's drumming, crisp, accurate, swinging, relevant and joyous. I went up on to the stage after the show had finished and told him so. And he's still swinging!

To top it all, at the end of August 2006 I was sitting in the Moldy Fig (this was at the time of the major refurbishments, with no jazz in the main club), and next to Doreen and me was a gentleman (!) who was obviously new to the club. We got chatting, and to cut a long story short (very!) I found my soul mate Norman Giller. He had lost his wife of 45 years a short while before, and had gone back to his first love – jazz – to get out and about (just like I had).

He made me laugh then, and still does, and we are now inseparable (although we live in separate locations!). I had been "happily divorced" for 18 years, and thought I would never meet anyone to share my passions (steady!) ... but, as the old saying goes, you never know.

Thanks, Mr G! Here's to the future, for us and for the Concorde Club, which now has an even more precious place in my heart. Thanks a million, Cole. While Norman has been working

Spike Robinson, American saxophone master who was beginning to see the light

on the book he has tried hard to find somebody willing to say something nasty about you. That would be like trying to get somebody to say something horrible about Santa Claus. You are beyond criticism, and we all love you.'

PHILIP G. COOK, Hedge End: 'A memory has come back to haunt me of the time when my wife and I and another couple were sitting in a sparse audience at the Concorde, with just a small group of jazz purists scattered around. The band was going at it hammer and tongs, and we had to shout to each other across the table to make ourselves heard.

Just as I opened my mouth and offered the shouted opinion that "this makes you worship silence, doesn't it" the band suddenly stopped playing. Everybody in the room heard my remark, and I felt obliged to apologise quickly. The response was a huge cheer and all-round applause, including from the band! They then went into their next number with renewed vigour, and we retreated in embarrassment.

Another moment that clunks to mind was when my wife and I took my mother and father-in-law to see Georgie Fame at the club. This was in the mid-to-late-80s. We were in the front row about two metres away from the band. With Georgie swinging away in typical style my mother-in-law suddenly slipped off into a sleep and started snoring. I don't think anyone noticed except Georgie, who struggled to stop himself laughing and desperately tried to avoid looking at us for the rest of the evening for the fear that he would again get a fit of the giggles.

I have been a Concorde member since 1971 and have had 37 years of wonderful entertainment.'

MAUREEN and BARRY HATCHER, West Byfleet, Surrey: 'We have been coming to the Club for the past 15 years or so, mainly for jazz events. To try and select the very best of these evenings is almost an impossible task but two such events do come to mind.

The first was back in October 1996 when the club presented the Frank Tate quintet featuring Harry Allen, Howard Alden, Dave McKenna, Frank Tate and Butch Miles. This was as good as it gets with Dave McKenna truly amazing, and if you don't believe us, listen to the Nagel Heyer CD (069) of the Frank Tate quintet 'Live in Belfast'!

The second event was an evening of the absolute best in British jazz by The Magnificent Seven, led by Alan Barnes, with Andy Panayi, Bruce Adams, Mark Nightingale, Dave Newton, Andy Cleyndert and Matt Home. This indeed was perfect home-grown jazz for a very special occasion – the celebration of a 70th birthday where we were joined by a number of our friends, many of whom stayed overnight and also enjoyed the delights of the Ellington Lodge.

We have been privileged to have visited many jazz clubs throughout Europe and the USA, but none of these can compare to the Concorde Club. This club is special, and we wish everyone involved the very best of good fortune for the next 50 years.'

PAM BUNDY, Southampton: 'There is so much to say about the Concorde I am not sure where to start! Probably quite a lot of it should be left unsaid now I think about it ... but moving on quickly .... I have always described the club as a place with many faces and a big heart. There has always been a different face to suit the mood of my life since I joined at 17 ... whoops, sorry was the minimum age 18 in those days? I didn't realise!

I did not experience the Bassett days, but have certainly enjoyed the current venue as it has grown and changed. From early days of disco nights and huge plates of chips with salad cream for 10p shared with several others. Friday cabaret nights when Joe Pasquale famously asked the cynical crowd: "'ave you lot ever been an audience before, you can laugh you know!?"

The opening of the Moldy Fig and celebrating my 40th birthday there with good friends and family. Getting to know and fall in love with Alan and failing spectacularly to keep our new relationship quiet, which culminated in Simon announcing our engagement to the whole club at a Pearly Kings and Queens evening!

That particular Saturday night at 1am when the much-missed Pat Sparling suggested to Alan that he had 'peaked' and she would get us a taxi home - an expression that the two of them debated at length for many years to follow! Wine Society evenings where fortunately the speakers seem somewhat relieved to have a noisy crowd to entertain and Lesley Monaghan seems to have a birthday every month!

The Summer Ball ... I just wish I would remember to wear comfortable shoes, but at least Alan has given up with white tux for his black one ... it doesn't show the red wine so much! Beaujolais day and the continual joy of watching first-timers' faces as the entertainment always amazes and amuses year on year.

The crazy pantos and that dreadful joke of Brian Kingsnorth's, which hard as I try I cannot forget! Sorry, the editor has censored it. I will leave others to talk more about the jazz for which the club is so famous ... we have met many people around the world who know the venue as performers or visitors. And of course those memorable personal events that only the Concorde can host with such assurance and style ... business celebrations, Christmas parties, Alan's 60th birthday in the garden on a glorious Sunday afternoon and both our retirement parties serenaded by Lucien ... the memories just go on and on!

It seems a long time since that 17 year old girl had the good sense to join Planet Concorde, but it was a move that has stood me in good stead ever since. Through good times and bad the comfort and pleasure of the Concorde Club has seen me through ... thank you to Cole, Pauline and their lovely family and staff and dogs – present and sadly some past!

I confess to having a tear at all these lovely memories ... and the thought of many more to come!❥

DENIS BUNDY, accomplished after dinner speaker, entertainer and a popular panto performer at the Concorde: ❦July 30 1966 – we won the World Cup and I have vivid memories of standing shoulder to shoulder with just enough room to hold a glass of cider while waving the free arm wildly about to live performances from Jimmy James and the Vagabonds and the like. Priceless. Rastus, Rosie and 'Dirty Den the Butcher' etc. in the legendary pantos that were even more fun for us than the audience! Not a bad memory in sight.❥

JOHN LINSDELL, Southampton: •I always remember the crap food, the warm beer, the unruly clientele, oh, sorry that was Simons Wine Bar!

I have so many fond memories of the Concorde Club. I was a member in the early days at The Bassett when beer was 2 shillings and 6 pence a pint (12.5p in new money). My social life seemed to include at least two drunken visits a week, usually on disco nights, as I could never understand jazz. We always told Cole that us disco goers subsidised the jazz members as they could make half a pint of bitter last all night! I can even remember as far back to when Simon Fodds was a DJ!

The Concorde had a great reputation for good music and trouble free nights. It was amazing how many people Cole could pack on the dance floor in the early days before fire regulations and Health and Safety rules.

Then there was the dress code! You could not get in if you were wearing earrings, hair bands, jeans, and body piercing or poncy aftershave. That would eliminate most of the Premiership footballers of today! I have rubbed shoulders in the gents' urinal with some famous names. Joe Pasquale, Bradley Walsh, Richard Digance, Alan Ball, Georgie Fame, Lonnie Donegan, Bob Kemp, just to name a few.

Congratulations and best wishes to Cole, Pauline, Fiona, Kirstie and Jamie in the Concorde's 50th year, and good luck for for the future. We've had a lot of laughs over a lot of years.•

JOE CROLL, Southampton: •After a long absence from the club – I had been living in America for 11 years and in London for six years – I returned home to Southampton. On arriving at the club on a Wednesday night in 1991, the young lady in reception politely asked me if I was a member. I replied: "I'm not quite sure." I then explained, producing my original 1957 membership card: "I've been away a lot lately."

The look on her face was priceless. It registered total disbelief as she informed me my membership was 34 years out of date and therefore it was not valid!

Once inside I noticed how the club had changed. The bandstand was now in the middle of the room, not at the far end as I remembered it. I was standing at the bar talking to Cole, and we were reminiscing about the old days. During our conversation I mentioned that I still had an original programme of the first Beaulieu Jazz Festival which featured Mick Mullgan's band with George Melly on the bill.

Cole said: "What a co-incidence, George is at the club next Wednesday with the John Chilton Feetwarmers. I'm sure he'd love to see the programme."

The following Wednesday I brought my treasured jazz possession of 35 years to the club for Mr. Melly to look at during the evening.

Cole introduced me to the great man, saying that I had the original Beaulieu Jazz Festival programme. 'Good Time George' promptly thanked me, and casually tucked my most treasured jazz possession in his pocket and walked off. I have not seen it since.

In 2007, George sadly "left the building" (as the death of a jazzman is now referred to).

No doubt a historian will find the programme and include it in research on British jazz in the future, thanking Mr. Melly for having the foresight to save such an important document.

I would like to close by saying it is thanks to Cole Mathieson's vision of 50 years ago and his love of jazz that many thousands of people have been able to hear and enjoy many of the world's greatest jazzmen and women, either at the original premises at the Bassett Hotel or at its present location at the Old School House in Stoneham Lane, which we now know and love as the famous Concorde Club.•

JAMES and SHARRON KARSENBARG, Ampfield: •Our Best Memory was when Cole and Pauline agreed to let us have our Wedding Reception at the Club on Saturday 28th May back in 1988! Cole and the team made the place look fabulous and Shirley Morgan sang for our first dance. We felt very privileged having our reception at the Club.

The local headlines, prompted by our performances in the Concorde pantomime, read "Cinderella marries local Farmer"! We staggered out and went on our merry way with all the panto cast, friends and family waving us off. It's true what they say about The Concorde affecting relationships. We have had 20 fantastic years since that one-off day! Thanks Cole and Pauline.•

TONY MULLETT goes right back to the early Concorde days and gives a fascinating eye-witness comparison of the old and the new: •I was a teenage seaman during the 50s when I first visited the Bassett. Which artistes were appearing were of no interest then, but I do recall how attractive Pauline was! Then in the early 60s when jazz music became a passion I used to push-bike there, leaving it propped against the wall, safe in the knowledge that nobody would steal it. On a hot night I could drink five pints of Watney's Mild at two shillings a pint, enjoy the music and almost freewheel home to the Millbrook Estate. Including the entrance fee, I would still have change from a pound note.

When I compare both Club venues over the past half century there have of course been many improvements to customer care, unrivalled parking, controlled temperatures, improved sound and gradually cleaner air. The change from wooden seats and floor boards to a carpet of such luxury that bare feet should be compulsory. One regular Sunday nighter cannot stay awake once he has sat for just a few minutes. But the earlier place had a certain informality where fans would sit at the same tables as their musical heroes, there being no Green Room.

The late great trumpeter and bandleader Alex Welsh once told me a sad tale of this most gorgeous female fan who showed him special attention right through the evening. They became more acquainted during the interval and after the show he was invited to her flat. She then tried to interest him in some religious sect. Not the sect he had in mind perhaps.

Later, at the present club, the band's drummer Lennie Hastings used to perform riotous solos dressed in an oversized German army trench coat and a helmet, which covered the top half of his face. The audience would try to be ready to join in when Lennie would stop playing in his drum break for a few beats to shout "Who Ya, Who Ya!"

Another band that played at both clubs and still does, is the Mission Hall. And they are still well received. They once had a clarinet player who would wander off somewhere out of the building during the session, not to appear again, leaving his instrument on the bandstand.

In the early years at Stoneham there were some fun coach trips to London. The old fashioned ones were without toilets. On one occasion the driver stopped where he could to let the males out. We were soon aboard again having been shouted at by some irate householder for mistaking his driveway for a quiet country lane. It's not easy to run fast and button one's flys at the same time.

Older jazzers will recall the black and white films that Cole used to entertain us with during the band intervals. Where are they now I wonder. There was one with that great personality Fats Waller seated at the piano, and wearing the familiar bowler-hat, striped waistcoat, thin moustache and with high-raised eyebrows. Turning to the camera, he said: "One never knows, do one." It became a catchphrase with those who watched the film at the Concorde.

Ah, so many marvellous memories and all revolving around The Concorde. I wonder what the next 50 years will bring? One never knows, do one …●

SUE SMITH, a lively member of the Concorde along with her husband Phil, makes two confessions: ●The first is a somewhat slightly embarrassing experience of mine: For many years we have been regulars at the Concorde Club and late into this particular Saturday evening, I found myself standing on my own in the middle of the Club.

Having consumed a good few glasses of wine I was quite happy watching the world go by when suddenly I felt something land on my foot. Well, you can imagine my horror when looking down I saw a 'chicken fillet' (aka boob enhancer) lying there – and it was mine! Looking quickly around I noted that no one else had appeared to see so in an instant I picked up the offending article, shoved it in my bag and made a quick retreat to the Ladies whereby the other one was instantly removed for fear of history repeating itself!

The second 'experience' occurred at the Summer Ball 2007. Prior to the event, Phil and I, along with our good friends Caroline and Nigel, made a plan that by the end of the evening we should all have obtained a small souvenir from the Ball.

Many, many drinks later and upon arrival back home the first person to show their 'freebie' was Phil who had a small 'No Smoking' sign. The second person, Caroline, had a once beautiful but now very crushed flower from one of the table displays. Nigel was up next and being slightly braver brought out an empty wine bottle.

Well, now it was my turn – with excitement I held aloft a gorgeous silver tissue box that had been 'borrowed' from the vanity area within the Ladies toilet! This was, of course, all well and good at the time but the big question now was how to get it back into the Club without giving a very lengthy explanation! I, of course, came clean and my prize was returned a couple of weeks later. But unfortunately by this time the hunt was on for the thief! Following my confession to Jamie and James, I thought the matter was closed, but, no!!

After a very enjoyable Friday night, I was just going to leave the Club when Jamie said: "I think I had better check your bag just in case." Well, knowing he would find nothing I flung it open and there looking at me was a bottle opener and a wine measuring cup!

How I laughed when I realised that – unknown to me, and having left my bag unattended on the bar – my favourite barman, Dougie, had proceeded to fill it up! That's the Concorde. Always good for a laugh.●

RON and DORRIE EYRES, Drayton, Portsmouth: ●We have so many happy memories of our visits spanning nearly all of those fifty years, but the highlight evening of them all for us was the night of that wonderful pianist Bill Cole's surprise 70th birthday celebrations on 23rd October 1989. We were co-conspirators who told Bill and his dear Mill that we were taking them out to dinner, not mentioning where. Ron, at the wheel, decided to take a long way round to the Concorde to put Bill 'off the scent.' Of course, Bill's sense of direction was always spot on and as we approached the club he said: "Oh, are we taking a look at the Concorde?" Ron replied: "Just thought we might take a look inside to see if anybody is in the Moldy Fig."

As we walked into the darkened room there was an outbreak of applause and cheers from Cole and all Bill's old friends and fellow musicians who had gathered to celebrate his birthday.

Bill then went on to play with bands from the 40s, 50s, 60s, 70s and 80s, and amazingly he remembered the original arrangements that he had put together years earlier. It was a tremendous Concorde evening, with Bill not only entertaining us with his piano playing but also his wit and his songs.

Our other 'top' evening was early in the Millennium when we attended Jamie Cullum's second visit to the Concorde, when he was quite early into his career. A spectacular voice and musicianship has established him as a huge favourite, and we were so pleased to be there virtually at the start. Thanks to Cole and the Concorde.●

Final word (despite protestations from Cole) to long-time member and highly regarded, now retired local trumpeter **GEORGE (BUNNY) AUSTIN**, Totton: ●The City of Southampton Council are allegedly looking for the 'WOW!' factor for the city. Well I've found it for them. It's called the Concorde Club in Stoneham Lane, Eastleigh! Here, the piano is always at concert pitch, the food and service excellent, and members and their guests get the chance to see and hear some of the greatest musicians and entertainers of all time.

Some of our local musicians – eg. Ray Ember, Teddy Layton, John Horler and Cuff Billett – would have graced many of the American bands that have appeared at the Concorde.

The man mainly responsible for the continuing success of the Club – Cole Mathieson – should be knighted for his services to the music world. Yes, arise Sir Cole!●

TIM TITHERIDGE, A MAN OF TRUST

TIM TITHERIDGE is the energetic chairman of the Wessex Cancer Trust, the charity we are hoping to boost with the sale of this book. He and Jane Carley – daughter of prominent Concorde member Gerry Seymour – have been a source of inspiration throughout the project. Tim has embarrassed Cole by insisting on the following contribution to the book:

*It is so typical of Cole Mathieson to make a donation to the Wessex Cancer Trust for every book he personally signs. Cole, I hope you wear yourself out signing your name.

Over the years he has done so much for charity, not only for Wessex Cancer but numerous other local charities, giving of his time and indeed the Concorde Club so unstintingly, enabling them to help others less fortunate. To have fun and to raise vast sums of money at the same time surely is what helping charity is all about.

It has been a pleasure knowing both Cole and his son, Jamie, and as Chairman of the Trustees of the Wessex Cancer Trust I thank them for what they have done for Charity over the last half century and I wish Cole, Pauline and their family, well for the next fifty years.*

Over to Cole: *As much as I appreciate Tim's kind words, I have to say he is thanking the wrong person. All the praise should be heaped on the Concorde members. I never cease to be amazed by their generosity, and time and time again they give their support to the worthy charities that the Concorde Club regularly supports.

I, with the help of a fantastic staff, do the easy organising bit. The members do the hard bit. They dig deep into their pockets to help those less fortunate. I am so proud of the kind heart that beats at the Concorde. We have raised thousands of pounds over the years, and we intend to continue the good work in the future. My personal thanks to everybody buying this book, helping to boost the Wessex Cancer Trust. And here's a brief word from my co-author ...*

NORMAN GILLER: *In the summer of 2007 I underwent emergency surgery at Chandler's Ford to have a cancerous tumour removed. My surgeon, Nicholas Beck, knowing my sportswriter background, reached for a sporting metaphor after the successful operation: "The tumour," he told me, "was as big as Mike Tyson's fist." I replied: "I'm just glad it wasn't as big as another part of his anatomy!" (and I've cleaned that up).

I vowed to try to do something to raise money for the Wessex Cancer Trust as a gesture for Nicholas Beck saving my life. When Cole and I first started discussing this book in the autumn of 2007, we agreed to bring in the Wessex Cancer Trust as a beneficiary, and so a £1 donation is being made to the WCT for every book sold. Thank you for your support, and if you are reading somebody else's copy, please pay a pound to the Trust.

I have good reason for liking the Concorde. It was in the Moldy Fig that I met my partner Jackie Jones on my first evening out as a widower. Perhaps I will write a book about it!*

THE CONCORDE CLUB: The First 50 Years
Cole Mathieson has THE LAST WORD

THANK you for getting this far in the book, or – if you are flicking from the back – enjoy the trip. They have been fifty unbelievable years of fun, frenzy, feasts, a fire, some frustration, a little fear and two more 'F' words, fellowship and friendship.

I have made so many good friends along the way, and I KNOW I have forgotten to mention a lot of them during my rambling memories. But you know who you are, and I hope you forgive me. They say that a clear conscience is a sign of a bad memory, and as I reach the autumn of my years my memory has become almost a blank sheet. All I hope is that in the following list of acknowledgements I have not left out somebody who deserves to be in ...

Firstly, thanks to our wonderful staff. Where would we be without the likes of Lynne, Jackie, Gill, Mark, Sue and the hotel team, James, Philippa, Liz, Teresa, Chris and her colleagues in the Moldy Fig – Olivier, Anna, Georgie, Helen, Donna, Heather and Sheila, cleaners Tina and Janine, our multi-lingual greeter-seater Pammi, the retiring but never work-shy Jim'll Fix-it and not forgetting an army of original loyal workers – Brian Kingsnorth, Jo Pearce, Pat Sparling, chefs Mike Smyth, Jane Mockford and Jenny Styan, Maureen Pickering (and daughters Karen and Louise), Miriam Hardingham, Heidi Bonnet, Debbie Thresher – and Val Anderson, Marlene Sant and Pat Masom who moved with us from the Bassett.

And is there any better catering anywhere outside the leading restaurants than that of Executive Chef David Ophaus with his team – Andy, Becky, Tasha, Emma, Mike, Adam, Kevin and Sue assisted by 'Aussie' Tony and his restaurant staff Stuart, Sarah and barman Dougie. David once played Tweedledee to my Tweedledum – much of what I have been through over the past 50 years would have fitted neatly into an *Alice in Wonderland* adventure!

There are many DJs who deserve thanks including pioneers Simon Foderingham, Jon Ferris and Joe Craen, the current team of Paul Mico, Ian James, Steve Phillips and Mike Christy and ever-helpful agent Terry Rolph.

I would also like to give a collective bow in the direction of the musicians, panto cast, cabaret and tribute artistes who have graced (and very occasionally disgraced) the Concorde stage over the years. Thanks as well to Gordon Sapsed, Ken Nutley and Jim Budd for help on the photographic front, and to Geoff Fisher for his printing advice.

A nod of appreciation to Tim Titheridge and Jane Carley of the Wessex Cancer Trust for their co-operation, and we hope the book makes a lot of money for a very deserving charity.

Most of all I am indebted to my family for being there for me – the miraculously recovered Pauline, Fiona, Kirstie and Jamie.

Thanks, too, to Norman Giller for knitting my memories into some sort of reasonable order and to our incredible archivist Maureen Chapman. She's on next.

And the last word: Thanks to all our members. It's YOU who made the Concorde. And to all those people who constantly ask me in the evening, "What do you do during the day?" I hope this book gives you a little insight into my *first* 50 years at the Concorde Club.

It's been a great journey, so far.

THE CONCORDE CLUB: The First 50 Years
The Performers A to Z – Collated by Maureen Chapman

OUR omniscient archivist Maureen Chapman (with help from Kirstie Mathieson) has listed most of the individual performers and bands (jazz, rhythm and blues, balladeer, cabaret and tribute artistes) who have appeared at the Concorde since the Club launched in 1957. Here is Maureen's A to Z breakdown, with decades in brackets:

A

A Band Called 'O' (70)
Abacus (70)
Abraham, Mick (60)
Action, The (60)
Acoustic Jazz (90-00)
Adams, Bruce (90-00)
Adderley, Nat (80)
Agerbeek, Rob (90-00)
Albatross (70)
Albion Jazz Band (90-00)
Albrektsson, Jesper (00)
Alden, Howard (90-00)
Alexander, Monty (00)
Allan, Alistair (90-00)
Allaway, Mark (00)
Allen, Bernie Jazz Band (70)
Allen, Brandon (00)
Allen, Harry (90-00)
Allen, Henry 'Red' (60)
Allen, Juliet (00)
Allen, Pete Band (70-90)
Allen, Verden (60)
Allena, Kerry (70)
Allison, Mose (70-90)
Allney, Dave (90)
Allred, Bill (80-90)
Allred, John (90-00)
Almeido, Laurindo (90)
Almond, John (60)
Amazing Blondell (70)
Amboy, Dave Big Band (60)
Amboy, Dukes (60)
Ambrose Slade - as Slade (60)
American Jazz All Stars (90-00)
Anderson, Keith (90)
Anderson, Miller (60-70)
Andrews, Alec (50-60-70)
Andrews, Revert (90)
Andrews, Ron (50-60)
Anglo American All Stars (00)
Annesley, Luke (00)
Antal, Tibor (90)

Anthony's, Dave Moods (60)
Anthony, John (60)
Antique Six (00)
Antolini, Charlie (90)
Antonia, Phil (00)
Antonia, Paul (90)
Apex Jazz Band (90-00)
Appleyard, Peter (80-90-00)
April Garden (70)
Aranov, Ben (90-00)
Archer, Pete (50-60)
Archer, Tony (90)
Argenziano, JJ (80)
Arlot, Dave (70)
Armageddon (70)
Armatage, John (60-80-00)
Armstrong, Denis (00)
Armstrong, Mark (90-00)
Arnold, PP and the Nice (60)
Arsenal, Lord (90)
Arthurs, Debbie (00)
Artwoods, The (60)
Ash, Vic (50-60-90-00)
Ashby, Harold (80)
Ashby, Clive (00)
Ashgar (70)
Ashman, Mickey Rag Time (60)
Ashman, Mickey (90-00)
Ashton, Gardner and Dyke (60-70)
Ashworth, Dominic (00)
Aspland, Robin (00)
Aston, Alan (70)
Atlantic Coast Jazz Band (80)
Atomic Rooster (60-70)
Auger, Brian (60-70)
Aukland, Joe (00)
Austen, John (90)
Aves, Pete (00)
Avon Cities Band (60-70-80)
Ayles, Tim (70-80-90)
Axelsson, Remis (00)

B

Babbidge, Roy (00)
Babbington, Roy (80-90-00)
Babylon (00)
Bach, Per (00)
Back O'Town Syncopators (60)
Back to Basie (00)
Backtracking (90)
Bagot, Tony (70-00)
Bailey, Dave (80)
Bailey, John (00)
Baines, Sera (00)
Baird, Edward (70)
Baker, Andy (90)
Baker, Ginger (60)
Baker, Kenny (50-60-70-80-90)
Bakerloo Blues Line (60)
Baldock, Ken (80-90-00)
Baldry, Long John (60-80)
Baldwin, Len (00)
Ball, Ray (60-00)
Ball, Kenny (60-80-90-00)
Bamsey, Spike (50-60)
Band of Joy (60)
Banham, Chris (60)
Bannister, Jeff (60)
Barati, Joe (00)
Barber, Chris (60-70-80-90-00)
Barbosa-Lima, Carlos (90)
Barby, Tony (00)
Barker, Brian (70)
Barker, Guy (90-00)
Barnard, Bob Jazz Band (80)
Barnard, Bob (80-90-00)
Barnes, Alan (80-90-00)
Barnes, John (60-70-80-90-00)
Barnes, Roger (90)
Baroque (70)
Barrett, Dan (90-00)
Barrett, Reg (60)
Barrett, Val (80)
Barry, Dave (90-00)
Barron, Leon (00)

Barron, Rob (00)
Barton, Cliff (60)
Basso, Gianni (80)
Bastable, John Chosen Six (70)
Bateman, Ian (90-00)
Bateman, Paul (00)
Bates, Barney (70-80)
Bates, Brian (00)
Bates, Colin (60-70-80)
Bates, Phil (60)
Batiste, Lionel (90)
Battrum, John (00)
Baughan, Charlie (80)
Baxter, Mally (00)
Bayliss, Tony (60)
Bayne, John (00)
BBC Big Band (90)
Beachcomers, The (90)
Beachey, Alan (00)
Beadle, Martin (00)
Beament, Ted (90-00)
Bean, George (60)
Bebeto (00)
Bee, Charlie (70)
Beecham, John (80)
Beiderbecke and All That Jazz (00)
Beirne, John (50-60)
Bell, Graeme Band (80)
Bell, John (70-80-90)
Bell, Pat (00)
Benford, Tommy (70)
Bennett, Betty (80)
Bennett, Cliff (70)
Bennett, Duster (60-70)
Bennett, John (60-80-90-00)
Bennett, Ken (50)
Bennett, Stuart (80-90-00)
Benson, John (80-90-00)
Bergeron, Chuck (00)
Bergeson, Boyd (80)
Bernhardt, Clyde (70)
Berry, Bill (90)
Bertini, Charlie (90)
Best, Lennie (80-90)
Best of British (90-00)
Best's, Bix Wolverines (60)
Bevin, Tony (80)
Beyer, Ralph (00)
Bickert, Ed (80)
Biella, Maurice (50)
Big Brother (80)
Big Chief (90, 00)
Big Town Playboys (90)
Big Red (00)
Bilk, Acker and His
 Paramount Jazz Band (60-70-80)
Bill Posters Will Be Band (80-00)
Billett, Cuff (60-70-80-90-00)
Birch, John (90)

Birchmore, Roscoe (00)
Bishop, Ken (50)
Birds, The (60)
Bitch (70)
Black Bottom Stompers (60-70)
Black Cat Bones (60)
Black Faith (70)
Black Watch, The (60)
Blackwell, Geoff (90)
Blackwell, Martin (80)
Blakesley, Mike (60-70-80-90-00)
Blannin, Pete (60)
Blossom Toes (60)
Blue Harlem (90-00)
Blue Honey (80)
Blue Notes (60-70)
Blue State (00)
Blue Three, The (80)
Bluesology (60)
Blues Incorporated (60)
Blundy, Gordon (70-80)
Bo Street Runners (60)
Body and Soul (70)
Boeren, Bert (90)
Bolan, Sean (00)
Bond, Joyce (60)
Bond, Graham (60-70)
Bonham, John (60)
Boogie Woogie Red (70)
Boston, Billie (00)
Boston, Johnny (00)
Boston Tea Party (00)
Bourbon Street Six (60)
Bourke, Stan (60-90-00)
Boutte, Lillian (80-90-00)
Bowden, Colin (80-00)
Bowden, Ron (60-80-90)
Bowen, Bertie (00)
Bowen, Dave (90-00)
Bowen, Lee (90)
Bower, Roy (00)
Bown, Alan Set (60)
Boyce, Gerry (80)
Boyd, Wayne (80)
Boz and the Boz People (60)
Braat, Adrie (90-00)
Bradley, Allan (90)
Bradley, Mike (90)
Braff, Ruby (70-90-00)
Breach, Joyce (00)
Breckman, Lee (90)
Breen, Bobby (60)
Brewers Droop (70)
Bray, Jim (60)
Briar, Quentin (80)
Bridge, Paul (80-90)
Briggs, Vic (60)
Brignola, Mike (00)
Brignola, Nick (90)

Brink, Han (00)
Briseno, Modesto (00)
Broadbent, Graham (00)
Bronco (70)
Brooks, Juanita (90)
Brooks, Elkie (00)
Brooks, Stuart (90)
Broomfield, Dave (70-80)
Brother Bung (60)
Brough, Harvey (00)
Brown, Andrew (90)
Brown, Andy (80)
Brown, Angela (90)
Brown, Arthur (90)
Brown, David (70)
Brown, Gerry (50-60-70-80-90-00)
Brown, Greg (90)
Brown, Jeremy (00)
Brown, Jimmy Sound (60)
Brown, Les (00)
Brown, Ricky (60)
Brown, Rod (90)
Brown, Rob (00)
Brown, Sam (00)
Brown, Sandy (60)
Brown, Steve (90-00)
Brown, Terry (60)
Bruce, Jack (60)
Bryant, Colin (60-70-90-00)
Bryant, Phil (70)
Bryant, Ritchie (70-90)
Bryden, Beryl (80-90)
Brymer, Jack (80)
BT Jazz Award Winners (90)
Buckley, 'Sir' Alan (90)
Budapest Ragtime Orchestra (90)
Budapest Ragtime Band (00)
Budd, Roy (90)
Budwig, Monty (90)
Bunch, John (90-00)
Burbidge, Graham (60-70)
Burgess, John (60-70-90-00)
Burgess, Stan (00)
Burich, Finn (00)
Burke, Chris (90)
Burman, David (80)
Burnap, Campbell (70-80-90-00)
Burns, Eddie 'Guitar' (70)
Burt, Michael (70)
Burton, Tommy (90)
Bury, Julian (00)
Bush, Lennie (80-90-00)
Bush, Ray (70)
Busiakiewicz, Richard (90-00)
Buta, Tiberiu (00)
Butcher, Mark (00)
Butterfield, Billy (70-80)
Button, Mike (00)
Byas, Don (60)
Byrd, Charlie (70-80-90)
Byrd, Joe (70)

Calderazzo, Gene (90)
Caldwell, Bob (00)
Callard, Pete (00)
Cambridge Jazz Band (80)
Campbell, Colin (90-00)
Campbell, Gordon (90-00)
Canale, Donna (00)
Candoli, Conti (90-00)
Candoli, Pete (00)
Caravan (70)
Carey, Roger (00)
Carisson, Niklas (00)
Carmello, Janusz (80-90)
Carmichael, Judy (00)
Carr, Ian (60)
Carr, Lesley (00)
Carr, Mike (60-70-80-90)
Carr, Stewart (00)
Carr, Tony (60)
Carroll, Liane (00)
Carson, Paul (70)
Carter, Benny (80)
Carter, Geoff (90)
Carter, Tony (90-00)
Carter-Dimmock, Sheila (60)
Cary, Dick (70)
Casey, Al (80)
Cash, Bernie (70)
Castle, Ian (60)
Castronari, Mario (80)
Caswell, Cas (00)
Catchpole, Tony (60)
Cater, Pete (90-00)
Cat Show, The (60)
Cave, Norman (60)
Cawley, Tom (00)
Chadwick, Brian (90)
Challis, Dave (70)
Chamberlain, Dave (00)
Chandler, Wayne (60)
Chapman, Peter (70)
Chapman, Roger (60)
Chappell, Roy (00)
Charleston Chasers (90-00)
Charlesworth, Dick Bands (60-70-90)
Chescoe, Laurie (60-70-80-90-00)
Chesterman, Chez (00)
Chicago Hush (60)
Childe, Sonny (60)
Childers, Buddy (90)
Chilton, John (60-70-80-90-00)
Chisholm, George (60-70-80)
Chisholm, Jo (80)
Chislett, Andy (00)
Chris and his Gang (80)
Christ, Herbert (00)

Christie, Keith (50)
Cirillo, James (90-00)
Clabby, Imelda (00)
Clapton, Eric (60)
Clare, Kenny (80)
Clark-Hutchinson Band (70)
Clarke, Billy Jazz Band (60-70)
Clarke, Erroll (80)
Clarke, Kenny (70)
Clarkson, Ian (00)
Clayton, Buck (60)
Clayton, Leon (90-00)
Clayton, Peter (80)
Clempson, Terry (70)
Cleverley, Adrian (00)
Cleyndert, Andy (80-90-00)
Cliff, Dave (70-90-00)
Cliff, Jimmy (60)
Clift, Dave (80)
Climax Jazz Band (60)
Clinton, Harry (50)
Clouds (60)
Clufton, Rob (00)
Clyne, Jeff (80)
Cocker, Joe (60)
Coe, Tony (60-80)
Cohen, Alan (70-80)
Cohen, Ben (80-90-00)
Cohn, Al (80)
Cohn, Joe (80)
Colane, Terry Quintet (50)
Cole, Bill (50-60-80)
Cole, Cyril (60)
Cole, Geoff (80-00)
Coleman, Bill - US (60)
Coleman, Bill - UK (70-00)
Coles, John (90)
Colianni, John (90-00)
Colicott, Graham (00)
Collett, Dave (70-80)
Collie, Max Rhythm Aces (60-70-80)
Collins, Colin (80-90)
Collins, Henry (00)
Collins, Roy (60)
Collinson, Jo (60-70)
Collinson, Ted (70)
Coloured Raisins (60)
Colton, Tony and the Crawdaddies (60)
Colville, Randy (70-80-90)
Colwell, Tim Jazz Friends (80)
Colyer, Ken (80)
Colyer, Ken Trust All Stars (90)
Committee (60)
Concorde Seven Plus (50)
Concorde Jazz Orchestra (90)
Connors, Gene 'Mighty Flea' (70)
Connor, Chas (80)
Continuam (70)
Contrast (00)

Cook, Dick (00)
Cook, Jez (90-00)
Cook, Peter (00)
Cooke, Micky (60-80-90)
Cooke, Mickey (00)
Coolman, Todd (80)
Cooney, Liz (00)
Cooper, Andy (60-80-90-00)
Cooper, Bob (90)
Cooper, Doug (80-90)
Cooper, Gomez (60)
Cooper, Nick (80)
Corn Rigs (80)
Costanzo, Sonny (90)
Cottee, Andrew (00)
Cotton, Brian (90)
Cotton Club Revue (00)
Cotton Club Years (00)
Cotton, Mike (60-70-90-00)
Coulbar, Dunstan (00)
Counts, The (60)
Courtley-Ross Group (60)
Courtley, Bert (50-60)
Courtney, Dave (60)
Cousin Joe from New Orleans (70)
Coutts, Andrew (00)
Coverdale, John (90)
Cowie, Dave (60-70-80)
Cox, Adrian (00)
Cox, Alan (90)
Cox, Dave (00)
Cox, Jim (80)
Cox, Mike (80-90-00)
Craen, Joe (90)
Craig, Jay (00)
Craig, Lorraine (00)
Crane, Ray (60-80)
Crawford, Hank (80)
Crawley, Harry (00)
Crazy World of Arthur Brown (60)
Cream, The (60)
Creese, Malcolm (90-00)
Crews, 'Red Hot Mama' Ruth (80)
Crimmins, Roy (80)
Critchinson, John (80-90-00)
Crocker, John (60-70-80-90-00)
Crombie, Tony (60-70-80)
Crooks, Mark (00)
Crow, Bill (90)
Crowdy, Andy (00)
Crumly, Pat (90)
Cubana Bop (00)
Cuenca, Sylvia (90)
Cullum, Jamie (00)
Cummings, Ben (00)
Cuss, Andy (90-00)
Cutler, Adge and the Wurzels (60-70)
Cutting Edge (80)
Cyril, Roy (00)

D

Dagley, Christopher (00)
Daley, Geoff (60)
Daley, Stan (90)
Dallas Dandies (90)
Dalton, Mitch (90-00)
Dandy, Allan (00)
Daniels, Andy (90-00)
Daniels, Maxine (80-90)
Daniels, Mike Delta Jazzmen (90)
Danish Radio Big Band (90)
Dankworth, Alec (80-90-00)
Dankworth, Jacqui (00)
Dankworth, Sir John (90-00)
Darling, Oliver (00)
Daughters of Time (70)
Davenport, RH (60)
Davern, Kenny (70-80-90-00)
Davey, Norman (00)
Davies, Henry Big Band (60)
Davies, Jerome (00)
Davies, Josephine (00)
Davini, Dave and the D-Men (60)
Davis, Cyril (60)
Davis, Dave (60-70-80-90-00)
Davis, Eddie 'Lockjaw' (70-80)
Davis, Gregory (90)
Davis, Henry (90)
Davis, Maggie (70)
Davis, Mick (00)
Davis, Nathan (80)
Davis, Ru (60-90)
Davis, Tony (00)
Davis, Troy (00)
Davis, Warren Monday Band (60)
Davison, Brian (60)
Davison, 'Wild' Bill (60-70-80)
Dawes, Tim (00)
Dawson, Nick (00)
Day, John (00)
Day, Tony (90-00)
De Franco, Buddy (80-90)
De Kort, Bert (00)
De Krom, Sebastian (00)
De Vore, Charles (80-90-00)
Dearie, Blossom (60)
Dedicated Men's Jug Band (60)
Dee, Brian (80-90-00)
Dee, Sonny All Stars (90)

Deep Soul (70)
Defferary, John (00)
Degville, Paul (00)
Dekker, Bob (90-00)
Delaney, Eric (90)
Delmar, Elaine (80-90-00)
Delta Jazzmen (00)
Demond, Frank (80)
Den Dulk, Terry (00)
Denham, Mike (00)
Denning, Barry (60)
Dennis, Maurice (00)
Derby Day Stompers (70)
Derrick, Andy (00)
Dibden, David (70)
Dickens, Andy Jump Jive
    And Wail (80-90)
Dickie, Neville (70-80-90-00)
Dickinson, Barney (00)
Dillinger, Spats and the
    Buzzin' Half Dozen (90)
Dirty Dozen Brass Band (90)
Disley, Diz (60-70-80)
Distel, Sacha (80)
Dixie Fellows (00)
Dixieland Syncopators (70)
Dixon, Iain (90)
Diz and the Doormen (80)
Dodds, Roy (00)
Donald, Keith (80)
Donaldson, John (90-00)
Donegan, Lonnie (80)
Dorman, Rex (90-00)
Dory, Keith (70)
Doug and Dory Riverside Band (90)
Dougan, Jackie (60)
Douglas, Alex (00)
Douglas, Jim (60-70-80-90-00)
Downliners Sect, The (60)
Downs, Efrem (90)
Doyle, Phil (00)
Drake, Ron (80-90-00)
Drevar, John Expression (60)
Drew, Martin (80-90-00)
Driscoll, Jimmy (60)
Driscoll, Julie (60)
Dubber, Goff (90-00)
Duddington, Alan (80-90-00)
Dunbar, Ainsley (60)
Duncan, Fiona Hot Five (80)
Duggan, Louisa (00)

Dunn, Michael (00)
Dunning, Barry (60)
Dunsford, Yona (00)
Dunstall, Clive (00)
Dupree, 'Champion' Jack (60-70)
Dupree, Simon (60)
Durham, Eddie (80)
Duston, Keith Jelly Roll Trio (90)
Dutch Swing College (70-80-90-00)
Dwight, Reg (Elton John) (60)
Dwyer, Bob Hot Seven (90-00)
Dyer, Pete Band (60-80)
Dyke, Johnny (00)

E

Eagle Brass Band (90)
Eales, Geoff (90-00)
Earth (60)
Earwaker, Brian (60)
Eastcott, John (90)
Easy Street (00)
Ebony Keyes (60)
Echoes of Ellington Jazz
    Orchestra (90-00)
Edison, Harry 'Sweets' Edison (70-80)
Edmonstone, Malcolm (00)
Edwards, Pete (60)
Edwards, Richard (80-90)
Effamy, Pete (00)
Efford, Bob (50)
Eire Apparent (60)
Elastic Band (70)
Eldridge, Paul (00)
Electric Soul People (70)
Ellefson, Art (50)
Elliott, Dennis (70)
Ellis, Dan (00)
Ellis, Desmond (60)
Ellis, Herb (70-80-90)
Elsdon, Alan (60-70-80-90-00)
Ember, Alvern (60-70-80-90-00)
Ember, Ray (60-70-80-90)
Emberson, Norman (80-90-00)
Emblow, Jack (00)
Emerson, Keith (60)
Emerson, Malcolm (00)
End, The (70)
English, Joe (50-60)
Enriquez, Bobby (80)

Episode Six (60)
Erickson, Eddie (00)
Erridge, Mick (60-70-80-90)
Escode, Christian (70)
Eshelby, Paul (80)
Essex, David (70)
Etheridge, John (90-00)
Eulry, Fabrice (90-00)
Euro Top 8 (00)
Evans, Dave (80-90)
Evans, James (00)
Evans, Rod (60)
Exall, Richard (00)
Excelsior Vintage Jazz Band (00)
Explosive Jimmy Cliff (60)
Eyden, Bill (70-80)
Eyles, Tim (00)

F

Fabulous Fats Jazz Show (90)
Fairground (70)
Fairweather, Digby (70-80-90-00)
Falana, Mike (60)
Falling Leaves (60)
Fallon, Jack (80)
Falkhall, Mike (00)
Fallon, John (00)
Fame, Georgie and the
    Blue Flames (60-70-80-90-00)
Famen, Dave (60)
Family, The (60)
Fantastics, The (60-70)
Farkas, Gabor (90)
Farkas, Jozsef (90)
Farler, Joe (00)
Farlow, Chris (60)
Farlow, Tal (80)
Farr, Gary and the T-Bones (60)
Fat Sams Band (90-00)
Fawcuss, Paul (00)
Fay, Don (60)
Fay, Mike (90)
Fays, Raphael Trio (80)
Fedchock, John (00)
Feeney, Frank (70-80)
Felix, Lennie (60)
Feltham, John (00)
Fenby, Ian (60)
Fenn, James (00)
Fenner, John (80-90-00)
Fenton, Clive (90-00)
Ferguson, Maynard (60-70)
Fergy's Friends Jazz Band (70)
Ferre, Boulou (90)

Field, Dennis (80)
Finch, Peter (80)
Findon, Ronnie (90)
Fingers, The (60)
Finian's Rainbow (70)
Finlayson, Tucker (60-70-00)
Fischer, Harold (80)
Fisher, Harold (00)
Fisher, Tony (00)
Fishwick, Matt (00)
Fitz, Wally (90)
Fitzgerald, Jim (00)
Five Proud Walkers (60)
Five Dimensions, The (60)
Five-A-Slide (80)
Flanagan, Kevin (90)
Flanigan, Phil (90)
Flavelle, Jackie (70)
Flaxman, Andy (90-00)
Fleetwood, Mick (60)
Fleming, Dave (90)
Fletcher, Marc (90-00)
Fleur De Lys (60)
Flint, Hughie (60)
Flory, Chris (80-00)
Flowers, Peter (70)
Flynn, Terry (60)
Fooks, Jo (00)
Foot, Rick (90-00)
Forbes, Shane (00)
Forcione, Antonio (80-90)
Fordham, John (00)
Forgie, Barry (90)
Foster, John (70)
Foster, Mick (00)
Four Kents, The (60)
Fourth Element (00)
Fowler, Robert (00)
Fox, Bobby (60-70-80-00)
Fox, Charlie (80)
Francis, Colin (00)
Francis, Joe (90)
Francis, Paul (90-00)
Frank, Christian (00)
Fraser, Andy (60)
Frazier, Cie (80)
Frederick, John (00)
Free, The (60)
Free At Last (60)
Freeman, Bud (60-70-80)
Friedman, Don (90)
Frog Island Jazz Band (70-90-00)
Frost, Jimmy (60-70-80)
Fry, Adrian (80-90-00)
Fuller, Jesse (60)
Fumble (70)
Fusion Road Show (60)

GB Jazz Band (60)
Gaillard, Slim (80)
Galbraith, Charlie All Stars (60)
Galloway, Jim (70-80-90-00)
Galper, Hal (80)
Gambit Jazzmen (90-00)
Gang, The (70)
Ganley, Allan (50-60-70-80-90-00)
Gardner, Simon (90)
Gare, Al (00)
Garfield, Loz (60)
Garforth, Jimmy (80)
Garland, Scott (90)
Garland, Tim (90)
Garnett, Alex (00)
Garnett, Willie (80-90)
Garrick, Christian (90-00)
Garrick, Michael (70-00)
Garside, Ernie (90)
Gascoyne, Geoff (90-00)
Gaskin, Leonard (80)
Gass, The (60)
Gateway Jazz Band (60-70-80)
Gay, Al (70-80-90-00)
Gayer, Ferenc (90)
Geesin, Ron (60)
Gelato, Ray (80-90-00)
Gelder, Bill (90)
Geller, Herb (90)
Genge, Martin (80)
Gentle Giant (70)
Giants (60)
Gibbs, Oliver (00)
Gibbs, Terry (90)
Gibson, Banu (80)
Gibson, Lee (00)
Gibson, Tony (60)
Gien, Bobby (70)
Gift, The (70)
Gilbert, Jack (60)
Gilbert, Jack Jumping
    Panama Jazz Band (90-00)
Gilbrook, Russell (90-00)
Gillan, Ian (60)
Gillespie, Dana Blues Band (90)
Gilmore, Peter Band (70)
Gilmore, Steve (80)
Giovannini, Davide (00)
Girl Talk (60)
Gladwin, John (70)
Glass Menagerie (60)
Glasser, Dave (90)
Gleaves, Ronnie (60)
Gledhill, Stuart (60-70-80-90)
Globe Show, The (60)

Glover, Roger (60)
Godber, John (90)
Goetz, Mike (90)
Goffe, Toni (60-70)
Goins, Herbie and The
    Night Timers (60)
Gold, Harry and His
    Pieces of Eight (80)
Golden, Chris (70)
Goldsmith, Adam (00)
Golson, Benny (80)
Gonella, Nat (50-60-70-80-90)
Gonzales (70-80)
Good, George (60)
Goodall, 'Bean' (50)
Goodhand-Tait, Philip (60)
Goodman, Benny Alumni (80)
Goodson, Andy (70)
Goodwin, Bill (80)
Gordon, Bobby (00)
Gordon, Don (50-60-70)
Gordon, Ron Orchestra (60)
Gordon, Tom (90-00)
Gordon-Walker, Bob (60)
Gospel Truth (70)
Gothic Jazz Band (60)
Gould, Helen (80)
Gould, Peter (60)
Gould, Sid (00)
Gough, Bob (00)
Gower, Chris (00)
Goykovic, Dusco (80)
Graham, Peter (00)
Graham, Steve (00)
Grainger, Dick (90)
Grand Dominion Band (80)
Grannies Intentions (60)
Grannies New Intentions (70)
Grappelli, Stephane (70-80)
Great American All Stars (90)
Great British Jazz Band (90-00)
Greatest Show on Earth (60)
Great Guitars (80)
Great Northern Jazz Band (00)
Grech, Rick (60)
Green, Benny (50-60-80-90)
Green, Benny - Pianist (90)
Green, Brian New Orleans
    Stompers (60)
Green, Dave (60-70-80-90-00)
Green, Gerry (90)
Green Leaf Band (60)
Green, Leo (00)
Green, Peter (60)
Green, Urbie (80)
Greenway, Sue (00)
Greening, Rollie (60)
Greene, Frank (00)
Greening, Leon (00)

Greenow, Bill (90)
Greenwood, Andy (00)
Gregory, Johnny (50)
Gregory, Tony (60)
Greig, Stan (60-70-80-90-00)
Grenfell, Kevin (90)
Grenn, Brian New Orleans
    Stompers (60)
Gresty, Alan/Brian White
    Ragtimers (90-00)
Greville, Keith (70-80)
Grey, Al (80)
Grey, Susan (60)
Griffen, Dale (60)
Griffin, Johnny (70)
Griffiths, Dave (00)
Griffiths, Derek (60)
Griffiths, Tony (70)
Grind, Jody (70)
Grinyer, Ken Quartet (80)
Groove Brothers (00)
Groove Juice (00)
Grosz, Marty (90-00)
Group One (60)
Gulliver, Ray (70)
Gutta Percha ElasticBand (60)

Habraken, Paul (00)
Hackett, Bobby Tribute (90)
Haggart, Bob (70-80)
Hagger, Tony (60)
Haggerty, Danny (60)
Haines, Jim Big Band (00)
Halcox, Pat (60-70-80-90-00)
Haldene, Stan (60)
Hale, Simon (90)
Hall, Adelaide (80)
Hall, Bob (70-80-00)
Hall, Ed (60)
Hall, Jim (80)
Hall, John (00)
Hall, Mike (00)
Hamill, Andy (90)
Hamilton, Jeff (90)
Hamilton, Mickey Band (80-90)
Hamilton, Scott (80-90-00)
Hamilton, Steve (90)
Hammer, Ian (60)
Hammer, Joe (70)
Hammond, John (00)
Hammond, Marshall (60)
Hammond, Roger (90)
Hammond, Steve (70)
Hampshire Jazz Appreciation
    Society (50-60)
Hampshire Jazz Orchestra (00)

Hampton, Slide (80)
Hands, Vicky (00)
Hanford, Mark (00)
Hanna, Jake (80-90-00)
Hanslip, Mark (00)
Happy Magazine (60)
Happy Tobacco (70)
Hardin and York (70)
Hardiman, Don (90)
Harding, 'Uncle' Bart (70)
Hardy, Cliff (00)
Harlem Blues Jazz Band (70)
Harlemania (00)
Harmony Express (70)
Harper, Cliff (60-70-80)
Harper, Janie (60-70-80)
Harrell, Tom (80)
Harriott, Joe (50-60)
Harriott, Joe Workshop (70)
Harris, Derek (60)
Harris, Gene (90)
Harris, Kevin (90)
Harris, Pedro Band (60-70)
Harrison, Henry (00)
Harrison, Kenny (50-60-80)
Harrison, Kenny Sidepipers (60)
Hart, Jim (00)
Hartley, Keef (60-70)
Hartley, Patrick (00)
Harvey, Eddie (50-60)
Harvey, Eddie Soul Band (60)
Harvey, Bill (00)
Harvey, Graham (00)
Hashim, Michael (90-00)
Hastie, Will (70-80)
Hastings, Jimmy (90-00)
Hastings, Lennie (60-70)
Hathaway, Martin (00)
Haveron, Andrew (00)
Hawkins, Annie (00)
Hawkins, Coleman (60)
Hayes, Steve (00)
Hayes, Tubby (50-60)
Hayson, Simon (00)
Haynes, Roy (70)
Hayward, Rachel (00)
Head (70)
Head, Hands and Feet (70)
Healey, Derek (90)
Healey, Gordon (70)
Healey, John (60)
Hearnshaw, Charlie Quartet (90)
Heart and Souls, The (60)
Heath, Jim (00)
Heath, Jimmy (00)
Heath, Percy (00)
Heath, 'Tootie' (00)
Heatherington, Ron (80)
Heatley, Spike (70-80-90)

Heckstall-Smith, Dick (60-80-90)
Hector (70)
Hedges, Chuck (80)
Heeley, Roger (00)
Hefty Jazz (80)
Helleny, Joel (90)
Hellraiser (70)
Hell's Children (70)
Hemmings, Bob (90)
Hemmings, Roy G (00)
Henderson, Doris (70)
Hendricks, Marcel (00)
Henry, Ian (00)
Henry, Michael (00)
Henry, Richard (00)
Henry's Bootblacks (60-80)
Henshaw, Elliott (00)
Herbert, Gwyneth (00)
Herd, The (60)
Herman, Woody Orchestra (00)
Hewitt, Dave (90-00)
Hibberd, John (90-00)
Hicks Jackie (00)
Hicks, John (90)
Higgins, Nick (00)
High Society Band (80)
Hill, Roger (80-00)
Hird, Karl (00)
Hirst, Robert and The
  Big Taste (60)
Hiseman, Jon (60)
Hitchcock, Nigel (00)
Hobbs, Steve (00)
Hobson, Helen (00)
Hodes, Art (80)
Hodges, Peter (60)
Hodgkinson, JW (70)
Hogan, Bill (70)
Hogg, Derek (70-80)
Hogh, Mike (00)
Hokum Jazz Band (00)
Holder, Noddy (60)
Holden, Butch (80-90-00)
Holly, Major (80)
Holloway, Laurie (90-00)
Holloway, 'Red' (90)
Holloway, Tony (60-70-80-90-00)
Holmes, Dave (90)
Holmes, Matt (00)
Home, Matt (00)
Homes, Mark (00)
Honkin' Hep Cats (90)
Hooker, John Lee (60)
Hooper, Jeff (90)
Horler, John (80-90-00)
Horler, Ronnie (60-70-80-90)
Horner, Johan (00)
Horn, Malcolm (80-90-00)
Horton, Joanne 'Pug' (80)

Horton, Julie (00)
Hot Antic Jazz Band (90)
Hot Cat Jazz Band (90)
Hot Strings (00)
Houghton, Ron (80)
Hour, The (70)
Houseshakers (70)
Howard-Davies, Serena (00)
Howard, Ian (60)
Howard, Jimmy (70)
Howard, Keith (70-80-90)
Howarth, Russell (00)
Howell, Peter (00)
Hucko, Peanuts (70-80-90)
Hugg, Mike (60-80)
Huggett, Jeremy (00)
Hughes, Grahame (00)
Hughes, Peter (00)
Hughes, Ronnie (80-90)
Hull, Geoff (90)
Humphries, Percy (80)
Humphries, Ron (90)
Humphries, Willy (80)
Hunky Dory (70)
Hunt, Bob (70-80-90-00)
Hunt, Fred (60-70-80)
Hunter, Ian (60)
Hunter, Joel (00)
Hunter-Randall, Ian (60-90)
Hurley, Vince (00)
Hurlock, Frank (60)
Hurricane Force Steel Band (90)
Hurst, Tony (60-70)
Husband, Gary (00)
Hutchings, Mike (70-80)
Hutton, Mick (90-00)
Hutton, Mike (50-60-70-80)
Hyams, Dudley (60-70)
Hyman, Dick (90)

I

Iawdselgn (60)
Iden, John (00)
If (70)
Ilett, Den (00)
Image Show, The (60)
Ind, Peter (80-00)
Ingham Keith (70-80-90-00)
Inkspots, The - Interview for TV (90)
Inness, Don (90-00)
Irving, Ian (90)
Ishihara, Eriko (00)

J

J-Parts, The (60)
Jab Jab (70)
Jackson, Alan (80-00)
Jackson, Bob (90)

Jackson, Duffy (90-00)
Jackson, Julian (00)
Jackson, Lee (60)
Jackson, Oliver (80)
Jackson, Ron (00)
Jacobs, Tony (90-00)
Jacobson, Pete (90)
Jaffe, Allan (80)
Jagers, Udo (00)
James, Ben (90)
James, George (70)
James, Jimmy and the
  Vagabonds (60-70)
James, Peter Collection (70)
James, Vance (80)
Jan and the Night People (60)
Janisch, Mike (00)
Janssen, Huub (80-90)
Jay, Barbara (60-90-00)
Jazz Bandits, The (70-80)
Jazz Committee (50)
Jazz Couriers, The (00)
Jazz Gitanes (00)
Jazz Guitars (90)
Jazz In Mind (00)
Jazz Journal Poll Winners Tour (90)
Jazzmakers, The (50)
Jazz Passengers (60)
Jazz Score (80)
Jazz West Coast (90)
JB Road Show (60)
Jeffries, Richard (90)
Jenkins, Terry (90-00)
Jennings, Tony (60)
Jenson, Ingrid (90)
Jessop, Paddy (50)
Jiear, Alison (00)
Jigsaw (70)
Jive Aces, The (00)
Jiving Lindy Hoppers (80-90-00)
John, Elton - Reg Dwight (60)
John, Freddie (90-00)
Johnson, Dave (80)
Johnson, Gus (70-80)
Johnson, Smokey (80)
Johnson, TJ (80-00)
Johnson, Steve (00)
Jolly, Pete (90)
Jones, Dave (90-00)
Jones, Dill (50-60-80)
Jones, Hank (80)
Jones, Oliver (80-90)
Jones, Paul (60-00)
Jones, Ronnie (60)
Jones, Salena (90)
Jones, Steve (00)
Jordan, Earl (70)
Judge, Phil (00)
Juklin, Bo (00)

You won't find Del Boy Trotter in our list of performers, but his clone Maurice Canham gate-crashed our 50th anniversary celebrations to give our respected accountant Graham Martin a few tips on how he would keep the books. Lovely jubbly, Graham.

July, The (60)
Jumping Jack's Panama
    Jazz Band (90)
Junco Partners (60)
Junction Jazz Band (60)
Junior Eyes (60)
Juris, Vic (80)
Jupp, Mickey (50)

Kaart, Dick (80)
Kaatee, Fritz (00)
Kaatee, George (00)
Kalderstat, Steve (00)
Kansas City Express (80)
Kaper, Bob (80-90-00)
Katch 22 (70)
Kavanagh, Gary (00)
Kaye, Alan (50-60)
Keane, Shake (60)
Keech, Dave (90)
Keene, Eric (60)
Kelby, Dave (90-00)
Kellard, Colin (90)
Kelly, Pete Solution (60)
Kelly, Sam (00)
Kelso, Jon-Erik (90-00)
Kemp, Mike (00)
Kendon, Adrian (80)
Kent, Clark (90)
Kent, Stacey (90-00)
Kerr, Anthony (90-00)
Kerr, Bob Whoopee Band (70-80-90-00)
Kerr, Pete Scottish All Stars (60)
Kerr, Trudi (00)
Kessel, Barney (70-80-90)
Keyworth, Terry (70-80-90)
Kidd, Carol (90)
Kilgore, Rebecca (00)
Kimball, Narvin (80)
Kimbara (90)
Kincaid, Tom (00)
Kinda Dixie Jazz Band (00)
King, Jim (60)
King Oliver Centennial Band (80-90)
King Ossy Disc Show (60)
King, Peter (60-70-80-90)
King Pleasure and The
    Biscuit Boys (80-90-00)
King, Reggie (60)
Kingwell, Colin Jazz Bandits (60-90-00)
Kinsey, Tony (80)
Kirke, Simon (60)
Kiss (70)
Klein, Harry (50-60)
Klink, Al (80)
Kliphuis, Tim (00)

Klippert, Jim (90)
Kole, Ronnie (80-90-00)
Konitz, Lee (80)
Korner Alexis Blues Incorporated (60)
Kossoff, Paul (60)
Kovacs, Ferenc (90)
Koven, Steve Trio (00)
Kronquest, Karl (90)
Kuc, Andy (00)
Kuermayr, Gunther (00)
Kyle, Bill (70)

L'Etienne, Thomas (00)
Lacey, Paul (90-00)
Lafertin, Fapy (80)
Lagrene, Birelli (80)
Laine, Dame Cleo (00)
Laine, Denny (60)
Lamb, Bert (00)
Lamb, Bobby (90)
Lamb, Bros and Co (60)
Lambe, Jeannie (90)
Lamond, Don (80)
Lamont, Duncan (60)
Land, Harold (90)
Lane, Steve (60)
Langham, Thomas 'Spats' (90-00)
Langford, Jill (00)
Langlan, Noel (90)
Lanham, Katherine (90)
Latham, Anne (80-90)
Laughlin, Tim (90)
Laurie, Cy (70-80)
Lawes, Pete (60)
Lawrence, Andy (90-00)
Lawrence, Denise (90-00)
Lawrence, Jamie (00)
Lawson, Yank (70-80-90)
Layton, Teddy (60-70-80-90)
Le Joindre, Emelio (00)
Le Sage, Bill (50-60-70-80-90)
Leadbeater, John (90)
Leake, Brian (50-70-80)
Leathertown Jazzmen (60)
Ledigo, Hugh (80-90-00)
Lee, Eggy Hotshots (80)
Lee, Crissy All Girl Big Band (90)
Lee, Phil (00)
Lee, Ranee (90)
Lee, Tony (70-80)
Lee, Justin (00)
Lee, Tony (80)
Legg, John (70)
Leggett, Andy (00)
Leigh, Carol (90)
Lemley, Ty (00)

Lemon, Brian (60-70-80-90-00)
Leonhart, Jay (00)
Lesberg, Jack (80)
Lewellyn, Huw (90)
Lewin, Dave (70-80-90-00)
Lewis, Juliet (90-00)
Lewis, Roger (60-90)
Lewis, Terry (00)
Lewitt, Ray (60)
Liddell, Davy (00)
Liddell, Simon (00)
Lightfoot, Adrian (50-60)
Lightfoot, Paddy (60)
Lightfoot, Terry (60-70-80-90-00)
Lighthouse All Stars (90)
Lightsey, Kirk (00)
Lightnin' Slim (70)
Limb, Jeremy (00)
Limehouse Jazz Band (00)
Limited Company Band (70)
Little, John (60)
Little Walter (60)
Littlejohn, Alan (90)
Litton, Martin (80-90-00)
Liverpool Scene (70)
Loch, Billy (60)
Lock, Mike (00)
Lock, Richard (90)
Lockjaw (70)
Locomotive (60)
Locket, Mornington (00)
Long, Gareth (90)
London City Soul Band (60)
London City Stompers (60)
London Jazz Big Band (80)
London Ragtime Orchestra (80)
London Vintage Orchestra (80)
Lonergan, Chris (00)
Long, Jimmy (90)
Long, Pete (90-00)
Lord, Jon (60)
Loose Ends, The (60)
Lord Napier Jazz Band (00)
Lotis, Denis (90)
Loughlin, Gerry (60)
Louisiana Jazzmen (90-00)
Louisiana Joymakers (90-00)
Louisiana Red (80)
Lovatt, Mike (00)
Lowe, Mundall (80)
Lowther, Henry (70-80)
Lucas (70)
Lucketts Travel Band (80)
Lumiere Puppets, The (70)
Lusher, Don (80-90-00)
Lynch, Jim (00)
Lyttelton, Humphrey (60-70-80-90-00)

M

M, Johnny (70-80-90)
M4 All Stars (90)
Mabon, Willie (70)
Mackenzie, Henry (80)
Mack, Freddie (60)
Macintosh, Adrian (80-90-00)
Mackintosh, Jim (60-00)
MacNicol, John (70)
Maddocks, John Bands (70-80-90-00)
Madrigal (70)
Maher, George (00)
Majority, The (60)
Malcolm, Austin (90)
Malett, Gavin (00)
Manatovani, Davide (00)
Mance, Junior (00)
Manfred Mann (60)
Mann-Hugg Blues Men (60)
Maniatt, Mark (90)
Mann, Tony (70-80)
Mannery, Paul Hot Five (90)
Mannix, Val (90-00)
Manone, Wingy (60-70)
Marable, Lawrence (90)
Mark, Jon (60)
Mark, Tom (00)
Marks, Roger Armada Band (90-00)
Marlow, Christine (60)
Marsden, Danny (00)
Marshall, Jenell (90)
Marshall, John (80)
Martin, Graham (70)
Martin, Juan Ensemble (80)
Martin, Kyd (60)
Martinique Jazz Band (70)
Martyn, Barry Bands (90-00)
Martyn, Ben (00)
Mason's, Phil New Orleans
   All Stars (60-90-00)
Mason, Rod Bands (70-80-90-00)
Masso, George (80-90-00)
Mathewson, Ron (80)
Mathieson, Cole (50-60 etc)
Mathieson, Kirstie (90-00)
May, Imelda (00)
May, Tina (90-00)
Mayall, John Blues Breakers (60)
Mays, Bill (90)
Maze, The (60)
Mazetier, Louis (90)
McCallum, John (70-80-90)
McCann, Colin (00)
McCarthy, Haydn (90-00)
McClear, Joe (90)
McConnell, Jim (60)

McCrary, Howard (90)
McDonald, Chris (00)
McGhee, Brownie (70)
McGriff, Jimmy (80)
McGuinness, Tom (60)
McIntyre, Gay (90)
McKay, Ron (60)
McKenna-Mendleson Band (60)
McKenna, Dave (90)
McKenzie, Henry (80)
McLaughlin, John (60)
McLaurin, Marcus (80-90)
McMurray, Fred (80-90-00)
McPartland, Jimmy (80)
McPartland, Emer (00)
McShann, Jay (80)
McVie, John (60)
Megger's Dixiecats (60)
Meggeson, Dave (60-70-80)
Melling, Steve (00)
Melly, Alan (00)
Melly, George (70-80-90-00)
Memphis Slim (60-80)
Merrett, Max and the Meteors (70)
Messinare, Andre (90-00)
Meyer, Peter (00)
Meyer, Ralph (00)
Michaux, Pascal (90-00)
Middleton-Pollock, Marilyn (90-00)
Midnite Follies Orchestra (70-80)
Midnite Ramblers (70)
Miles, Butch (80-90-00)
Miles, Matt (90-00)
Miller, Clarence 'Big' (90)
Miller, Colin (00)
Miller, Dominic (00)
Miller, 'Sing' (80)
Millet, Neil (60)
Mills, Eddie (60)
Mills, John (60)
Mills, Martin (00)
Millward, Nick (90-00)
Milverton, Craig (90-00)
Milward, Ady (00)
Mince, Johnnie (80)
Mingus, Charlie (70)
Minter, Keith (00)
Mires, Trevor (00)
Mission Hall Band (70-80-90-00)
Mitachelli, Anthony (00)
Mitchell, Alan (00)
Moffat, Ian (00)
Mohammed, Idris (80)
Money, Zoot (60-80-90)
Monkford, John (00)
Monnery, Ian (00)
Montgomery, Alan (70)
Montgomery, Marion (80-90)
Mooch (60)

Moody Bosh (50-60-70)
Moody, James (80)
Moon, The (70)
Moore, Michael (90-00)
Morcom, Peter (00)
Mordue, Eddie (90)
Morgan, Chuck (00)
Morgan, Dave Band (70)
Morgan, Lanny (00)
Morgan, Mark (00)
Morgan, Paul (70-80-90-00)
Morgan, Shirley - nee Alexander
(60-70-80-90-00)
Morris, Sonny Delta Band (80-90-00)
Morrissey, Dick (60-70-80-90)
Morrison, 'Stu' (60-70)
Mortimer, John (60-70-90-00)
Mortimer, Malcolm (90)
Morton, Bennie (70)
Morton, Clive (80)
Morwood, Dave (90)
Moseley, Snub (70)
Moss, Danny (60-80-90-00)
Moss, Danny Jnr (00)
Moss, Nick (00)
Most, Abe (80)
Motivation (60)
Mott The Hoople (60)
Moule, Sarah (00)
Moyland, Paul (00)
Moyses, Sean (90-00)
Mud (70)
Mudge, Bill (00)
Mullen, Jim (80-90-00)
Mullins, Winston (00)
Mumford, John (60-00)
Munns, Roger (80)
Murphy, Malc (00)
Murphy, Sky (00)
Musselwhite, John (60)
Myers, Pete (00)
Myers, Terry (80-90)
Myerscough, Roger (00)

N

Namyslowski Zbiegnkw
   Polish Quartet (60)
Napoleon, Marty (80)
Nash, Denny (50-60)
Nash, Derek (90-00)
N.Y.J.O. (80-90)
Nesbitt, James (00)
Neuhauser, Ed (00)
New Antonians Swing Orchestra (00)
New Beachcombers Band (00)
New Black Eagle Band (90-00)
New Couriers, The (00)

My lovely sister Jan (now Mrs Derek Jones) was a big help to me in the Bassett days, and is seen here giving a warm welcome to Acker Bilk during one of his visits to the original Concorde Club.

New Era Band (60-70)
New Europa Jazz Band (70-80-90-00)
New Excelsior Band (00)
New Forest Rhythm Kings (80-90)
New Gateway Band (60-90-00)
New Iberia Stompers (60)
New Orleans Heat (00)
New Orleans Hot Shots (00)
New Orleans Serenaders (00)
New Sedalia Band (60)
New Stompers (00)
New Sydney Stompers (90)
New Temperance Seven (70)
New Zenith Stompers (90)
Newman, Joe (80)
Newton, Dave (80-90-00)
Newton, Pete 'Slim' (60-70-80)
Newton, Tad Jazz Friends (90)
Nice, The (60)
Nicholas, Andy (00)
Nichols, Al (90-00)
Nichols, Geoff (70-80)
Nichols, Keith Bands (70-80-90-00)
Niebla, Eduardo (80)
Niece, Steve (00)
Nightingale, Mark (80-00)
Nile, Bill Bands (60)
Nimitz, Jack (90)
Nistico, Sal (80)
Nite People (60-70)
Nobes, Roger (70-80-90-00)
Nolan, Jason (00)
Northern Jazz Orchestra (90)
Norvo, Red (80)
Nugent, John (00)
Nyman, Olle (00)

O'Regan, Matt (00)
Okey All Stars (00)
Olney, Dave (00)
Orange Rainbow (70)
Original Dixieland Syncopators (70)
Original Downtown Syncopators (60)
Original Gateway Band (60)
Original Jubilee Band (90)
Original Society Syncopators (80)
Ornberg, Tomas (00)
Orr, Bobby (80)
Osbourne, Jim (00)
Oufram, Mike (00)
Our Band (80)
Outfit, The (00)
Over, Geoff (90-00)
Oxley, Colin (90-00)
O'Grady, Rosie Good Time Band (80)
O'Higgins, Dave (90)
O'List, David (60)

Packman, Dave (00)
Paice, Ian (60)
Painter, Greg (50-60-90-00)
Panayi, Andy (90-00)
Papa Joe All Stars (90-00)
Paris Barcelona Swing
    Connection (90)
Parker, Brian (70)
Parker, Johnny (70-80)
Parnell, Jack (80-90)
Parrott, Nicki (00)
Pasadena Roof Orchestra (70-00)
Patterson, George (90-00)
Patton, Jeb (00)
Pearce, Bob Blues Band (70-00)
Pearce, Dick (80-00)
Pearce, John (90-00)
Pearce, Ken (80)
Pearce, Steve (90)
Pearson, James (00)
Peberdy, Jack (60)
Peeters, Joep (00)
Pelland, Bob (90)
Pellett, Roy (70-80-90)
Pendulum (70)
Penny Peeps (60)
Peplowski, Ken (90-00)
Percival, John (90-00)
Perdido Street Band (60)
Perkins, Bill (80-90)
Perry, John (00)
Percer, Percy (00)
Person, Houston (00)
Peters, Colin Band (60)
Peters, Nelson (60)
Peters, Robin (60)
Petley, Gary (70)
Petrocca, David (00)
Petters, John Bands (80-90)
Peyer, Ralph (00)
Phillips, Wayne (70)
Phoenix Jazz Band (80-00)
Picard, John (60-80-00)
Pied Piper Quintet (80)
Pierce, Nat (80)
Pine City Stompers (60-70)
Piotrowski, Dcato (00)
Pite, Richard (00)
Pitt, Tony (60-70-80-90-00)
Pitt, Vic (60-70-80-90-00)
Pizza Express All Stars (80-90-00)
Pizzarelli, Bucky (90-00)
Pizzarelli, John (90)
Pla, Roberta (90)
Plant, Robert (60)

Plater, Alan (00)
Playfoot, Andy (00)
Pod, Peter and the Peas (00)
Polcer, Ed (90)
Poole, Malcolm (60)
Pope, Ted (90)
Porter-Robinson Big Band (80)
Potter, Gary (90-00)
Potts, Ted (60)
Powell, James (90-00)
Powell, Jane (00)
Powell, Jimmy Bands (60-70)
Powell, Robert (00)
Powell, Tristan (90-00)
Preservation Hall Band (80)
Preston, Nick (00)
Price, Alan Bands (60-80-90)
Price, 'Red' (50)
Priseman, Dave (00)
Pritchard, Sarah (90)
Pritchard, Bill (90)
Pritchard, Guy (00)
Privin, Bernie (70)
Proud, Geoff (50)
Puddy, James (00)
Purbrook, Colin (80-90)
Pure 8 (00)
Purnell, Alton (60)
Pyne, Mick (70-80-90)

Quincy, Dave (70-00)
Quinton, Bob (50-60)
Rae, Ronnie (60)
Ralphs, Mick (60)
Ram Jam Band (60)
Ramirez, Ram (70)
Randall, Alan (80-90)
Randall, Freddie (60)
Ravell, Andrew (00)
Ravell, Patti (00)
Read, Graham (80-90-00)
Reading, Bertice (80)
Real Ale and Thunder Band (70-80-90)
Red Onion Jazz Band (60)
Red River Jazz Band (70)
Reece, Dizzy (50)
Rees-Jones, John (90-00)
Reid, Rayna (00)
Reinhardt, Babik (80)
Reinhart, Randy (00)
Relf, Keith Renaissance (60)
Rendell, Don (50-60-70-90)
Resurrection (00)
Rhapsody, Miss (70)
Rhythm Aces, The (80)
Richards, Terry (90)

Richardson, Jim (70-80-90-00)
Richardson, Johnny (70-80-90-00)
Richardson, Tony (60)
Richmond, Dave (60)
Rickenburg, Rob (00)
Ricki Hi-Lites (60)
Rimington, Sammy
   Bands (70-80-90-00)
Rio Grande Hot Tango Orchestra (80)
Ripper, Peter (00)
Riverside Jazz Band (80)
Roberts, Grahame (00)
Roberts, Tony (60-70-80)
Robinson, Eddie (00)
Robinson, Spike (80-90-00)
Robson, Phil (00)
Roche, Jimmy (80-00)
Roche, Martine (60)
Rockett 88 (80-00)
Roden, Jess (60)
Roger on the Piano (00)
Rogers, Andy (00)
Rogers, Ken (70)
Rogers, Paul (60)
Rogers, Shorty (80-90)
Rolfe, Mel (70)
Rollercoaster (80)
Rollins, Winston (90-00)
Rose, Gerry (00)
Rosengarden, Bobby (80)
Ross, Annie (80)
Ross, Ronnie (50-60)
Royal Garden Jazz Band (70)
Royen, John (90-00)
Rubin, Ron (60-70-80-90)
Rucker, Ellyn (80-90-00)
Running Wild (90-00)
Rushden, Steve (90-00)
Russo, Sonny (70)

S

Sadler, Mike (60)
Salmins, Ralph (90-00)
Salmons, Murray (90)
Salmons, Pete (00)
Sam Apple Pie (60-70)
Samuel, Keith (60-70-80-90-00)
Sanders, Tom (80)
Sanderson, Hayley (00)
Sanchez, Mike (90-00)
Sanderson, Hayley (00)
Sandke, Randy (80-90-00)
Satisfaction (70)
Satterley, Chris (60-70-90)
Sauer, Warren (80-90)
Savage, Padriac (00)
Savannah Jazz Band (00)

Saville, Dave (70-80)
Savoy Brown Blues Band (60)
Schilperoort, Peter (80-90)
Scott, Gary (90)
Scott, Johnny (60)
Scott, Johnny (00)
Scott, Nina (00)
Scott, Rae (50-60)
Scott, Ronnie (50-60-70-80)
Scott-Taylor, Ian (90)
Scriven, Graham (80)
Sealey, Paul (80-90-00)
Seaman, John (90-00)
Seaman, Phil (60)
Second Line Jazz Band (00)
Seidel, David (00)
Seidel, Janet (00)
Senersiti, Bernie (80)
Shades of Kenton Orchestra (90)
Shag Connors and the
   Carrot Crunchers (70)
Shakin' Stevens and the Sunsets (70)
Shane, Mark (80-90)
Shank, Bud (80-90)
Sharp, Karen (00)
Shaw, Hank (60-70)
Shaw, Sam (00)
Shaw, Steve (00)
Shea, Ray (00)
Shepherd, Dave (80-90-00)
Shepherd, Jim (80-90)
Sherman, Daryl (90)
Sherry, Ed (00)
Shew, Bobby (80)
Shinn, Don (70)
Shipton, Alyn (80)
Siefert, Matthias (00)
Siegal, Julian (00)
Sims, Ken Dixie Kings (90)
Sisto, Dick (00)
Skeat, Bill (80)
Skeat, Len (70-80-90-00)
Skelton, Matt (90-00)
Skidmore, Alan (60-90-00)
Skidmore, Jimmy (50-60)
Skinner, Colin (00)
Skivington, Pete (60-70-80-90-00)
Slade – as Ambrose Slade (60)
Slater, Holly Quartet (90)
Slaughter, John (70-80-90-00)
Smalls, Clifford (80)
Smiling Hard (70)
Smith, Betty (50-60-70)
Smith, Carey (80)
Smith, Colin (70-80-90)
Smith, Dave (00)
Smith, Derek (80-00)
Smith, Dick (60)
Smith, Don (80)

Smith, Keith (50-60-70-80-90)
Smith, Ken (60)
Smith, Mark (00)
Smith, Marvin (80)
Smith, Mike (00)
Smith, Pete (90)
Smith, Richard Guitar Trio (90)
Smith, Terry (70-80)
Snell, Frank (00)
Snelling, Tony (60)
Snelling, Mike (90-00)
Solent City Jazzmen (60-70-80-90)
Solberg, Nils (00)
Some Like It Hot (70)
Soul Agents, The (60)
Soul Sounds and Lucas (70)
South, Harry (60-80)
Southampton All Stars (70-80)
Southern Union Jug Band (60)
Spencer's Washboard Kings (60)
Spike's Young Lions (00)
Spillett, Simon (00)
Sportiello, Rossano (00)
Sporting House Strings (00)
Squires, Rosemary (90-00)
Stacey, Neil (90-00)
Staff, Freddy Orchestra (90)
Stane Street Jazz Band (70-80)
Stansfield, Andy (90-00)
Steam Packet, The (60)
Steele, Mick Band (60)
Stewart, Ian (80-00)
Stewart, Louis (70)
Stewart, Rex (60)
Stewart, Rod (60)
Stewart, Slam (80)
Stiles, Paul (90-00)
Stitt, Sonny (60)
Stobart, Kathy (50-60-70-80-90-00)
Stockley, Brian (70)
Stoneham Stompers (70-90)
Storeyville Tickle (80-90-00)
Strange, Pete (60-70-80-90-00)
Stringle, Julian Marc (80-90-00)
Strutters, Harry Hot Rhythm
   Orchestra (70-80-90-00)
Stuart, Mike Span (60)
Sudhalter, Dick (90)
Sullivan, Maxine (70-80)
Sunnyland Slim (70)
Sunset Café Stompers (00)
Sunshine, Monty Band (70-80-90)
Sussex Jazz Kings (00)
Sutch, 'Screaming Lord'
   and the Savages (70)
Sutton, John (80-00)
Sutton, Ralph (70-80-90-00)
Sutton, Roger (80-00)
Swedish Jazz Kings (00)

Kathy Stobart playing at the original Concorde where we made her the Club President

Sweet Substitute (70-80)
Swegas (70)
Swift, Duncan (60-90)
Swing Affair Show (90)
Swing Time Orchestra (90-00)
Sykes, Katherine (00)

T-Bone Walker (60)
Tailgate Six (00)
Taste, The (60)
Tate, Buddy (70-80)
Tate, Frank (90)
Taylor, Bob (70-80)
Taylor, Eddie (60-80-90-00)
Taylor, Gordon (00)
Taylor, John (70-80)
Taylor, Mark (80-90)
Taylor, Martin (70-80-90-00)
Taylor, Mick (60)
Taylor, Rusty (80)
Taylor, Sid (90-00)
Teal, Clare (00)
Temperance Seven (70-80)
Temperley, Joe (60-90)
Terry, Clark (80-90)
Terry, Sonny (70)
Thacker, Clive (80)
Thain, Gary (60-70)
Thames City Band (60)
Theman, Art (80)
Thompson, Barbara (70)
Thompson, Butch (80-90-00)
Thompson-Clark, Robin (00)
Thompson, Eddie (50-60-70-80)
Thorne, Shady (60)
Thorpe, Mel (80)
Thorpe, Simon (00)
Tia Juana Band (60-70-80)
Tiberi, Frank (00)
Toast, The (60)
Tobin, Louise (80-90)
Tomasso, Enrico (90-00)
Tomkins, Trevor (70-80-90)
Tomlinson, Jim (90-00)
Topgaard, Svenne (00)
Torfe, Brian (80)
Townley, Simon (00)
Tracey, Clark (80-90-00)
Tracey, Sheila (90)
Tracey, Stan (80-00)
Traves, Chris (00)
Treend, Mike (70-80)
Trinity College Big Band (90)
Trinity, Julie Driscoll and
  Brian Auger (60)

Troy, Doris and Gospel
  Truth (70)
Tucker, Mickie (80)
Turner, 'Big' Joe (60)
Turner, Bruce (60-70-80-90)
Turner, Sandy Quartet (50)
Turnock, Brian (90-00)
Tyle, Chris (90)
Tyrrell, Christine (90-00)

Vache, Warren (80-90-00)
Valenti, Carla (00)
Van Berteijk, Ton (00)
Van Der Linden, Dirk (00)
Van Drakestein, Henk Bosch (80)
Van Duin, Sytze (90)
Van Epps, George (80)
Van Pool, Jack (90)
Varekamp, Michael (90)
Varoo, Johnny (80)
Vasconcelos, Monica (00)
Vass, Olaf (70-80)
VerPlanck, Marlene (90-00)
Vernon, Richard (90)
Verrell, Ronnie (80-90-00)
Vickers, Mike (50-60)
Vintage Hot Five (00)
Vintage Jazz (90-00)
Vintner, Andy (90-00)
Vinten, Jonathan (90-00)
Voxtet (00)

Wade, Pat (50-60)
Wadham, John (80-90)
Wagner, Robert (00)
Walker, Chris (60-70-80-90-00)
Wallace, Simon (00)
Waller, Chris (70)
Waller, Tony (00)
Wallis, Bob (60-70)
Walters, Chris (00)
Walton, Peter (90-00)
Ward, Arthur (50-60-70-80-90-00)
Wareham, Pete (00)
Warren, Alistair (00)
Warren, Baby Boy (70)
Wasen, Anders (00)
Washington, Gino (60)
Washington, Kenneth (60)
Waso (80)
Wasser, Stan (50)
Waters, Ben Boogie Band (90-00)

Waters, Benny (70-80)
Wates, Matt (90)
Wates, Bill (90)
Watts, Lennie (60)
Watts, Pete (60)
Watts, Steve (00)
Weatherburn, Ron (60)
Weaver, Mick (60-70)
Web, The (60)
Webb, George Dixielanders (70-80)
Webster, Ben (60)
Webster, Eric (00)
Webster, Julian (00)
Weedon, Bert (60)
Weldon, Nick (80-90-00)
Weller, Don (80-90-00)
Wellins, Bobby (90-00)
Wells, Dickie (60)
Wells, Spike (80)
Wellstood, Dick (70-80)
Welsh, Alex Band (60-70-80)
Wess, Frank (90)
West Jesmond Rhythm Kings (00)
Weston, Harvey (60-70-80-90)
Whatmough, John (80-90)
Wheatley, Jon (00)
Wheatley, Martin (00)
Wheeler, Doug (50-60-90)
Wheeler, Ian (60-70-80-90)
Wheeler, Kenny (70)
Whigham, Jiggs (80-90)
White Brian/Alan Gresty (70-90-00)
White Hot Airmen (70)
White, Jimmy (80)
White, Johnny (50-60-70-80)
White, Mac (70-80)
White, Roy (50-60-70-80-90-00)
Whiting, Trevor (00)
Whitfield, Dory (60)
Whitfield, Doug (60)
Whittaker, Pete (00)
Whittle, Tommy (50-60-70-80-90-00)
Wickett, Alan 'Sticky' (80-90-00)
Widdowson, John (00)
Wilbur, Bob (70-80-90)
Wilby, Olly (00)
Wild Angels (60-70)
Wiles, Darren (00)
Williams, Howard (60)
Williams, Jessica Trio (90)
Williams, Jackie (90)
Williams, Martin (00)
Williams, Roy (60-70-80-90-00)
Williams, Trefor (00)
Williamson, Sonny Boy (60)
Willox, Roy (90-00)
Wilson, Bob (90-00)
Wilson, Chuck (90)
Wilson, John Orchestra (00)
Wilson, Teddy (70)

Wiseman, Val (90-00)
Witherspoon, Jimmy (80)
Wood, Andy (00)
Wood, Art (60)
Wood, Georgie (60)
Woodard, Ricky (90-00)
Woolf, Simon (90-00)
Woolley, Bob Jazzmen (60)

Wordsworth, Ray (90-00)
World's Greatest Jazz Band (70)
Worlock, Monty (50-60-70-80-90)
Worth, Bobby (90-00)
Wright, Denny (80)
Ydstie, Jim (00)
York, Pete (70-80-90-00)
Zenith Hot Stompers (00)

Zewada, Jan (00)
Zottola, Glen (80-90)
Zwingenberger, Axel (90-00)
4th International Guitar Festival (80)
9.20 De Luxe (90-00)
10th Avenue Jazz Band (90)
100 Club Festival All Stars (90)
100 Club All Stars (90)

The Balladeer (1961-1967)

Bailey, Roy
Bailey, Val
Baldry, Long John
Balladeers, The
Black Glove Band
Benbow, Steve
Bradford, Geoff
Cambell, Alex
Campbell, Ian
Campbell, Lorna
Carthy, Martin
Carter, Sydney
Clarke, Brian
Collins, Shirley
Davenport, Bob
Davey, Graham
Davis, Cyril
Davis, Tony
Denver, Nigel

Dorita-Y-Pepe
Dudley
Dunkerley, John
Friedman, Jill
Gerlach, Fred
Graham, Davy
Groves, Mick
Hall, Cliff
Jones, Hugh
Kelly, Stan
Killen, Lou
Korner, Alexis
Laughlan, Gerry
McColl, Ewan
McEwan, Alex
McNeill, Paul
McPeake, Family
Moxham, John
Mumming Play

Nelson, Pat
Paley, Tom
Portsmouth Singers
Rhodes, Frank
Roud, Peter
Russell, Ian
Sadler, Christine (later Williams)
Seeger, Peggy
Spinners, The
Sunny Hill Square Dancers
Swarbrick, Dave
Tawney, Cyril
Walker, Pete
West, Hedy
Willaby, Dr Constance
Williams, Dave
Wilton, Vic
Woods, Rollo Band
Young, Gerald

The Cabaret Artistes

Andre, David (80-90)
Ardra, Robin (90)
Austin, Neil (80-90)
Ayling, Will (70-80)
Azela (70)
Ball, Alan (90)
Bassett, Dave 'Harry' (00)
Battie, David (90)
Bayfield, Martin (00)
Benali, Francis (90)
Bentine, Michael (80)
Big Brother Soul (90)
Bremner, Rory (90)
Brown, Adger (00)
Brutus, Tony (70-80)
Bryan, Ted & Col W Possum (70)
Bull, Micky John (90)
Butler, Dave (80-90)
Butler, Nick (80-90)
Bylett, Chris (80)
Camelfoot, Humphrey (80)
Carla, Mia (80-90)
Cartridge, Richard (00)

Channon, Mick (90)
Charles, Roy and Sue (90)
Clown, Bluey (90-00)
Cole, Dave (70-80-90)
Colinski (80-90)
Corres, The (90)
Crosse, Tony (80-90)
Dahli (70-80)
Danata, Michael (70-80)
Darren, Colin (80-90)
Dave and Amos (80-90)
Davine, Lola (70)
Day, Adam (80-90)
De Milles, The (70)
Deception Unlimited (80)
Denton, Terry (70-80-90)
Digance, Richard (90-00)
Downton and Hendricks (90)
Edge of Darkness (90)
Fielding, Alan (80-90)
Fred the Ted (80-90-00)
Fredricks, Paul (80)
Fresh 11 (90)

Fuller, Danny (80)
Gold, Mike (80-90)
Gutbucket, Arnold (70-80-90)
Hague, Andrew (90)
Henry, Michael (80)
Hercules (80)
Ismay, Dave (70-80)
James, Ian (90-00)
James, Paul (90)
Jamie, Jay and Kim (80)
Jay, Janie (80-90)
Jerome, Mike (80-90)
Just Adger (80-90)
Kingstons, The (70)
Kirk, Ian (90)
Klegg, Dave (80-90)
La Rue, Danny (90)
Leach Billy J and The Humbugs (90)
Leach, Andy (90)
Lees, Ian 'Sludge' (70-80)
Le Tissier, Matt (00)
Lennon, Hugh (80)
Lovell, Simon (80)

No, not Nana Mouskouri and Demis Rousos tribute artistes but my daughter, Kirstie, with the singing chef David Ophaus during a pantomime performance

Lowen, Phil (80-90)
Lucas, Pete (80-90)
Lyndricks, The (70-80)
M, Barney (00)
Martin, Ron (80)
Massiah, Ted (90)
McCabe, Mike (90-00)
McMenemy, Lawrie (00)
Melanie (70-80)
Mellors, Mel (00)
Mike, Miran and Terry (80)
Miller, Willie (80-90)
Mooney, Pat (90)
Moore, Sir Patrick (00)
Moroni, Toni (80-90)
Nikki (80-90)
One Nation (90)

Ophaus, David (80-90-00)
Osgood, Peter (90)
Pasquale, Joe (80-90)
Potts, Mike (00)
Plumb, Maxell (90)
Price, Peter (80)
Prince, James (90-00)
Quinn, Jimmy (00)
Quinn, Tommie (70-80-90)
Rae, Leslie (70)
Rae, Keith (70)
Reed, Alan (80-00)
Richards, Ian (80-90)
Roberts, Chris (70)
Rogers, Greg (80-90)
Scherazade (80-90)
Shakira (80)

Simpson, Stan (70)
Smith, Chris (70-80)
Spencer, Olly (80-90)
Stevenson, Jeff (90)
Sweet and Simple (80)
Tamley, Tony (80)
Tandy, Steve (90)
Taylor, Lou (90)
Tensai (80-90-00)
Townsend, Andy (00)
Turner, Ray (80-90)
Van Dyke, Roy (70)
Walsh, Bradley J (80-90)
Westlake, Peter (70-80-90)
Wild, Fire (70-80)
Woodward, Christopher (80)
Woolley, Shep (70-80-90)

The Tribute Artistes

Abba - Abba Rival
Abba - Ultimate Abba
A-Ha - The A-Ha Tribute Band
Beach Boys, The - Total Beach Boys
Beach Boys, The - Boys on the Beach
Beach Boys, The - Endless Summer
Beatles, The - The Silver Beatles
Beatles, The - Phoney Beatles
Bee Gees - Taste of Honey
Bee Gees - The Tribute
Bill Haley and the Comets - Phil
Hayley and his Comments
Blondie - Bootleg Blondie
Blues Brothers - B'hmn Blues Brothers
Blues Brothers - Blues Brothers Uncut
Bob Marley - Bob Bailey and the Jailers
Bon Jovi - B Jovi Steve
Rolling Stones - Bog Rolling Stones
Boy George - Boy George Experience
Britney Spears - Jeni Jaye
Buddy Holly and the Crickets - Marc
Robinson and the Counterfeit Crickets
Celine Dion - Tracie Shield
Cher - Deadringers
Cher - Catherine Mary Carter
Christina Aguilera - Jeni Jaye
Cliff Richard - Jimmy Jermain
Coldplay - Coolplay
Dave Bowie - Bootleg Bowie
David Essex - Christopher Nott
Diane Ross - Diane Shaw
Dire Straits - Money for Nothing
Dirty Dancing - A Night of Dirty
    Dancing - a tribute to the film

Eagles, The - The Flyin' Eagles
ELO - The ELO Experience
Elton John - John Ellis
Elvis - Alvin
Eric Clapton - Claptonite
Everly Brothers - Walk Right Back
Frank and Dean Show - A Rat Pack
Tribute
Gene Pitney - Sounds of Gene Pitney
George Benson - Dave Tiwary
George Michael - Andrew Browning
George Michael - Rob Lamberti
Grease - Grease is the Word
Girls Aloud - Girls 'R' Aloud
Hot Chocolate - Kennie Simon
Infantasia - The Ultimate Tribute Band
James Brown - Buzz
Jimi Hendrix - Gimme Hendrix
Johnny Cash - John Verity
Jools Holland Orchestra - Bootleg Jools
Holland Orchestra
Karen Carpenter - Karen Barnett
Kylie Minogue - Joanne Steel
Kylie Minogue - Ultimate Kylie
Lionel Richie - Hamilton Browne
Luther Vandross - Harry Cambridge
Madness - Ultimate Madness
Madonna - Sally Moore
Meatloaf - Deadringers
Michael Jackson - Mikki Jay
Michael Jackson - Navi
Mick Hucknall - Darren Alboni
Mr Soul Drifters - Roy G Hemmings -
    ex leader of The Drifters

Neil Diamond - Ian Scott
Phil Collins - Rob Lewis
Pussycat Dolls - Pussycat Babes
Queen - The Queens
Queen - Monarchy
Rat Pack - David Alacey, Harry
Crawley, Rahul D'Mello
Robbie Williams - Paul Warren
Rolling Stones - Bog Rolling Stones
Rod Stewart - Stan Terry
Ronan Keating - Paul Sutton
Roy Orbison - Barry Steele
Status Quo - Status Clone
Shania Twain - Terri Anne
Shirley Bassey - Milli Munro
Spice Girls, The - Spicey Girls
Stevie Wonder - Shenton Dixon
Supreme Soul Show - Diane Shaw
Take That - Fake That
Take That - Take This
The Soul Divas - Diane Shaw
Tina Turner - Milli Munro
Tom Jones - Tom Canning
T Rex - Get It On
U2 - U2UK
UB40 - RU40
Village People - Village Boyz
Westlife - Westlike
Whitney Houston - Milli Munro
70s Disco – Groovejuice
80s Night – Total Electric

PREVIOUS BOOKS BY NORMAN GILLER
(Thanks for letting me share this one with you, Cole)

Banks of England (with Gordon Banks)
The Glory and the Grief (with George Graham)
Football And All That (an irreverent history of the game)
The Seventies Revisited (with Kevin Keegan)
The Final Score (with Brian Moore) **ABC of Soccer Sense** (Tommy Docherty)
Billy Wright, A Hero for All Seasons (official biography)
The Rat Race (with Tommy Docherty) **Denis Compton** (The Untold Stories)
McFootball, the Scottish Heroes of the English Game
The Book of Rugby Lists (with Gareth Edwards)
The Book of Tennis Lists (with John Newcombe)
The Book of Golf Lists **TV Quiz Trivia** **Sports Quiz Trivia**
Know What I Mean (with Frank Bruno) **Eye of the Tiger** (with Frank Bruno)
From Zero to Hero (with Frank Bruno) **The Judge Book of Sports Answers**
Watt's My Name (with Jim Watt) **My Most Memorable Fights** (with Henry Cooper)
How to Box (with Henry Cooper) **Henry Cooper's 100 Greatest Boxers**
Mike Tyson Biography **Mike Tyson, the Release of Power** (Reg Gutteridge)
Crown of Thorns, the World Heavyweight Championship (with Neil Duncanson)
Fighting for Peace (Barry McGuigan biography, with Peter Batt)
World's Greatest Cricket Matches **World's Greatest Football Matches**
Golden Heroes (with Dennis Signy) **The Judge** (1,001 arguments settled)
The Great Football IQ Quiz Book (The Judge of *The Sun*)
The Marathon Kings **The Golden Milers** (with Sir Roger Bannister)
Olympic Heroes (with Brendan Foster)
Olympics Handbook 1980 **Olympics Handbook 1984**
Book of Cricket Lists (Tom Graveney) **Top Ten Cricket Book** (Tom Graveney)
Cricket Heroes (Eric Morecambe) **Big Fight Quiz Book** **TVIQ Puzzle Book**
Lucky the Fox (with Barbara Wright) **Gloria Hunniford's TV Challenge**
Comedy novels: **Carry On Doctor** **Carry On England** **Carry On Loving**
Carry On Up the Khyber **Carry On Abroad** **Carry On Henry**
A Stolen Life (novel) **Mike Baldwin: Mr Heartbreak** (novel) **Hitler's Final Victim** (novel)
Affairs (novel) **The Bung** (novel) **Footballing Fifties**

Books in collaboration with **RICKY TOMLINSON**
Football My Arse **Celebrities My Arse** **Cheers My Arse**
Reading My Arse (The Search for the Rock Island Line)
PLUS books in collaboration with **JIMMY GREAVES**:
This One's On Me **The Final** (novel) **The Ball Game** (novel)
The Boss (novel) **The Second Half** (novel)
Let's Be Honest (with Reg Gutteridge) **Greavsie's Heroes and Entertainers**
World Cup History **GOALS!** **Stop the Game, I Want to Get On**
The Book of Football Lists **Taking Sides** **Funny Old Games**
Sports Quiz Challenge **Sports Quiz Challenge 2**
It's A Funny Old Life **Saint & Greavsie's World Cup Special**
The Sixties Revisited **Don't Shoot the Manager**